SCHAUM'S OUTLINE OF

Theory and Problems of

PRINCIPLES OF ACCOUNTING I

Fifth Edition

·

JOEL J. LERNER, M.S., P.D.

Former Chairman, Faculty of Business
Sullivan County Community College

JAMES A. CASHIN, M.B.A., CPA

Emeritus Professor of Accounting
Hofstra University

Schaum's Outline Series

McGRAW-HILL

New York   San Francisco   Washington, D.C.   Auckland   Bogotá   Caracas
Lisbon   London   Madrid   Mexico City   Milan   Montreal   New Delhi
San Juan   Singapore   Sydney   Tokyo   Toronto

JOEL LERNER is a retired Professor and former Chairman of the Business Division at Sullivan County Community College, Loch Sheldrake, New York. He received his B.S. from New York University and his M.S. and P.D. from Columbia University. He has coauthored the Schaum's Outlines of *Principles of Accounting II* and *Business Mathematics* and is the sole author of *Bookeeping and Accounting* and McGraw-Hill's publication of *Financial Planning for the Utterly Confused*, now in its fifth edition. Professor Lerner is also a financial lecturer to several Fortune 500 firms, has produced his own TV and radio series for fifteen years, and addresses thousands of people annually on finances.

JAMES A. CASHIN was Emeritus Professor of Accounting at Hofstra University, where he was formerly Chairman of the Accounting Department. He was a coauthor of several accounting textbooks, of the Schaum's Outlines of *Principles of Accounting II* and *Cost Accounting*, and he was Editor-in-Chief of the *Handbook for Auditors*. Professor Cashin was a Certified Public Accountant and a Certified Internal Auditor. He held a B.S. degree in Accounting from the University of Georgia and an M.B.A. from New York University. He taught in the Graduate School of City University of New York and New York University.

Schaum's Outline of Theory and Problems of
PRINCIPLES OF ACCOUNTING I

10 11 12 13 14 15 16 17 18 19 20   CUS CUS   0 9 8 7

ISBN 0-07-038149-6

Sponsoring Editor: Barbara Gilson
Production Supervisor: Pamela Pelton
Editing Supervisor: Maureen B. Walker

Library of Congress Cataloging-in-Publication Data

Lerner, Joel J.
    Schaum's outline of theory and problems of principles of
accounting I / Joel J. Lerner, James A. Cashin. — 5th ed.
        p.   cm. — (Schaum's outline series)
    Includes index.
    Spine title: Principles of accounting I.
    ISBN 0-07-038149-6
    1. Accounting—Problems, exercises, etc.   I. Cashin, James A.
II. Title.   III. Title: Principles of accounting I.   IV. Series.
HF5661.C37   1998
657'.076—dc21   98-35909
                                                           CIP

McGraw-Hill

A Division of The McGraw-Hill Companies

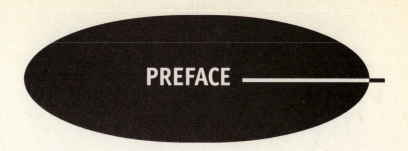

PREFACE

The fifth edition of *Principles of Accounting I* brings to the study of accounting the same *solved-problems approach* which has proved so successful in the disciplines of engineering and mathematics. In contrast to previous supplementary materials, which have been little more than summary textbooks, the Schaum's Outline Series in Accounting is organized around the *practical application* of basic accounting concepts. By providing the student with

1. Concise definitions and explanations, in easily understood terms
2. Fully worked-out solutions to a large range of problems (against which the student can check his or her own solutions)
3. Review questions
4. Sample examinations typical of those used by two-year and four-year colleges

these books help the student to develop the all-important know-how for solving problems—on the CPA examination and in professional practice.

Principles of Accounting I and its sequel, *Principles of Accounting II*, parallel the full-year introductory course offered in most colleges and universities. Subject matter in this newly revised edition has been carefully coordinated with the leading textbooks, so that any topic can easily be found from the table of contents or the index. In addition, this book should prove a valuable supplement to other accounting courses and to individual study. Today, there are an increasing number of programs offering college credit by examination, such as the College Level Examination Program (CLEP) and the New York College Proficiency Examination. Advanced placement, too, is now possible. People who may have taken introductory accounting some years ago will find much-needed aid in brushing up for the next course

JOEL J. LERNER

CONTENTS

CHAPTER 1

Accounting Concepts

1.1 NATURE OF ACCOUNTING

Every element of society—from the individual to an entire industry or government branch—has to make decisions on how to allocate its resources. *Accounting is the process that aids these decisions by (1) recording, (2) classifying, (3) summarizing, and (4) reporting business transactions and interpreting their effects on the affairs of the business entity*. This definition makes it clear that the recording of data, or *bookkeeping*, is only the first and simplest step in the accounting process.

1.2 BASIC ELEMENTS OF FINANCIAL POSITION: THE ACCOUNTING EQUATION

The financial condition or position of a business enterprise is represented by the relationship of assets to liabilities and capital.

Assets. Properties used in business that are owned and have monetary value; for instance, cash, inventory, buildings, equipment.

Liabilities. Amounts owed to outsiders, such as notes payable, accounts payable, bonds payable. These are known as claims to creditors. Liabilities may also include certain deferred items, such as income taxes to be allocated.

Owner's Equity. The interest of the owners in an enterprise.

These three basic elements are connected by a fundamental relationship called the accounting equation. This equation expresses the equality of the assets on one side with the claims of the creditors and owners on the other side:

$$\text{Assets} = \text{Liabilities} + \text{Owner's Equity}$$

According to the accounting equation, a firm is assumed to possess its assets subject to the rights of the creditors and owners.

EXAMPLE 1

Assume that a business owned assets of $100,000, owed creditors $70,000, and owed the owner $30,000. The accounting equation would be

$$\begin{array}{ccc} \textbf{Assets} & = \textbf{Liabilities} + & \textbf{Owner's Equity} \\ \$100,000 = & \$70,000 + & \$30,000 \end{array}$$

1

If over a certain period the firm had a net income of $10,000, the equation would then be

$$\textbf{Assets} \ = \textbf{Liabilities} + \textbf{Owner's Equity}$$
$$\$110,000 = \ \$70,000 \ + \ \ \ \ \$40,000$$

We shall call any business event that alters the amount of assets, liabilities, or owner's equity a *transaction*. In Example 1, the net changes in asset groups were discussed; in Example 2, we show how the accountant makes a meaningful record of a series of transactions, reconciling them step by step with the accounting equation.

EXAMPLE 2

During the month of January, Mr. Alan Bagon, lawyer,

1. Invested $5,000 to open his law practice
2. Bought supplies (stationery, forms, pencils, etc.) for cash, $300
3. Bought office equipment from Altway Furniture Company on account, $2,500
4. Received $2,000 in fees earned during the month
5. Paid office rent for January, $500
6. Paid salary for part-time help, $200
7. Paid $1,000 to Altway Furniture Company on account
8. After taking an inventory at the end of the month, found that he had used $200 worth of supplies
9. Withdrew $300 for personal use

These transactions might be analyzed and recorded as follows:

Transaction (1). Mr Bagon invested $5,000 to open his law practice. There are two accounts that are affected: The asset Cash is increased, and the capital of the firm is increased by the same amount.

	Assets	=	Liabilities	+	Owner's Equity
	Cash				A. Bagon, Capital
(1)	+$5,000	=			+$5,000

Transaction (2). Bought supplies for cash, $300. In this case, Mr. Bagon is substituting one asset for another: He is receiving (+) the asset Supplies and paying out (−) the asset Cash. Note that the capital of $5,000 remains unchanged, but there is still equality.

	Assets			=	Liabilities	+	Owner's Equity
	Cash	+	Supplies				A. Bagon, Capital
	$5,000						$5,000
(2)	−300		+$300				
	$4,700	+	$300	=			$5,000

Transaction (3). Bought office equipment from Altway Furniture Company on account, $2,500. He is receiving the asset Equipment but is not paying for it with the asset Cash. Instead, he will *owe* the money to the Altway Furniture Company. Therefore, he is *liable* for this amount in the future, thus creating the liability Accounts Payable.

	Assets					=	Liabilities	+	Owner's Equity
	Cash	+	Supplies	+	Equipment		Accounts Payable		A. Bagon, Capital
	$4,700		$300						$5,000
(3)					+$2,500		+$2,500		
	$4,700	+	$300	+	$2,500	=	$2,500	+	$5,000

Transaction (4). Received $2,000 in fees earned during the month. Because he received $2,000, the asset Cash increased and also his capital increased. It is important to note that he labels the $2,000 *Fees Income* to show its origin. This is known as Revenue or Income.

	Cash +	**Assets** Supplies +	Equipment	=	**Liabilities** Accounts Payable	+	**Owner's Equity** A. Bagon, Capital	
	$4,700	$300	$2,500		$2,500		$5,000	
(4)	+2,000						+2,000	Fees Income
	$6,700 +	$300 +	$2,500	=	$2,500	+	$7,000	

Transaction (5). Paid office rent for January, $500. When the word "paid" is stated, you know that it means a deduction from Cash, since he is paying *out* his asset Cash. Payment of expense is a reduction of capital. It is termed *Rent Expense*.

	Cash +	**Assets** Supplies +	Equipment	=	**Liabilities** Accounts Payable	+	**Owner's Equity** A. Bagon, Capital	
	$6,700	$300	$2,500		$2,500		$7,000	
(5)	−500						−500	Rent Expense
	$6,200 +	$300 +	$2,500	=	$2,500	+	$6,500	

Transaction (6). Paid salary for part-time help, $200. Again the word "paid" means a deduction of cash and a reduction in capital. This time it refers to *Salaries Expense*.

	Cash +	**Assets** Supplies +	Equipment	=	**Liabilities** Accounts Payable	+	**Owner's Equity** A. Bagon, Capital	
	$6,200	$300	$2,500		$2,500		$6,500	
(6)	−200						−200	Salaries Expense
	$6,000 +	$300 +	$2,500	=	$2,500	+	$6,300	

Transaction (7). Paid $1,000 to Altway Furniture Company on account. Here Mr. Bagon is reducing the asset Cash because he is paying $1,000, and reducing the liability Accounts Payable. He will now owe $1,000 less.

	Cash +	**Assets** Supplies +	Equipment	=	**Liabilities** Accounts Payable	+	**Owner's Equity** A. Bagon, Capital	
	$6,000	$300	$2,500		$2,500		$6,300	
(7)	−1,000				−1,000			
	$5,000 +	$300 +	$2,500	=	$1,500	+	$6,300	

Transaction (8). After taking an inventory at the end of the month, Mr. Bagon found that he had used $200 worth of supplies. The original amount of supplies purchased has been reduced to the amount that was found to be left at the end of the month. Therefore, the difference was the amount used ($300 − $100 = $200). This reduces the asset Supplies by $200, and reduces his Capital by the same amount. It is termed *Supplies Expense*.

	Cash +	**Assets** Supplies +	Equipment	=	**Liabilities** Accounts Payable	+	**Owner's Equity** A. Bagon, Capital	
	$5,000	$300	$2,500		$1,500		$6,300	
(8)		−200					−200	Supplies Expense
	$5,000 +	$100 +	$2,500	=	$1,500	+	$6,100	

Transaction (9). Withdrew $300 for personal use. The withdrawal of cash is a reduction not only in Mr. Bagon's cash position but also in his capital. This is not an expense but a personal withdrawal, a reduction of the amount invested.

	Assets				=	Liabilities	+	Owner's Equity
	Cash	+	Supplies	+	Equipment		Accounts Payable		A. Bagon, Capital
	$5,000		$100		$2,500		$1,500		$6,100
(9)	−300								−300 Drawing
	$4,700	+	$100	+	$2,500	=	$1,500	+	$5,800

Summary of Transactions
Month of January 19X8

	Assets				=	Liabilities	+	Owner's Equity
	Cash	+	Supplies	+	Equipment		Accounts Payable		A. Bagon, Capital
(1)	+$5,000					=		+	$5,000
(2)	−300	+	$300	+					
	$4,700	+	$300			=			$5,000
(3)					+$2,500		+$2,500		
	$4,700	+	$300	+	$2,500	=	$2,500	+	$5,000
(4)	+2,000								+2,000 Fees Income
	$6,700	+	$300	+	$2,500	=	$2,500	+	$7,000
(5)	−500								−500 Rent Expense
	$6,200	+	$300	+	$2,500	=	$2,500	+	$6,500
(6)	−200								−200 Salaries Expense
	$6,000	+	$300	+	$2,500	=	$2,500	+	$6,300
(7)	−1,000						−1,000		
	$5,000	+	$300	+	$2,500	=	$1,500	+	$6,300
(8)			−200						−200 Supplies Expense
	$5,000	+	$100	+	$2,500	=	$1,500	+	$6,100
(9)	−300								−300 Drawing
	$4,700	+	$100	+	$2,500	=	$1,500	+	$5,800

Summary

1. The four phases of accounting are _____, _____, _____, and _____.

2. The accounting equation is _____ = _____ + _____.

3. Items owned by a business that have monetary value are known as _____ .

4. _____ is the interest of the owners in a business.

5. Money owed to an outsider is a(n) _____ .

6. The difference between assets and liabilities is _____ .

7. Financial events that occur in a business are termed _____ .

8. An investment in the business increases _____ and _____ .

9. To purchase "on account" is to create a(n) _____ .

10. When the words "paid on account" occur, it means a reduction of the asset _____ and reduction of the liability _____ .

11. Income increases net assets and also _____ .

12. A withdrawal of cash reduces cash and _____ .

Answers: 1. recording, classifying, summarizing, reporting; 2. assets, liabilities, owner's equity; 3. assets; 4. owner's equity; 5. liability; 6. owner's equity; 7. transactions; 8. assets, owner's equity; 9. liability; 10. Cash, Accounts Payable; 11. owner's equity; 12. capital

Solved Problems

1.1. What effect do the transactions below have on the owner's equity (capital)?

(*a*) Fran Johnson invested $5,000 in the business.
(*b*) She bought equipment on account, $2,400.
(*c*) She paid half of the bill owed to the creditor.
(*d*) She received $2,000 in fees.
(*e*) She paid salaries for the week, $800.
(*f*) She withdrew $400 from the business.
(*g*) She paid rent for the month, $900.
(*h*) Inventory of supplies decreased $350 during the month.

SOLUTION

(*a*) increase	(*c*) no effect	(*e*) decrease	(*g*) decrease
(*b*) no effect	(*d*) increase	(*f*) decrease	(*h*) decrease

1.2.   Compute the amount of the missing element:

	Assets	**Liabilities**	**Owner's Equity**
(a)	$24,000	$19,000	?
(b)	$16,500	?	$12,300
(c)	?	$2,700	$14,000
(d)	$15,665	$9,406	?

SOLUTION

(a)	$5,000	($24,000 − $19,000)
(b)	$4,200	($16,500 − $12,300)
(c)	$16,700	($2,700 + $14,000)
(d)	$6,259	($15,665 − $9,406)

1.3.   Transactions completed by J. Epstein, M.D., appear below. Indicate increase (+), decrease (−), or no change (0) in the accompanying table.

		Assets	=	Liabilities	+ Owner's Equity
(a)	Paid rent expense for month				
(b)	Paid biweekly salary for lab assistant				
(c)	Cash fees collected for the week				
(d)	Bought medical equipment, paying cash				
(e)	Bought equipment on account				
(f)	Paid a creditor (liability) money owed				

SOLUTION

		Assets	=	Liabilities	+ Owner's Equity
(a)	(reduction of cash and capital)	−		0	−
(b)	(reduction of cash and capital)	−		0	−
(c)	(increase in cash and capital)	+		0	+
(d)	(increase in equipment, reduction in cash)	+ −		0	0
(e)	(increase in equipment and in accounts payable)	+		+	0
(f)	(decrease in cash and in accounts payable)	−		−	0

1.4.   Mr. Allen begins business, investing $4,000 in cash, equipment valued at $12,000, and $1,000 worth of supplies. What is the equity of the firm?

SOLUTION

$$\textbf{Assets = Liabilities + Owner's Equity}$$

$$\begin{array}{l} \$\ 4,000 \\ 12,000 \\ \underline{1,000} \\ \$17,000 = \qquad 0 \quad + \quad \$17,000 \end{array}$$

Mr. Allen's Owner's Equity is $17,000, the total of all his assets less his liabilities (0).

1.5.   If Mr. Allen had included a $6,000 note payable (written liability), in Prob. 1.4, what would then have been his Owner's Equity?

SOLUTION

$$\textbf{Assets} = \textbf{Liabilities} + \textbf{Owner's Equity}$$
$$\$17,000 = \quad \$6,000 \quad + \quad \$11,000$$

The total assets of $17,000, reduced by liabilities of $6,000, results in $11,000 owner's equity. Stated a different way:

$$\text{Assets } (\$17,000) = \text{Liabilities } (\$6,000) + \text{Owner's Equity } (?)$$
$$17,000 = 6,000 + ?$$
$$17,000 = 6,000 + 11,000$$

1.6. Supplies had a balance of $2,400 at the beginning of the year. At the end of the period, its inventory showed $1,400. How is this decrease recorded?

SOLUTION

Assets = Liabilities + Owner's Equity

Supplies		
$2,400		$2,400
−1,000		−1,000 Supplies Expense
$1,400		$1,400

1.7. Illustrate the difference between *Supplies* and *Supplies Expense*.

SOLUTION

Supplies is an asset and represents the value of supplies *owned* (supplies on hand). *Supplies Expense* is the value of supplies *used* during the period and is a reduction of capital.

Supplies (asset)	$2,400	(beginning)
Supplies Expense	−1,000	(used during year)
Supplies (asset)	$1,400	(end)

The value of supplies at the end of the period is the difference between the beginning balance and the amount that has been used.

1.8. The Supplies account had a balance of $3,850 at the beginning of January. At the end of the month, it was discovered that $1,425 remained.

(*a*) What was the *Supplies Expense* for the month?

(*b*) What was the *balance* of the asset Supplies?

SOLUTION

(*a*)

$3,850	Supplies, Jan. 1 (asset)
−1,425	Supplies, Jan. 31 (asset)
$2,425	Supplies Expense (used during month)

(*b*) $1,425. This is the amount that remains at the end of the month and is considered an asset.

1.9. The Supplies account had a balance of $3,850 at the beginning of January. At the end of the month, it was discovered that $1,425 had been used.

(*a*) What was the *Supplies Expense* for the month?

(*b*) What was the *balance* of the asset, Supplies?

SOLUTION

(*a*) $1,425. This is the amount that has been used.

(*b*)

$3,850	Supplies, Jan. 1 (asset)
−1,425	Supplies Expense (used)
$2,425	Supplies, Jan. 31 (asset)

1.10. Record the following transaction in the space provided: Bought equipment for $22,000, paying $6,000 in cash and owing the balance.

	Assets			=	**Liabilities**	+	**Owner's Equity**
	Cash	+	Equipment	=	Accounts Payable	+	Capital
Balance	$30,000						$30,000
Entry (?)							
Balance (?)							

SOLUTION

1. Reduce the Cash account by the amount paid, $6,000.
2. Record the purchase of the equipment at its cost, $22,000.
3. Increase Accounts Payable for the amount owed, $16,000.

	Assets			=	**Liabilities**	+	**Owner's Equity**
	Cash	+	Equipment	=	Accounts Payable	+	Capital
Balance	$30,000						$30,000
Entry	−6,000		+$22,000		+$16,000*		
Balance	$24,000	+	$22,000	=	$16,000	+	$30,000

*$22,000	(equipment)
−6,000	(paid in cash)
$16,000	(balance owed)

1.11. Based on the information in Prob. 1.10, what effect does the purchase of the equipment on account have on capital?

SOLUTION

No effect.

	Assets			=	**Liabilities**	+	**Owner's Equity**
	Cash	+	Equipment	=	Accounts Payable	+	Capital
Balance	$30,000						$30,000
Entry	−6,000		+$22,000		+$16,000		
Balance	$24,000	+	$22,000	=	$16,000	+	$30,000

Note that the capital before and after the transaction remains the same. The only areas that are affected are assets and liabilities.

1.12. In Prob. 1.10, what effect does the payment of the liability in full have on the capital account?

SOLUTION

No effect.

	Assets		=	Liabilities	+	Owner's Equity
	Cash	+ Equipment	=	Accounts Payable	+	Capital
Balance	$24,000	$22,000		$16,000		$30,000
Entry	−16,000			−16,000		
Balance	$8,000 +	$22,000	=			$30,000

The reduction of cash is accompanied by an equal reduction of the accounts payable.

1.13. The summary data of the Buntz Taxi Company for May are presented below in equation form. Describe each of the transactions that occurred during the month.

	Assets			=	Liabilities	+	Owner's Equity	
	Cash	+ Supplies	+ Equipment	=	Accounts Payable	+	Capital	
(1)	+$6,600						+$6,600	Investment
(2)	−3,200		+$3,200					
(3)	−500	+$500						
(4)			+2,000		+$2,000			
(5)	+2,500						+2,500	Fares Income
(6)	−1,100						−1,100	Salaries Expense
(7)	−500				−500			
(8)	−300						−300	Drawing
	$3,500 +	$500 +	$5,200		$1,500	+	$7,700	

SOLUTION

(1) An investment was made by the owner.

(2) Equipment was bought and *paid* for.

(3) Supplies were bought and *paid* for.

(4) Additional equipment was bought *on account*, thus creating the liability.

(5) Income from taxi fares was recorded.

(6) Salaries were paid to the company's drivers.

(7) Cash was paid to reduce the amount owed.

(8) Owner *withdrew* funds for his personal use.

1.14. Determine what accounts are affected, by how much, and if it is an increase (+), decrease (−), or there is no effect (0).

Nov. 5 Invested $7,000 cash and $400 of supplies into the business

7 Received $4,200 for services rendered

9 Purchased equipment on account, $3,700

11 Paid $750 for supplies

14 Paid salaries, $2,100

16 Paid $3,500 for land

17 Paid $2,000 on account from Nov. 9 transaction

19 Paid utilities, $200

20 Paid $300 for supplies and $700 for equipment

   21   Received $4,700 for services rendered
   25   Withdrew $2,000 cash for personal use
   30   Inventory of supplies showed $600 of supplies on hand

Record the effect of each transaction in the following table:

	Cash	Supplies	Equipment	Land	Accounts Payable	Capital
Nov. 5						
7						
9						
11						
14						
16						
17						
19						
20						
21						
25						
30						

SOLUTION

	Cash	Supplies	Equipment	Land	Accounts Payable	Capital
Nov. 5	+$7,000	+$400	0	0	0	+$7,400
7	+ 4,200	0	0	0	0	+ 4,200
9	0	0	+$3,700	0	+$3,700	0
11	− 750	+ 750	0	0	0	0
14	− 2,100	0	0	0	0	− 2,100
16	− 3,500	0	0	+$3,500	0	0
17	− 2,000	0	0	0	− 2,000	0
19	− 200	0	0	0	0	− 200
20	− 1,000	+ 300	+ 700	0	0	0
21	+ 4,700	0	0	0	0	+ 4,700
25	− 2,000	0	0	0	0	− 2,000
30	0	− 850	0	0	0	− 850

1.15. On June 1, Bob Friedland started his lawn care service. Listed below are the transactions for the month of June. Record the transactions on the blank form which follows.

June 1   Invested $2,200 cash and equipment with a book value of $3,500
      5   Received $375 for lawn care service
      7   Received $1,100 for lawn care service
    11   Purchased equipment for $2,000, paying $1,000 cash and giving a note for $1,000 for the remainder
    15   Paid gas bill, $275
    19   Withdrew $200 cash for personal use
    21   Purchased supplies for $100 on account
    25   Paid $400 on outstanding note (see June 11 transaction)
    30   Received $925 for lawn care service

Bob Friedland Lawn Care Service

	Cash +	Supplies +	Equipment =	Accounts Payable +	Notes Payable +	Capital
June 1						
June 5						
Balance						
June 7						
Balance						
June 11						
Balance						
June 15						
Balance						
June 19						
Balance						
June 21						
Balance						
June 25						
Balance						
June 30						
Balance						
June 30						

SOLUTION

Bob Friedland Lawn Care Service

	Cash +	Supplies	+ Equipment =	Accounts Payable +	Notes Payable +	Capital	
June 1	+$2,200		$3,500 =			+$5,700	
June 5	+ 375					+ 375	Lawn Income
Balance	$2,575		$3,500 =			$6,075	
June 7	+ 1,100					+ 1,100	Lawn Income
Balance	$3,675		$3,500 =			$7,175	
June 11	− 1,000		+ 2,000		+$1,000		
Balance	$2,675		$5,500 =		$1,000	$7,175	
June 15	− 275					− 275	Gas Expense
Balance	$2,400		$5,500 =		$1,000	$6,900	
June 19	− 200					− 200	Drawing
Balance	$2,200		$5,500 =		$1,000	$6,700	
June 21		+$100					
Balance	$2,200	$100	$5,500 =	$100	+$1,000	$6,700	
June 25	− 400				− 400		
Balance	$1,800	$100	$5,500 =	$100	$ 600	$6,700	
June 30	+ 925					+ 925	Lawn Income
Balance	$2,725	$100	$5,500 =	$100	$ 600	$7,625	
June 30							

1.16. The following transactions were engaged in during the month of March by Dr. Scott Braunstein:

(1) Opened his practice by investing $50,000 in the business

(2) Bought office equipment for $27,000 on account from Medical Products, Inc.

(3) Paid $2,000 for various medical supplies for the office

(4) Received $11,600 in fees earned during the first month of operations

(5) Paid office rent for the month, $900

(6) Paid medical assistant salary for the month, $1,800

(7) Paid Medical Products, Inc., $3,000 on account

(8) Withdrew $1,500 for personal use

Enter each transaction in the following form:

	Assets			=	Liabilities	+	Owner's Equity
	Cash	+ Supplies	+ Equipment	=	Accounts Payable	+	Capital
(1)							
(2)	_____	_____	_____		_____		_____
Balance							
(3)	_____	_____	_____		_____		_____
Balance							
(4)	_____	_____	_____		_____		_____
Balance							
(5)	_____	_____	_____		_____		_____
Balance							
(6)	_____	_____	_____		_____		_____
Balance							
(7)	_____	_____	_____		_____		_____
Balance							
(8)	_____	_____	_____		_____		_____
Balance							

SOLUTION

	Assets			=	Liabilities	+	Owner's Equity	
	Cash	+ Supplies	+ Equipment	=	Accounts Payable	+	Capital	
(1)	+$50,000			=			+$50,000	Investment
(2)			+$27,000		+$27,000			
Balance	$50,000		$27,000	=	$27,000		$50,000	
(3)	−2,000 +	+$2,000						
Balance	$48,000 +	$2,000 +	$27,000	=	$27,000	+	$50,000	
(4)	+11,600						+$11,600	Fees Income
Balance	$59,600 +	$2,000 +	$27,000	=	$27,000	+	$61,600	
(5)	−900						−900	Rent Expense
Balance	$58,700 +	$2,000 +	$27,000	=	$27,000	+	$60,700	
(6)	−1,800						−1,800	Salaries Expense
Balance	$56,900 +	$2,000 +	$27,000	=	$27,000	+	$58,900	
(7)	−3,000				−3,000			
Balance	$53,900 +	$2,000 +	$27,000	=	$24,000	+	$58,900	
(8)	−1,500						−1,500	Drawing
Balance	$52,400 +	$2,000 +	$27,000	=	$24,000	+	$57,400	

1.17. Summary financial data for the Nu-Look Dry Cleaning Co. for November are presented below in transaction form.

(1)   Opened a business bank account, depositing $12,000

(2)   Purchased supplies for cash, $220

(3)   Purchased dry cleaning equipment from Hill Cleaning Equipment, Inc., for $3,500, paying $1,500 in cash with the balance on account

(4)   Paid rent for the month, $825

(5)   Cash sales for the month totaled $1,850

(6)   Paid salaries of $375

(7)   Paid $500 on account to Hill Cleaning Equipment, Inc.

(8)   The cost of supplies used was determined to be $60.

   Record the transactions and running balances in the following form.

	Cash	+	**Assets** Supplies	+	Equipment	=	**Liabilities** Accounts Payable	+	**Owner's Equity** Nu-Look Capital
(1)									
(2)	____		____		____		____		____
Balance									
(3)	____		____		____		____		____
Balance									
(4)	____		____		____		____		____
Balance									
(5)	____		____		____		____		____
Balance									
(6)	____		____		____		____		____
Balance									
(7)	____		____		____		____		____
Balance									
(8)	____		____		____		____		____
Balance	════		════		════		════		════

SOLUTION

	Cash	+	**Assets** Supplies	+	Equipment	=	**Liabilities** Accounts Payable	+	**Owners' Equity** Nu-Look Capital	
(1)	$12,000					=			$12,000	Investment
(2)	−220	+	+$220							
Balance	$11,780	+	$220			=			$12,000	
(3)	−1,500	+			$3,500		+$2,000			
Balance	$10,280	+	$220	+	$3,500	=	$2,000	+	$12,000	
(4)	−825								−825	Rent Expense
Balance	$ 9,455	+	$220	+	$3,500	=	$2,000	+	$11,175	
(5)	+1,850								+1,850	Cleaning Income
Balance	$11,305	+	$220	+	$3,500	=	$2,000	+	$13,025	
(6)	−375								−375	Salaries Expense
Balance	$10,930	+	$220	+	$3,500	=	$2,000	+	$12,650	

(7)		−500						−500		
Balance	$10,430	+	$220	+	$3,500	=	$1,500	+	$12,650	
(8)			−60						−60	Supplies Expense
Balance	$10,430	+	$160	+	$3,500	=	$1,500	+	$12,590	

1.18. John Silver started the Good Cleaning Service on July 1, 19X8. Record the following transactions in the blank form which follows.

July 1 Started business; invested $10,000 cash and equipment with book value of $2,500
5 Purchased $300 of cleaning supplies on account
7 Received $2,700 for cleaning services (Fees Income)
9 Paid $200 of the $300 owed for purchase of cleaning supplies from July 5 transaction
13 Paid $810 rent for month
15 Paid employee 2 weeks' wages of $940 (Salaries Expense)
21 Purchased new cleaning machines for $3,000 on account
24 Withdrew $1,000 for personal use (use Drawing)
30 Took inventory; found he had $125 worth of supplies left ($300 − $175 = $125)

Good Cleaning Service

	Cash	+	Supplies	+	Equipment	=	Accounts Payable	+	Capital
July 1									
July 5									
Balance									
July 7									
Balance									
July 9									
Balance									
July 13									
Balance									
July 15									
Balance									
July 21									
Balance									
July 24									
Balance									
July 30									
Balance, July 31									

SOLUTION

Good Cleaning Service

	Cash	+	Supplies	+	Equipment	=	Accounts Payable	+	Capital	
July 1	+$10,000				+$2,500				+$12,500	
July 5			+$300				+$ 300			
Balance	$10,000		$300		$2,500		$ 300		$12,500	
July 7	+ 2,700								+ 2,700	Fees Income
Balance	$12,700		$300		$2,500		$ 300		$15,200	
July 9	– 200						– 200			
Balance	$12,500		$300		$2,500		$ 100		$15,200	Rent Expense
July 13	– 810								– 810	
Balance	$11,690		$300		$2,500		$ 100		$14,390	
July 15	– 940								– 940	Salaries Expense
Balance	$10,750		$300		$2,500		$ 100		$13,450	
July 21					+ 3,000		+ 3,000			
Balance	$10,750		$300		$5,500		$3,100		$13,450	
July 24	– 1,000								– 1,000	Drawing
Balance	$9,750		$300		$5,500		$3,100		$12,450	
July 30			– 175						+ 175	Supplies Expense
Balance, July 31	$9,750		$125	+	$5,500	=	$3,100	+	$12,275	

1.19 Rocco Burday operates a shoe repair shop known as the Repair Center. The balances of his accounts on June 1 of the current year were as follows:

Cash	$5,400
Supplies	600
Equipment	3,200
Accounts Payable	3,000
Capital	6,200

The transactions during the month of June appear below.

(1) Paid salaries of $350
(2) Paid creditors on account $2,000
(3) Bought additional equipment on account for $3,100
(4) Received cash from customers for repair service, $3,600
(5) Paid delivery expense, $140
(6) Inventory of supplies at the end of the month was $275
(7) Mr. Burday withdrew for his personal use $250

Record the transactions in the form provided.

	Assets			=	Liabilities +	Owner's Equity
	Cash +	Supplies +	Equipment		Accounts Payable +	R. Burday, Capital
Balance, June 1	$5,400	$600	$3,200		$3,000	$6,200
(1)	_____	_____	_____		_____	_____
Balance						
(2)	_____	_____	_____		_____	_____
Balance						
(3)	_____	_____	_____		_____	_____
Balance						
(4)	_____	_____	_____		_____	_____
Balance						
(5)	_____	_____	_____		_____	_____
Balance						
(6)	_____	_____	_____		_____	_____
Balance						
(7)	_____	_____	_____		_____	_____
Balance, June 30						

SOLUTION

	Assets			=	Liabilities +	Owner's Equity
	Cash +	Supplies +	Equipment		Accounts Payable +	R. Burday, Capital
Balance, June 1	$5,400 +	$600 +	$3,200	=	$3,000 +	$6,200
(1)	−350					−350 Salaries Expense
Balance	$5,050 +	$600 +	$3,200	=	$3,000 +	$5,850
(2)	−2,000				−2,000	
Balance	$3,050 +	$600 +	$3,200	=	$1,000 +	$5,850
(3)			+3,100		+3,100	
Balance	$3,050 +	$600 +	$6,300	=	$4,100 +	$5,850
(4)	+3,600					+3,600 Repair Income
Balance	$6,650 +	$600 +	$6,300	=	$4,100 +	$9,450
(5)	−140					−140 Delivery Expense
Balance	$6,510 +	$600 +	$6,300	=	$4,100 +	$9,310
(6)		−325*				−325 Supplies Expense
Balance	$6,510 +	$275 +	$6,300	=	$4,100 +	$8,985
(7)	−250					−250 Drawing
Balance, June 30	$6,260 +	$275 +	$6,300	=	$4,100 +	$8,735

*$600 (beginning inventory) − $275 (ending inventory) = $325 (amount used, or supplies expense).

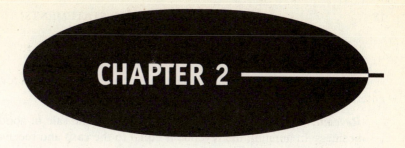

CHAPTER 2

Financial Statements

2.1 INTRODUCTION

The two principal questions that the owner of a business asks periodically are:

(1) What is my net income (profit)?

(2) What is my equity?

The simple balance of assets against liabilities and owner's equity, provided by the accounting equation, is insufficient to give complete answers. For (1) we must know the type and amount of income and the type and amount of each expense for the period in question. For (2) it is necessary to obtain the type and amount of each asset, liability, and owner's equity account at the end of the period. This information is provided by (1) the *income statement* and (2) the *balance sheet*.

EXAMPLE 1

After the transactions for the month of January have been recorded in the books of Mr. Alan Bagon (see Example 2 in Chap. 1), the accounts show the following balances:

Accounts	Assets	Liabilities and Owner's Equity
Cash	$4,700	
Supplies	100	
Equipment	2,500	
Accounts Payable		$1,500
A. Bagon, Capital		5,800
Total	$7,300	$7,300

It can be seen that the assets of the business changed from the original $5,000 invested by Mr. Bagon at the beginning of January to $7,300 at the end of January. Does that represent the amount of profit earned? It does not, because (1) liabilities have changed and (2) some of the transactions affecting capital were related to his investment; that is, he withdrew some of his original investment. It is apparent that his liabilities increased: They are now $1,500 more than the beginning liabilities (the balance due on the equipment).

His net assets or his capital is now $5,800, an increase of $800 over the beginning amount. That would represent his profit if he had not withdrawn some of his investment.

2.2 FINANCIAL STATEMENTS

(A) The Income Statement

The income statement may be defined as *a summary of the revenue, expenses, and net income or net loss of a business entity for a specific period of time*. This may also be called a profit and loss statement, operating statement, or statement of operations. Let us review the meanings of the elements entering into the income statement.

Revenue. The increase in capital resulting from the sale of goods or rendering of services by the business. In amount, the revenue is equal to the cash and receivables gained in compensation for the goods sold or services rendered.

Expenses. The decrease in capital caused by the business's revenue-producing operations. In amount, the expense is equal to the value of goods and services used up or consumed in obtaining revenue.

Net income. The increase in capital resulting from profitable operation of a business. It is the excess of revenues over expenses for the accounting period.

Net loss. The decrease in capital resulting from the operations of a business. It is the excess of expenses over revenue for the accounting period.

It is important to note that a cash receipt qualifies as revenue only if it serves to increase capital. Thus, for instance, borrowing cash from a bank does not contribute to revenue. Similarly, a cash payment is an expense only if it decreases capital.

EXAMPLE 2

Mr. A. Bagon's total January income and the totals for his various expenses can be obtained by analyzing the transactions shown under the heading "A. Bagon, Capital" in Example 2, Chap. 1. The income from fees amounted to $2,000, and the expenses incurred to produce this income were: rent, $500; salaries, $200; and supplies, $200. The formal income statement can now be prepared. Note that the heading of a financial statement answers the questions Who? What? and When? In the situation below, Who? (Alan Bagon), What? (Income Statement), and When? (month of January 19X8) are all answered.

Alan Bagon
Income Statement
Month of January 19X8

Fees Income		$2,000
Operating Expenses		
Rent Expense	$500	
Salaries Expense	200	
Supplies Expense	200	
Total Operating Expenses		900
Net Income		$1,100

In many companies there are hundreds and perhaps thousands of income and expense transactions in one month. To lump all these transactions under one account would be very cumbersome and would, in addition, make it impossible to show relationships among the various items. For example, we might wish to know the relationship of selling expenses to sales and whether the ratio is higher or lower than in previous periods. To solve this problem, we leave the investment or permanent entries in the capital account and then set up a *temporary* set of income and expense accounts. The net difference of these accounts, the net profit or net loss, is then transferred as one figure to the capital account.

Because an income statement pertains to a definite period of time, it becomes necessary to determine just *when* an item of revenue or expense is to be accounted for. Under the *accrual basis of accounting*, revenue is recognized only when earned and expense is recognized only when incurred. This differs significantly from the *cash basis of accounting*, which recognizes revenue and expense generally with the receipt and payment of cash. Essential to the accrual basis is the *matching* of expenses with the revenue that they helped produce. Under the accrual system, the accounts are adjusted at the end of the accounting period to properly reflect the revenue earned and the costs and expenses applicable to the period.

Most business firms use the accrual basis, while individuals and professional people generally use the cash basis. Ordinarily the cash basis is not suitable when there are significant amounts of inventories, receivables, and payables.

(B)   The Balance Sheet

The information needed for the balance sheet items is the net balances at the end of the period, rather than the total for the period as in the income statement. Thus, management wants to know the balance of cash in the bank and the balance of inventory, equipment, etc., on hand at the end of the period.

The balance sheet may then be defined as *a statement showing the assets, liabilities, and owner's equity of a business entity at a specific date*. This statement is also called a statement of financial position or statement of financial condition.

In preparing the balance sheet, it is not necessary to make any further analysis of the data. The needed data—that is, the balances of the asset, liability, and owner's equity accounts—are already available.

EXAMPLE 3   Report Form

Alan Bagon
Balance Sheet
January 31, 19X8

ASSETS			
Cash			$4,700
Supplies			100
Equipment			2,500
Total Assets			$7,300
LIABILITIES AND OWNER'S EQUITY			
Liabilities			
Accounts Payable			$1,500
Owner's Equity			
Balance, January 1, 19X8		$5,000	
Net Income for January	$1,100		
Less: Withdrawals	300		
Increase in Owner's Equity		800	
Total Owner's Equity			5,800
Total Liabilities and Owner's Equity			$7,300

The close relationship of the income statement and the balance sheet is apparent. The net income of $1,100 for January, shown as the final figure on the income statement of Example 2, is also shown as a separate figure on the balance sheet of Example 3. The income statement is thus the connecting link between two balance sheets. As discussed earlier, the income and expense items are actually a further analysis of the Capital account.

The balance sheet of Example 3 is arranged in *report form*, with the liabilities and owner's equity sections shown below the asset section. It may also be arranged in *account form*, with the liabilities and owner's equity sections to the right of, rather than below, the asset section, as shown in Example 4.

EXAMPLE 4   Account Form

Alan Bagon
Balance Sheet
January 31, 19X8

ASSETS			LIABILITIES AND OWNER'S EQUITY			
Cash	$4,700		Liabilities			
Supplies	100		Accounts Payable			$1,500
Equipment	2,500		Owner's Equity			
			Balance, January 31, 19X8		$5,000	
			Net Income for January	$1,100		
			Less: Withdrawals	300		
			Increase in Owner's Equity		800	
			Total Owner's Equity			5,800
Total Assets	$7,300		Total Liabilities and Owner's Equity			$7,300

(C)   The Statement of Owner's Equity

Instead of showing the details of the Capital account in the balance sheet, we may show the changes in a separate form called the Statement of Owner's Equity. This is the more common treatment.

EXAMPLE 5

Alan Bagon
Statement of Owner's Equity
Month of January 19X8

Capital, January 1, 19X8		$5,000
Add: Net Income	$1,100	
Less: Drawing	300	
Increase in Capital		800
Capital, January 31, 19X8		$5,800

(D)   Financial Statement Summary

The three financial statements from Examples 3, 4, and 5 are all interrelated and appear below in Example 6.

EXAMPLE 6

Income Statement

Fees Income		$2,000
Expenses		
Rent Expense	$ 500	
Salaries Expense	200	
Supplies Expense	200	
Total Expenses		900
Net Income		$1,100

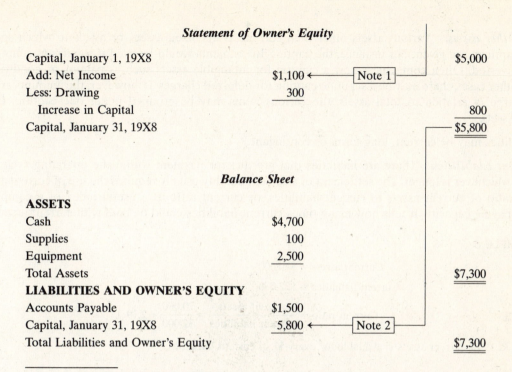

Statement of Owner's Equity

Capital, January 1, 19X8		$5,000
Add: Net Income	$1,100 ← Note 1	
Less: Drawing	300	
Increase in Capital		800
Capital, January 31, 19X8		$5,800

Balance Sheet

ASSETS

Cash	$4,700	
Supplies	100	
Equipment	2,500	
Total Assets		$7,300

LIABILITIES AND OWNER'S EQUITY

Accounts Payable	$1,500	
Capital, January 31, 19X8	5,800 ← Note 2	
Total Liabilities and Owner's Equity		$7,300

Note 1. The net income from the income statement, $1,100, is transferred to the statement of owner's equity.

Note 2. The capital is summarized in the statement of owner's equity and the final balance is included in the balance sheet.

2.3 CLASSIFIED FINANCIAL STATEMENTS: THE BALANCE SHEET

Financial statements become more useful when the individual items are classified into significant groups for comparison and financial analysis. The classifications relating to the balance sheet will be discussed in this section, while the classification of the income statement will be shown in Chap. 8.

The balance sheet becomes a more useful statement for comparison and financial analysis if the asset and liability groups are classified. For example, an important index of the financial state of a business, derivable from the classified balance sheet, is the ratio of current assets to current liabilities. This *current ratio* ought generally to be at least 2:1; that is, current assets should be twice current liabilities. For our purposes we will designate the following classifications.

Assets	**Liabilities**
Current	Current
Fixed	Long-term
Other	Contingent

Assets include the following:

Current assets. Assets reasonably expected to be converted into cash or used in the current operation of the business. (The current period is generally taken as 1 year.) Examples are cash, notes receivable, accounts receivable, inventory, and prepaid expenses (prepaid insurance, prepaid rent, etc.).

Fixed assets. Long-lived assets used in the production of goods or services. These assets, sometimes called *plant assets*, are used in the operation of the business rather than being held for sale, as are inventory items.

Other assets.   Various assets other than current assets, fixed assets, or assets to which specific captions are given. For instance, the caption Investments would be used if significant sums were invested. Often companies show a caption for intangible assets such as patents or goodwill. In other cases, there may be a separate caption for deferred charges. If, however, the amounts are not large in relation to total assets, the various items may be grouped under one caption, Other Assets.

Liabilities may be current, long-term, or contingent.

Current Liabilities.   There are liabilities that are due for payment within the operating cycle or 1 year, whichever is longer. The settlement of a current liability usually requires the use of current assets. The ratio of current assets to current liabilities, or current ratio, is a useful index of a company's debt-paying capacity. It tells how many times current liabilities could be paid with current assets.

EXAMPLE 8

$$\text{Current assets} = \$70,000$$

$$\text{Current liabilities} = \$32,000$$

$$\text{Current ratio} = \frac{\text{current assets}}{\text{current liabilities}} = \frac{70,000}{32,000} = 2.19:1$$

Thus, $2.19 of current assets is available for every $1 of current liabilities.

Following are the seven principal types of current liabilities.

1. *Notes payable.* Liabilities evidenced by a written promise to pay at a later date.

2. *Accounts payable.* Liabilities for goods or services purchased on account, trade payables, and also nontrade obligations.

3. *Accrued liabilities.* Liabilities that have accumulated but are not yet due, as payment does not coincide with the end of the period. These are *expenses* and are shown on the income statement under

Salaries and Wages	Payroll Taxes
Commissions	Sales Taxes
Insurance	Income Taxes
Interest	Pensions
Property Taxes	Royalties

4. *Withholdings.* Amounts that have been withheld from employees' pay and are to be turned over to government agencies, insurance companies, etc. These are *not* expenses of the company but must be properly safeguarded until they are transmitted to the specified agency. These include income taxes, social security taxes, unemployment taxes, hospitalization, group insurance, and pensions.

5. *Dividends payable.* Dividends become payable only as declared by the board of directors of the company. They do not accrue, or accumulate, as does interest on bonds.

6. *Unearned revenues.* Sometimes revenue is received in advance, such as magazine subscriptions or rent. These are liabilities, as they represent claims against the enterprise. Generally they are settled by delivery of goods or services in the next accounting period. Where these are long-term advances extending well beyond the next period, they should be classed on the balance sheet as noncurrent.

7. *Portion of long-term debt.* The portion of long-term debt payable in the next 12 months should be included in the current liabilities category. This includes amounts due on bonds, mortgages, or long-term notes.

Long-Term Liabilities.   Where funds are needed for a long-term purpose such as construction of a building, a long-term liability account would be used. Presumably, increased earnings would be used to retire the debt. Almost always, long-term liabilities are interest-bearing and have a fixed due date.

Following are the principal types of long-term liabilities:

1. ***Long-term notes payable.*** The company may be able to obtain the needed amount from one lender rather than by issuing bonds for sale to the public. Sometimes notes may be issued to await better terms for issuing bonds.

2. ***Mortgages payable.*** The terms of a mortgage generally pledge the property of the company as security. The mortgage involves a lien on the property, not a transfer of title.

3. ***Bonds payable.*** If the amount of funds needed is larger than a single lender can supply, bonds may be sold to the investing public, splitting the loan into thousands of units. A bond is a written promise to pay the face amount, generally $1,000, at a future date and to make interest payments semiannually at a stipulated rate of interest. Interest payments on bonds are deductible as expense for income tax purposes, but dividends paid on preferred or common stock are not. This is an important consideration in deciding whether to use stocks or bonds for long-term financing.

Contingent Liabilities.   These are potential liabilities arising from past events. For example, when a note receivable is endorsed and transferred to another person, no liability is created. However, there is a possibility that a liability could exist in the future, because the maker of the note might not honor it. If that were to happen, the business that endorsed the note would be required to make payment. Some other examples of contingent liabilities are additional tax assessments, product guarantees, pending lawsuits, and litigation.

It is not necessary to prepare an entry until the potential liability becomes an actuality. However, it cannot be ignored. Therefore, a contingent liability should be reflected in the balance sheet in a footnote describing the possibility of the loss. This will give the reader a more accurate picture of the financial position of the firm.

Example 10 shows a classified balance sheet of typical form, based upon the information in the statement of owner's equity in Example 9.

EXAMPLE 9

J. Ales
Statement of Owner's Equity

J. Ales, Capital, January 1		$4,750
Net Income for the year	$3,000	
Less: Withdrawals	2,000	
Increase in Capital		1,000
J. Ales, Capital, December 31		$5,750

EXAMPLE 10

J. Ales
Balance Sheet

ASSETS

Current Assets

Cash	$5,400	
Accounts Receivable	1,600	
Supplies	500	$ 7,500
Total Current Assets		

Fixed Assets

Land	$4,000	
Building	8,000	
Equipment	2,000	
Total Fixed Assets		14,000
Total Assets		$21,500

LIABILITIES AND OWNER'S EQUITY

Current Liabilities

Notes Payable	$1,750	
Accounts Payable	2,000	
Total Current Liabilities		$ 3,750
Long-Term Liabilities		
Mortgage Payable		12,000
Total Liabilities		$15,750
Capital, December 31		5,750
Total Liabilities and Owner's Equity		$21,500

Corporate Equity Section

Although covered in part in Chap. 11 and fully in Accounting II, it is important to mention the corporation's equity section. A corporation is a legal entity organized in accordance with state or federal laws, with ownership represented by shares of stock. The applicable laws require that a distinction be made between the amount invested in a corporation by its owners (stockholders) and the subsequent changes due to profits or losses. Because of these requirements, the stockholders' equity is shown in at least two parts. If there is more than one class of stock, such as preferred and common, there may be more parts in the stockholders' equity section.

STOCKHOLDERS' EQUITY

Capital Stock	$100,000	
Retained Earnings	25,000	$125,000

The principal equity accounts for a corporation are those for capital stock, dividends, and retained earnings, but that is a discussion for Chap. 11.

RULES GOVERNING THE BALANCE SHEET

Clearly, such rules must exist, for otherwise it would be necessary to state for each financial statement the specific assumptions used in preparing it. Over the years, certain principles have been developed on the basis of experience, reason, custom, and practical necessity. We call these *generally accepted accounting principles*, better known as GAAP.

Business entity. Accounts are kept for business entities rather than for the persons who own or are associated with the business.

Continuity. Unless there is strong evidence to the contrary, it is assumed that the business will continue to operate as a going concern. If it were not to continue, then liquidation values, generally much lower, would apply.

Unit of measure. It is assumed that the most practical unit of measure is money and that changes in investment and income will be measured in money. So far, no better unit of measure has been found.

Time period. An essential function of accounting is to provide information for decision making. To accomplish this, it is necessary to establish accounting periods, or systematic time intervals, so that timely accounting data can be developed.

Cost. The properties and services acquired by an enterprise are generally recorded at cost (the cash or its equivalent given to acquire the property or service). The cost is spread over the accounting periods that benefit from the expenditure.

Revenue. Revenue relates to the output of goods and services. In most cases revenue is recognized when goods are delivered or services rendered. In some cases revenue is recognized (1) during production, (2) when production is completed, or (3) when cash is collected.

Matching. In determining the proper periodic income, it is necessary to match related costs and expenses to revenue for the period. The cost of the product sold and all expenses incurred in producing the sale should be matched against the revenue.

Objectivity. Accounting entries should be based on objective evidence to the fullest extent possible. Business documents originating outside the firm provide the best evidence. Estimates should be supported by verifiable objective data.

Consistency. A standard method of treatment is necessary if periodic financial statements are to be compared with one another. Where a different method will state results and financial position more fairly, the change may be made if the effect on the statements is clearly disclosed.

Disclosure. Financial statements and notes to financial statements should contain all relevant data of a material nature. They should disclose such things as a change in accounting methods, contingent liabilities, etc.

Materiality. The accountant must be practical and must consider the relative importance of data. The decision as to what is material and what is unimportant requires judgment rather than inflexible rules.

Conservatism. Accountants necessarily make many value judgments that affect financial statements. In these judgments, it is desirable that they provide for all possible losses and not anticipate profits as yet unrealized.

Summary

1. The income statement and balance sheet are known as _____ .

2. The statement that shows net income for the period is known as the _____ statement.

3. The statement that shows net loss for the period is known as the _____ statement.

4.   Two groups of items on the income statement are _____ and _____ .

5.   The difference between income and expense is known as _____ .

6.   Withdrawal of money by the owner is not an expense but a reduction of _____ .

7.   To show the change in the owner's equity of a business, the statement of _____ is used.

8.   The balance sheet contains _____ , _____ , and _____ .

9.   Assets must equal _____ .

10.   Expense and income must be matched in the same _____ .

Answers: 1. accounting statements; 2. income; 3. income; 4. income, expense; 5. net income; 6. capital; 7. owner's equity; 8. assets, liabilities, owner's equity; 9. liabilities and owner's equity; 10. year or period

Solved Problems

2.1.   Prepare an income statement based on the following information: Fees Income, $38,000; Supplies Expense, $16,000; Salaries Expense, $12,000; Miscellaneous Expense, $7,000.

SOLUTION

Income Statement		
Fees Income		$38,000
Expenses		
Supplies Expense	$16,000	
Salaries Expense	12,000	
Miscellaneous Expense	7,000	
Total Expenses		35,000
Net Income		$ 3,000

2.2. Based on Prob. 2.1, what would the net income or net loss be if, in addition to the listed expenses, there was an additional expense of $5,000 charged to Rent?

SOLUTION

Income Statement		
Fees Income		$38,000
Expenses		
Supplies Expense	$16,000	
Salaries Expense	12,000	
Rent Expense	5,000	
Miscellaneous Expense	7,000	
Total Expenses		40,000
Net Loss		$ 2,000

Note: When expenses exceed income, a net loss results. This will have the effect of reducing capital.

2.3. The following information was taken from an income statement: Fees Income, $14,000; Rent Expense, $2,000; Salaries Expense, $5,000; Miscellaneous Expense, $1,000. If the owner withdrew $2,000 from the firm, what is the increase or decrease in capital?

SOLUTION

There are two steps to solving this problem:

1. Prepare an income statement.
2. Determine increases or decreases in capital by subtracting the drawing (withdrawal) from the net income.

Fees Income		$14,000
Expenses		
Rent Expense	$2,000	
Salaries Expense	5,000	
Miscellaneous Expense	1,000	
Total Expenses		8,000
Net Income		$ 6,000
Net Income	$6,000	
Drawing	2,000	
Increase in Capital	$4,000	

2.4. Based on the information in Prob. 2.3, if the withdrawal were $9,000 instead of $2,000, what would the increase (decrease) become?

SOLUTION

If the withdrawal is larger than the net income, a decrease in capital will result.

Net Income	$6,000
Drawing	9,000
Decrease in Capital	$3,000

2.5. If the Capital account has a balance on January 1 of $32,000, what will be the balance on December 31 (*a*) based on Prob. 2.3? (*b*) based on Prob. 2.4?

SOLUTION

(*a*)	Capital, January 1		$32,000
	Net Income	$6,000	
	Less: Drawing	2,000	
	Increase in Capital		4,000
	Capital, December 31		$36,000
(*b*)	Capital, January 1		$32,000
	Net Income	$6,000	
	Less: Drawing	9,000	
	Decrease in Capital		3,000
	Capital, December 31		$29,000

2.6. Based on the following information, determine the capital as of December 31, 19X8: Net Income for period, $18,000; Drawing, $6,000; Capital (January 1, 19X8), $20,000.

SOLUTION

Capital, January 1, 19X8		$20,000
Net Income	$18,000	
Less: Drawing	6,000	
Increase in Capital		12,000
Capital, December 31, 19X8		$32,000

2.7. Based on the following information, determine the capital as of December 31: Capital (January 1), $26,000; Net Income, $18,000; Drawing, $20,000.

SOLUTION

Capital, January 1		$26,000
Net Income	$18,000	
Drawing	20,000	
Decrease in Capital		2,000
Capital, December 31		$24,000

Note: It is possible to withdraw more than net income, provided that your beginning capital has an adequate balance. This will result in a decrease in capital, which will be subtracted from the beginning capital.

2.8. Determine the capital as of December 31, given the following information: Capital (January 1), $30,000; Net Loss for period, $18,000; Drawing, $4,000.

SOLUTION

Capital, January 1		$30,000
Net Loss	$18,000	
Drawing	4,000	
Decrease in Capital		22,000
Capital, December 31		$ 8,000

2.9. Based on the following information, determine the capital on December 31:

Cash	$6,000
Supplies	400
Equipment	8,000
Accounts Payable	4,500
Notes Payable	2,500

SOLUTION

ASSETS		LIABILITIES AND OWNER'S EQUITY	
Cash	$ 6,000	Accounts Payable	$ 4,500
Supplies	400	Notes Payable	2,500
Equipment	8,000	Total Liabilities	$ 7,000
		Capital	7,400*
Total Assets	$14,400	Total Liabilities and Owner's Equity	$14,400

*$14,400(Assets) − $7,000(Liabilities) = $7,400(Owner's Equity).

2.10. Selected accounts of the Ruez Company produced the following balances:

	January 1	January 31
Assets	$16,000	$19,000
Liabilities	4,000	3,000

What was the net income of the firm, assuming that there were no withdrawals?

SOLUTION

Capital, January 1	$12,000*
Capital, January 31	16,000**
Increase in Capital	$ 4,000

Because there was no drawing, $4,000 must also be the net income, because net income minus drawing equals increase in capital.

*($16,000 − $4,000). Based on the concept assets − liabilities = owner's equity.
**($19,000 − $3,000). Based on the concept, assets − liabilities = owner's equity.

2.11. Based on the information in Prob. 2.10, determine the net income if $1,500 was withdrawn from the company.

SOLUTION

Capital, January 1	$12,000
Capital, January 31	16,000
Increase in Capital	$ 4,000

We know that net income − drawing = increase in capital.
Therefore, net income − $1,500 = $4,000. Net income must be $5,500.

2.12. Below are the financial statements for Lucky Dip Ice Cream Consulting. Certain key figures have been left out. Place the correct amount needed in each of the blanks.

Lucky Dip Ice Cream Consulting		
Income Statement		
Year Ended December 31, 19X8		
Fees Income		66,700
Operating Expenses		
Wages Expense	$31,500	
Rent Expense	7,200	
Supplies Expense	700	
Miscellaneous Expense	900	
Total Operating Expenses		(*a*)
Net Income		(*b*)

Lucky Dip Ice Cream Consulting		
Statement of Owner's Equity		
Year Ended December 31, 19X8		
Capital, January 1, 19X8		$18,000
Net Income for the Year	(*c*)	
Less: Withdrawals	$20,000	
Increase in Capital		(*d*)
Capital, December 31, 19X8		(*e*)

Lucky Dip Ice Cream Consulting		
Balance Sheet		
December 31, 19X8		
ASSETS		
Current Assets		
Cash	$11,000	
Accounts Receivable	(*f*)	
Supplies	5,700	
Total Current Assets		$29,700
LIABILITIES		
Accounts Payable	$2,500	
Notes Payable	2,800	
Total Liabilities		(*g*)
OWNER'S EQUITY		
John Sweet, Capital		(*h*)
Total Liabilities and Owner's Equity		(*i*)

SOLUTION

(a) $40,300

(b) $26,400

(c) See Net Income from income statement

(d) $6,400

(e) $24,400

(f) $13,000

(g) $5,300

(h) $24,400 (John Sweet, Capital, December 31, 19X8)

(i) $29,700

2.13. Prepare a statement of owner's equity and balance sheet as of December 31, 19X8, from the following data:

Accounts Payable	$ 3,000
Cash	4,000
Equipment	16,000
Notes Payable	12,000
Supplies	200
Net Income	11,400
Drawing	10,200
Capital, January 1, 19X8	4,000

Statement of Owner's Equity		
Capital, January 1, 19X8		
Net Income		
Drawing		
Increase in Capital		
Capital, December 31, 19X8		

Balance Sheet		
ASSETS		
Cash		
Supplies		
Equipment		
Total Assets		
LIABILITIES AND OWNER'S EQUITY		
Notes Payable		
Accounts Payable		
Total Liabilities		
Capital, December 31, 19X8		
Total Liabilities and Owner's Equity		

SOLUTION

Statement of Owner's Equity		$ 4,000
Capital, January 1, 19X8	$11,400	
Net Income	10,200	
Drawing		1,200
Increase in Capital		$ 5,200
Capital, December 31, 19X8		

Balance Sheet		
ASSETS		
Cash		$ 4,000
Supplies		200
Equipment		16,000
Total Assets		$20,200
LIABILITIES AND OWNER'S EQUITY		
Notes Payable	$12,000	
Accounts Payable	3,000	
Total Liabilities		$15,000
Capital, December 31, 19X8		5,200
Total Liabilities and Owner's Equity		$20,200

2.14. Classify the following accounts by placing a check mark in the appropriate column.

		Current Asset	Fixed Asset	Current Liability	Long-Term Liability
(1)	Accounts Receivable				
(2)	Accounts Payable				
(3)	Notes Payable				
(4)	Mortgage Payable				
(5)	Cash				
(6)	Supplies				
(7)	Salaries Payable				
(8)	Bonds Payable				
(9)	Equipment				
(10)	Land				

SOLUTION

		Current Asset	Fixed Asset	Current Liability	Long-Term Liability
(1)	Accounts Receivable	✓			
(2)	Accounts Payable			✓	
(3)	Notes Payable			✓	
(4)	Mortgage Payable				✓
(5)	Cash	✓			
(6)	Supplies	✓			
(7)	Salaries Payable			✓	
(8)	Bonds Payable				✓
(9)	Equipment		✓		
(10)	Land		✓		

2.15. From the information that follows, prepare a classified balance sheet as of December 31.

Cash	$ 6,000
Accounts Receivable	3,000
Supplies	1,000
Equipment	14,000
Accounts Payable	2,500
Notes Payable	1,500
Mortgage Payable	12,000
Capital, December 31	8,000

ASSETS		
Current Assets		
Total Current Assets		
Fixed Assets		
Total Assets		
LIABILITIES AND OWNER'S EQUITY		
Current Liabilities		
Total Current Liabilities		
Long-Term Liabilities		
Total Liabilities		
Capital		
Total Liabilities and Owner's Equity		

SOLUTION

ASSETS		
Current Assets		
Cash	$6,000	
Accounts Receivable	3,000	
Supplies	1,000	
Total Current Assets		$10,000
Fixed Assets		
Equipment		14,000
Total Assets		$24,000
LIABILITIES AND OWNER'S EQUITY		
Current Liabilities		
Notes Payable	$1,500	
Accounts Payable	2,500	
Total Current Liabilities		$ 4,000
Long-Term Liabilities		
Mortgage Payable		12,000
Total Liabilities		$16,000
Capital		8,000
Total Liabilities and Owner's Equity		$24,000

2.16. What is the current ratio in Prob. 2.15?

SOLUTION

$$\text{Total current assets} = \$10,000$$
$$\text{Total current liabilities} = \$4,000$$
$$\frac{10,000}{4,000} = 2.5:1$$

The firm has $2.50 in current assets for every $1 in current liabilities.

2.17. Complete the chart by writing in the appropriate column the name of the account group in which the particular account belongs and check the appropriate column for the classification of each balance sheet item.

	Income Statement	Balance Sheet	Current Asset	Fixed Asset	Current Liability	Long-Term Liability
Accounts Payable						
Accounts Receivable						
Advertising Expense						
Cash						
Capital						
Equipment						
Fees Income						
Machinery						
Mortgage Payable						
Notes Receivable						
Other Income						
Salaries Expense						
Supplies						
Supplies Expense						

SOLUTION

	Income Statement	Balance Sheet	Current Asset	Fixed Asset	Current Liability	Long-Term Liability
Accounts Payable		Liability			✓	
Accounts Receivable		Asset	✓			
Advertising Expense	Expense					
Cash		Asset	✓			
Capital		Owner's Equity				
Equipment		Asset		✓		
Fees Income	Income					
Machinery		Asset		✓		
Mortgage Payable		Liability				✓
Notes Receivable		Asset	✓			
Other Income	Income					
Salaries Expense	Expense					
Supplies		Asset	✓			
Supplies Expense	Expense					

2.18. Prepare (*a*) an income statement and (*b*) a balance sheet, using the data of Prob. 1.16.

(*a*)

Dr. S. Braunstein		
Income Statement		
Month of March		

(*b*)

Dr. S. Braunstein		
Balance Sheet		
March 31		
ASSETS		
LIABILITIES AND OWNER'S EQUITY		

SOLUTION

(a)

Dr. S. Braunstein		
Income Statement		
Month of March		
Fees Income		$11,600
Expenses		
Rent Expense	$ 900	
Salaries Expense	1,800	
Total Expenses		2,700
Net Income		$ 8,900

(b)

Dr. S. Braunstein		
Balance Sheet		
March 31		
ASSETS		
Cash	$52,400	
Supplies	2,000	
Equipment	27,000	
Total Assets		$81,400
LIABILITIES AND OWNER'S EQUITY		
Accounts Payable	$24,000	
Capital	57,400*	
Total Liabilities and Owner's Equity		$81,400

*If a statement of owner's equity is not required, capital is computed as follows:

Capital (beginning)		$50,000
Add: Net Income	$8,900	
Less: Drawing	1,500	
Increase in Capital		7,400
Capital (ending)		$57,400

2.19. Below are the account balances as of December 31, 19X8, of Mr. R. Gregg, owner of a movie theater.

Accounts Payable	$11,400
Admissions Income	34,200
Capital, January 1, 19X8	16,000
Cash	7,500
Drawing	5,400
Equipment	18,500
Film Rental Expense	6,000
Miscellaneous Expense	4,000
Notes Payable	1,000
Rent Expense	10,000
Salaries Expense	7,000
Supplies	4,200

Prepare (a) an income statement, (b) a statement of owner's equity, (c) a balance sheet.

(a)

R. Gregg		
Income Statement		
Year Ended December 31, 19X8		

(b)

R. Gregg		
Statement of Owner's Equity		
Year Ended December 31, 19X8		

(c)

R. Gregg		
Balance Sheet		
December 31, 19X8		

SOLUTION

(a)

R. Gregg		
Income Statement		
Year Ended December 31, 19X8		
Income		$34,200
Expenses		
Rent Expense	$10,000	
Salaries Expense	7,000	
Film Rental Expense	6,000	
Miscellaneous Expense	4,000	
Total Expenses		27,000
Net Income		$ 7,200

(b) The statement of owner's equity is needed to show the capital balance at the end of the year. Mr. Gregg's capital balance above is the balance at the beginning. Net income increases capital, and drawing reduces capital.

R. Gregg		
Statement of Owner's Equity		
Year Ended December 31, 19X8		
Capital, January 1, 19X8		$16,000
Add: Net Income	$ 7,200	
Less: Drawing	5,400	
Increase in Capital		1,800
Capital, December 31, 19X8		$17,800

(c)

R. Gregg		
Balance Sheet		
December 31, 19X8		
ASSETS		
Cash	$ 7,500	
Supplies	4,200	
Equipment	18,500	
Total Assets		$30,200
LIABILITIES AND OWNER'S EQUITY		
Accounts Payable	$11,400	
Notes Payable	1,000	
Total Liabilities		$12,400
Capital		17,800
Total Liabilities and Owner's Equity		$30,200

2.20. Listed below are the year-end balances of the Sun Shine Service Company, which is owned by Mort Sunshine. Prepare the year-end classified financial statements.

Fees	$37,600
Wages Expense	17,400
Rent Expense	9,300
Drawing	4,000
Supplies Expense	7,200
Miscellaneous Expense	750
Cash	11,600
Capital, January 1, 19X8	17,100
Accounts Receivable	7,400
Supplies	1,300
Prepaid Insurance	1,200
Land (fixed asset)	4,200
Equipment (fixed asset)	3,700
Accounts Payable	2,950
Notes Payable	6,150
Mortgage Payable (long-term)	4,250

Sun Shine Service Company		
Income Statement		
Year Ended December 31, 19X8		

Sun Shine Service Company		
Statement of Owner's Equity		
Year Ended December 31, 19X8		

Sun Shine Service Company		
Balance Sheet		
December 31, 19X8		
ASSETS		
LIABILITIES		
OWNER'S EQUITY		

SOLUTION

Sun Shine Service Company		
Income Statement		
Year Ended December 31, 19X8		
Fees Income		$37,600
Operating Expenses		
Wages Expense	$17,400	
Rent Expense	9,300	
Supplies Expense	7,200	
Miscellaneous Expense	750	
Total Expenses		34,650
Net Income		$ 2,950

Sun Shine Service Company		
Statement of Owner's Equity		
Year Ended December 31, 19X8		
Capital, January 1, 19X8		$17,100
Net Income for the Year	$ 2,950	
Less: Withdrawals	4,000	
Decrease in Capital		1,050
Capital, December 31, 19X8		$16,050

Sun Shine Service Company		
Balance Sheet		
December 31, 19X8		
ASSETS		
Current Assets		
Cash	$11,600	
Accounts Receivable	7,400	
Supplies	1,300	
Prepaid Insurance	1,200	
Total Current Assets		$21,500
Fixed Assets		
Land	$ 4,200	
Equipment	3,700	
Total Fixed Assets		7,900
Total Assets		$29,400
LIABILITIES		
Current Liabilities		
Accounts Payable	$ 2,950	
Notes Payable	6,150	
Total Current Liabilities		$ 9,100
Long-Term Liabilities		
Mortgage Payable		4,250
Total Liabilities		$13,350
OWNER'S EQUITY		
Mort Sunshine, Capital		16,050
Total Liabilities and Owner's Equity		$29,400

2.21. The balances of the accounts of Dr. J. Hoflich, Dentist, appear as follows:

Accounts Payable	$ 2,800
Accounts Receivable	3,600
Building	12,000
Capital, January 1, 19X8	19,000

Cash	12,200
Dental Income	38,000
Drawing	6,000
Equipment	15,000
Furniture	3,000
Mortgage Payable	10,000
Miscellaneous Expense	2,000
Notes Payable	2,000
Supplies	6,000
Salaries Expense	8,000
Supplies Expense	4,000

Using the forms provided below, prepare (*a*) an income statement, (*b*) a statement of owner's equity, and (*c*) a classified balance sheet.

(*a*)

Dr. J. Hoflich		
Income Statement		
Year Ended December 31, 19X8		
Income from fees		
Expenses		
Total Expenses		
Net Income		

(*b*)

Dr. J. Hoflich		
Statement of Owner's Equity		
Year Ended December 31, 19X8		
Capital, January 1, 19X8		
Add: Net Income		
Less: Drawing		
Increase in Capital		
Capital, December 131, 19X8		

(c)

Dr. J. Hoflich Balance Sheet December 31, 19X8		
ASSETS		
Current Assets		
Total Current Assets		
Fixed Assets		
Total Fixed Assets		
Total Assets		
LIABILITIES AND OWNER'S EQUITY		
Current Liabilities		
Total Current Liabilities		
Long-Term Liabilities		
Total Liabilities		
Capital		
Total Liabilities and Owner's Equity		

SOLUTION

(a)

Dr. J. Hoflich Income Statement Year Ended December 31, 19X8		
Income from Fees		$38,000
Expenses		
Salaries Expense	$ 8,000	
Supplies Expense	4,000	
Miscellaneous Expense	2,000	
Total Expenses		14,000
Net Income		$24,000

(b)

Dr. J. Hoflich		
Statement of Owner's Equity		
Year Ended December 31, 19X8		
Capital, January 1, 19X8		$19,000
Add: Net Income	$24,000	
Less: Drawing	6,000	
Increase in Capital		18,000
Capital, December 31, 19X8		$37,000

(c)

Dr. J. Hoflich		
Balance Sheet		
December 31, 19X8		
ASSETS		
Current Assets		
Cash	$12,200	
Accounts Receivable	3,600	
Supplies	6,000	
Total Current Assets		$21,800
Fixed Assets		
Building	$12,000	
Equipment	15,000	
Furniture	3,000	
Total Fixed Assets		30,000
Total Assets		$51,800
LIABILITIES AND OWNER'S EQUITY		
Current Liabilities		
Accounts Payable	$ 2,800	
Notes Payable	2,000	
Total Current Liabilities		$ 4,800
Long-Term Liabilities		
Mortgage Payable		10,000
Total Liabilities		$14,800
Capital		37,000
Total Liabilities and Owner's Equity		$51,800

CHAPTER 3

Analyzing and Classifying Transactions

3.1 INTRODUCTION

Preparing a new equation $A = L + OE$ after each transaction would be cumbersome and costly, especially when there are a great many transactions in an accounting period. Also, information about a specific item, such as cash, would be lost as successive transactions were recorded. This information could be obtained by going back and summarizing the transactions, but that would be very time-consuming.

A much more efficient way is to classify the transactions according to items on the balance sheet and income statement. The increases and decreases are then recorded according to type of item by means of a summary called an *account*.

3.2 THE ACCOUNT

A separate account is maintained for each item that appears on the balance sheet (assets, liabilities, and owner's equity), and on the income statement (revenue and expense). Thus an account may be defined as *a record of the increases, decreases, and balances in an individual item of asset, liability, owner's equity, revenue, or expense.*

The simplest form of the account is known as the "T" account because it resembles the letter "T". The account has three parts: (1) the name of the account and the account number, (2) the debit side (left side), and (3) the credit side (right side). The increases are entered on one side, the decreases on the other. Which change goes on which side will be discussed in Sec. 3.3. The balance (the excess of the total of one side over the total of the other) is inserted near the last figure on the side with the larger amount.

EXAMPLE 1

		Cash	
	700		600
	400		200
	600		
900	1,700		800

Note that the left side of the account adds up to $1,700 while the right side totals $800. The $1,700 and $800 totals, respectively, are written in smaller type and are known as footings. The difference between the total amounts is $900 and is called the ending balance. Since the larger total, $1,700, appears on the left side of the account, the ending balance of $900 is placed there. Had the right side total been greater than the left, the ending balance would have appeared on the right side.

3.3 DEBITS AND CREDITS: THE DOUBLE-ENTRY SYSTEM

When an amount is entered on the left side of an account, it is a *debit* and the account is said to be *debited*. When an amount is entered on the right side, it is a *credit* and the account is said to be *credited*. The abbreviations for debit and credit are Dr. and Cr., respectively.

Whether an increase in a given item is credited or debited depends on the category of the item. By convention, asset and expense increases are recorded as debits, whereas liability, capital, and income increases are recorded as credits. Asset and expense decreases are recorded as credits, whereas liability, capital, and income decreases are recorded as debits. The following tables summarize the rule.

Assets and Expenses		Liabilities, Owner's Equity, and Income	
Dr.	Cr.	Dr.	Cr.
+	−	−	+
(Increases)	(Decreases)	(Decreases)	(Increases)

EXAMPLE 2

Let us reexamine the transactions that occurred in Mr. Bagon's law firm during the first month of operation. These are the same as in Chap. 1, except that accounts are now used to record the transactions.

Transaction (1). **Mr. Bagon opened his law practice, investing $5,000 in cash.** The two accounts affected are Cash and Capital. Remember that an increase in an asset (cash) is debited, whereas an increase in capital is credited.

Cash		Capital	
Dr.	Cr.	Dr.	Cr.
+	−	−	+
(1) 5,000			5,000 (1)

Transaction (2). **Bought supplies for cash, $300.** Here we are substituting one asset (cash) for another asset (supplies). We debit Supplies, because we are receiving more supplies. We credit Cash, because we are paying out cash.

Cash		Supplies	
Dr.	Cr.	Dr.	Cr.
+	−	+	−
5,000	300 (2)	(2) 300	

Transaction (3). **Bought equipment from Altway Furniture Company on account, $2,500.** We are receiving an asset (equipment), and therefore we debit Equipment to show the increase. We are not paying cash, but creating a new liability, thereby increasing the liability account Accounts Payable.

Equipment		Accounts Payable	
Dr.	Cr.	Dr.	Cr.
+	−	−	+
(3) 2,500			2,500 (3)

Transaction (4).   Received $2,000 in fees earned during the month. In this case, we are increasing the asset account Cash, as we have received $2,000. Therefore, we debit it. We are increasing the owner's equity, yet we do not credit Capital. It is better temporarily to separate the income from the capital and create a new account, Fees Income (revenue).

Cash		Fees Income	
Dr.	Cr.	Dr.	Cr.
+	−	−	+
5,000	300		2,000 (4)
(4) 2,000			

Transaction (5).   Paid office rent for January, $500. We must decrease the asset account Cash, because we are paying out money. Therefore, we credit it. It is preferable to keep expenses separated from capital. Therefore, we open a new account for the expense involved, Rent Expense. The $500 is entered on the left side, as expenses decrease owner's equity.

Cash		Rent Expense	
Dr.	Cr.	Dr.	Cr.
+	−	+	−
5,000	300	(5) 500	
2,000	500 (5)		

Transaction (6).   Paid salary for part-time help, $200. Again, we must reduce our asset account Cash because we are paying out money. Therefore, we credit the account. Bagon's owner's equity was reduced by an expense, and we open another account, Salaries Expense. A debit to this account shows the decrease in owner's equity.

Cash		Salaries Expense	
Dr.	Cr.	Dr.	Cr.
+	−	+	−
5,000	300	(6) 200	
2,000	500		
	200 (6)		

Transaction (7).   Paid $1,000 to Altway Furniture Company, on account. This transaction reduced our asset account (Cash), since we are paying out money. We therefore credit Cash. We also reduce our liability account Accounts Payable by $1,000; we now owe that much less. Thus, we debit Accounts Payable.

Cash		Accounts Payable	
Dr.	Cr.	Dr.	Cr.
+	−	−	+
5,000	300	(7) 1,000	2,500
2,000	500		
	200		
	1,000 (7)		

Transaction (8). **After taking inventory at the end of the month, Mr. Bagon found that he had used $200 worth of supplies.** We must reduce the asset account Supplies by crediting it for $200. Supplies Expense is debited for the decrease in owner's equity. This is computed as follows: beginning inventory of $300, less supplies on hand at the end of the month $100 indicates that $200 must have been used during the month.

Supplies		Expense	
Dr.	Cr.	Dr.	Cr.
+	−	+	−
300	200 (8)	(8) 200	

Transaction (9). **Withdrew $300 for personal use.** The withdrawal of cash means that there is a reduction in the asset account Cash. Therefore, it is credited. The amount invested by the owner is also $300 less. We must open the account Drawing, which is debited to show the decrease in capital.

Cash		Drawing	
Dr.	Cr.	Dr.	Cr.
+	−	+	−
5,000	300	(9) 300	
2,000	500		
	200		
	1,000		
	300 (9)		

An account has a debit balance when the sum of its debits exceeds the sum of its credits; it has a credit balance when the sum of the credits is the greater. In *double-entry accounting*, which is in almost universal use, there are equal debit and credit entries for every transaction. When there are only two accounts affected, the debit and credit amounts are equal. If more than two accounts are affected, the total of the debit entries must equal the total of the credit entries (see Example 5).

3.4 THE LEDGER

The complete set of accounts for a business entity is called a *ledger*. It is the "reference book" of the accounting system and is used to classify and summarize transactions and to prepare data for financial statements. It is also a valuable source of information for managerial purposes., giving, for example, the amount of sales for the period or the cash balance at the end of the period. Depending on what method of data processing is used, the ledger may take the form or a bound book with a page for each account, or magnetic tapes or disks. In any case, the accounting principles are the same.

3.5 THE CHART OF ACCOUNTS

It is desirable to establish a systematic method of identifying and locating each account in the ledger. The *chart of accounts*, sometimes called the *code of accounts*, is a listing of the accounts by title and numerical designation. In some companies the chart of accounts may run to hundreds of items. In designing a numbering structure for the accounts, it is important to provide adequate flexibility to permit expansion without having to revise the basic system. Generally, blocks of numbers are assigned to various groups of accounts, such as assets, liabilities, etc. There are various systems of coding, depending on the needs and desires of the company.

EXAMPLE 3

A simple chart structure is to have the first digit represent the major group in which the account is located. Thus accounts that have numbers beginning with 1 are assets; 2, liabilities; 3, capital; 4, income; and 5, expenses. The second or third digit designates the position of the account in the group.

In the more common two-digit system, assets are assigned the block of numbers 11–19, and liabilities 21–29. In larger firms a three-digit (or more) system may be used, with assets assigned 101–199 and liabilities 201–299. Following is an example of the numerical designations for the account groups under both methods.

Account Group	Two-Digit	Three-Digit
1. Assets	11–19	101–199
2. Liabilities	21–29	201–299
3. Capital	31–39	301–399
4. Income	41–49	401–499
5. Expenses	51–59	501–599

Thus Cash may be account 11 under the first system and account 101 under the second system. The Cash account may be further broken down as: 101, Cash—First National Bank; 102, Cash—Second National Bank; etc.

3.6 THE TRIAL BALANCE

As every transaction results in an equal amount of debits and credits in the ledger, the total of all debit entries in the ledger should equal the total of all credit entries. At the end of the accounting period we check this equality by preparing a schedule called a *trial balance*, which compares the total of all *debit balances* with the total of all *credit balances*. The procedure is as follows:

1. List account titles in numerical order.
2. Record the balance of each account, entering debit balances in the debit column and credit balances in the credit column. (*Note*: Asset and expense accounts are debited for increases and would normally have debit balances. Liabilities, capital, and income accounts are credited for increases and would normally have credit balances.)
3. Add the columns and record the totals.
4. Compare the totals. They must both be the same.

If the totals agree, the trial balance is in balance, indicating the equality of the debits and credits for the hundreds or thousands of transactions entered in the ledger. Although the trial balance provides *arithmetic* proof of the accuracy of the records, it does not provide *theoretical* proof. For example, if the purchase of equipment was incorrectly charged to Expense, the trial balance columns may agree, but theoretically the accounts would be wrong, as Expense would be overstated and Equipment understated. In addition to providing proof of arithmetic accuracy in accounts, the trial balance facilitates the preparation of the periodic financial statements.

EXAMPLE 4

The summary of the transactions for Mr. Bagon (see Example 2), and their effect on the accounts, is shown below. The trial balance is then taken. Note that each account now has a numerical designation, in this case using a two-digit base.

		Assets					*Liabilities*					*Owner's Equity*		

Assets

Cash   11

(1)	5,000	300	(2)
(4)	2,000	500	(5)
4,700	*7,000*	200	(6)
		1,000	(7)
		300	(9)
		2,300	

Supplies   12

(2)	300	200	(8)
100			

Equipment   13

(3)	2,500	

Liabilities

Accounts Payable   21

(7)	1,000	2,500	(3)
		1,500	

Owner's Equity

A. Bagon, Capital   31

	5,000	(1)

Drawing   32

(9)	300	

Fees Income   32

	2,000	(4)

Rent Expense   51

(5)	500	

Salaries Expense   52

(6)	200	

Supplies Expense   53

(8)	200	

A. Bagon, Lawyer
Trial Balance
January 31, 19X8

	Dr.	Cr.
Cash	$4,700	
Supplies	100	
Equipment	2,500	
Accounts Payable		$1,500
A. Bagon, Capital		5,000
Drawing	300	
Fees Income		2,000
Rent Expense	500	
Salaries Expense	200	
Supplies Expense	200	
	$8,500	$8,500

EXAMPLE 5

As stated on page 49, if more than two accounts are affected in a transaction, the total of the debit entries must equal the total of the credit entries. For example,

(*a*) Bought a $3,000 piece of equipment, paying $1,000 cash and owing the balance.

Cash		Equipment		Accounts Payable		Capital	
Bal. 10,000	1,000 (*a*)	(*a*) 3,000			2,000 (*a*)		10,000 Bal.

Summary

1. To classify and summarize a single item of an account group, we use a form called a(n) _____ .

2. The accounts make up a record called a(n) _____ .

3. The left side of the account is known as the _____ , whereas the right side is the _____ .

4. Increases in all asset accounts are _____ .

5. Increases in all liability accounts are _____ .

6. Increases in all equity accounts are _____ .

7. Increases in all income accounts are _____ .

8. Increases in all expense accounts are _____ .

9. Expenses are debited because they decrease _____ .

10. The schedule showing the balance of each account at the end of the period is known as the _____ .

Answers: 1. account; 2. ledger; 3. debit side, credit side; 4. debited; 5. credited; 6. credited; 7. credited; 8. debited; 9. owner's equity; 10. trial balance

Solved Problems

3.1. Revenue and expense accounts are designated as *temporary* or *nominal* accounts (accounts in name only). Explain.

SOLUTION

The increase in owner's equity resulting from revenue is temporary, since owner's equity will be reduced by expenses in the same period. These accounts are closed out at the end of the accounting period, and the net balance (for example, the excess of revenue over expenses for the period) is then transferred to the Capital account.

The *permanent* or *real account* balances—assets, liabilities, and capital—are not closed out at the end of the accounting period. For example, the cash or inventory balance at the end of one period becomes the beginning balance in the following period.

3.2. Interpret the balance in the Supplies account at the end of the period.

SOLUTION

The book figure before adjustment is the amount on hand at the beginning of the period plus the amount purchased during the period. The sum is the total amount that was available during the period and was either used up or is still on hand. When an inventory count is made at the end of the period, the amount still on hand is determined, and the difference between that amount and the available amount above represents what was used during the period, which is an expense (supplies expense). The balance on hand is an asset (supplies on hand).

3.3. In each of the following types of T accounts, enter an increase (by writing +) and a decrease (by writing −).

Assets		Liabilities		Owner's Equity	
Dr.	Cr.	Dr.	Cr.	Dr.	Cr.

Income		Expenses	
Dr.	Cr.	Dr.	Cr.

SOLUTION

Assets		Liabilities		Owner's Equity	
Dr.	Cr.	Dr.	Cr.	Dr.	Cr.
+	−	−	+	−	+

Income		Expenses	
Dr.	Cr.	Dr.	Cr.
−	+	+	−

3.4. Indicate in the columns below the increases and decreases in each account by placing a check in the appropriate column.

		Debit	Credit
(a)	Capital is increased		
(b)	Cash is decreased		
(c)	Accounts Payable is increased		
(d)	Rent Expense is increased		
(e)	Equipment is increased		
(f)	Fees Income is increased		
(g)	Capital is decreased (through drawing)		

SOLUTION

(a) Cr. (b) Cr. (c) Cr. (d) Dr. (e) Dr. (f) Cr. (g) Dr.

3.5. For each transaction in the table below, indicate the account to be debited and the account to be credited by placing the letter representing the account in the appropriate column.

Name of Account	Transaction	Dr.	Cr.
(a) Accounts Payable	1. Invested cash in the firm		
(b) Capital	2. Paid rent for month		
(c) Cash	3. Received cash fees for services		
(d) Drawing	4. Paid salaries		
(e) Equipment	5. Bought equipment on account		
(f) Fees Income	6. Paid 1/2 balance on equipment		
(g) Notes Payable	7. Bought supplies on account		
(h) Rent Expense	8. Borrowed money from bank, giving a note in exchange		
(i) Salaries Expense	9. Supplies inventory showed 1/3 used during the month		
(j) Supplies	10. Withdrew cash for personal use		
(k) Supplies Expense			

SOLUTION

	Dr.	Cr.
1.	(c)	(b)
2.	(h)	(c)
3.	(c)	(f)
4.	(i)	(c)
5.	(e)	(a)
6.	(a)	(c)
7.	(j)	(a)
8	(c)	(g)
9.	(k)	(j)
10.	(d)	(c)

3.6.   Record each separate transaction in the accompanying accounts.

(*a*)   Bought supplies for cash, $700.

Supplies		Cash	
		Bal. 2,000	

(*b*)   Bought equipment for $2,700, paying 1/3 down and owing the balance.

Equipment		Cash		Accounts Payable	
Bal. 600		Bal. 1,400			

(*c*)   Gave a note in settlement of transaction (*b*).

Accounts Payable		Notes Payable	
	Bal. 1,800		

(*d*)   Received $800 in plumbing fees.

Cash		Fees Income	
Bal. 500			

SOLUTION

(*a*)

Supplies		Cash	
700		Bal. 2,000	700

(*b*)

Equipment		Cash		Accounts Payable	
Bal. 600		Bal. 1,400	900		1,800
2,700					

(*c*)

Accounts Payable		Notes Payable	
1,800	Bal. 1,800		1,800

(*d*)

Cash		Fees Income	
Bal. 500			800
800			

3.7. The 10 accounts that follow summarize the first week's transactions of the Willis Taxi Company.

	Cash	11
(a) 14,000	10,000	(b)
(e) 1,000	200	(d)
	300	(f)
	500	(g)
	100	(h)
	2,000	(i)
	300	(j)

	Supplies	12
(d) 200		

	Equipment	13
(b) 10,000		
(c) 6,000		

	Accounts Payable	21
(i) 2,000	6,000	(c)

	Capital	31
	14,000	(a)

	Drawing	32
(h) 100		

	Fees Income	41
	1,000	(e)

	Salaries Expense	51
(f) 300		

	Rent Expense	52
(g) 500		

	Gasoline Expense	53
(j) 300		

Complete the form below. (The analysis of the first transaction is given as a sample.)

	Transaction	Account Debited	Effect of Debit	Account Credited	Effect of Credit
(a)	Invested $14,000 in firm	Cash	Increased asset	Capital	Increased capital
(b)					
(c)					
(d)					
(e)					
(f)					
(g)					
(h)					
(i)					
(j)					

SOLUTION

	Transaction	Account Debited	Effect of Debit	Account Credited	Effect of Credit
(a)	Invested $14,000 in firm	Cash	Increased asset	Capital	Increased capital
(b)	Bought equipment for cash	Equipment	Increased asset	Cash	Decreased asset
(c)	Bought additional equipment on account	Equipment	Increased asset	Accts. Payable	Increased liability
(d)	Paid $200 for supplies	Supplies	Increased asset	Cash	Decreased asset
(e)	Received $1,000 in fees	Cash	Increased asset	Fees Income	Increased income
(f)	Paid $300 for salaries	Salaries Expense	Increased expense	Cash	Decreased asset
(g)	Paid $500 for rent	Rent Expense	Increased expense	Cash	Decreased asset
(h)	Withdrew $100 for personal use	Drawing	Decreased capital	Cash	Decreased asset
(i)	Paid $2,000 on account	Accounts Payable	Decreased liability	Cash	Decreased asset
(j)	Paid $300 for gasoline	Gasoline Expense	Increased expense	Cash	Decreased asset

3.8. Rearrange the following list of accounts as they would appear in the ledger and assign a numerical designation for each one based on a two-digit system.

Fees Income	Accounts Payable
Salaries Expense	Notes Payable
Supplies Expense	Capital
Supplies	Equipment
Cash	Drawing
Accounts Receivable	

SOLUTION

Account	Designated Number	Account	Designated Number
Cash	11	Capital	31
Supplies	12	Drawing	32
Accounts Receivable	13	Fees Income	41
Equipment	14	Salaries Expense	51
Accounts Payable	21	Supplies Expense	52
Notes Payable	22		

3.9. Rearrange the alphabetical list of the accounts and produce a trial balance.

Accounts Payable	$ 6,000	General Expense	$ 1,000
Accounts Receivable	14,000	Notes Payable	11,000
Sarah Hudson, Capital	32,000	Rent Expense	5,000
Cash	20,000	Salaries Expense	8,000
Sarah Hudson, Drawing	4,000	Supplies	6,000
Equipment	15,000	Supplies Expense	2,000
Fees Income	26,000		

SOLUTION

	Dr.	Cr.
Cash	$20,000	
Accounts Receivable	14,000	
Supplies	6,000	
Equipment	15,000	
Accounts Payable		$ 6,000
Notes Payable		11,000
Sarah Hudson, Capital		32,000
Sarah Hudson, Drawing	4,000	
Fees Income		26,000
Salaries Expense	8,000	
Rent Expense	5,000	
Supplies Expense	2,000	
General Expense	1,000	
	$75,000	$75,000

3.10. In the following trial balance for R. Romez Company, certain accounts have been recorded improperly; therefore it does not balance. Prepare a corrected trial balance.

R. Romez Company
Trial Balance
December 31, 19X8

	Debit	Credit
Cash	$ 26,000	
Accounts Receivable	14,000	
Supplies		$ 6,000
Equipment	12,000	
Accounts Payable	14,000	
R. Romez, Capital	30,000	
R. Romez, Drawing		4,000
Fees Income		38,000
Rent Expense	6,000	
Supplies Expense	2,000	
Salaries Expense		12,000
	$104,000	$60,000

	Debit	Credit

SOLUTION

	Debit	Credit
Cash	$26,000	
Accounts Receivable	14,000	
Supplies	6,000	
Equipment	12,000	
Accounts Payable		$14,000
R. Romez, Capital		30,000
R. Romez, Drawing	4,000	
Fees Income		38,000
Rent Expense	6,000	
Supplies Expense	2,000	
Salaries Expense	12,000	
	$82,000	$82,000

3.11. The trial balance of Greg Johnson presented below does not balance. In reviewing the ledger, you discover the following:

1. The debits and credits in the Cash account total $24,100 and $21,400, respectively.
2. The $400 received in settlement of an account was not posted to the Accounts Receivable account.
3. The balance of the Salaries Expense account should be $200 less.
4. No balance should exist in the Notes Payable account.
5. Each account should have a normal balance.

Prepare a corrected trial balance.

Greg Johnson, Lawyer
Trial Balance
December 31, 19X8

	Dr.	Cr.
Cash	$ 3,000	
Accounts Receivable	11,800	
Supplies		$ 800
Equipment	18,500	
Accounts Payable		1,500
Notes Payable		300
Greg Johnson Capital		15,400
Greg Johnson, Drawing		500
Fees Income		29,000
Salaries Expense	8,200	
Rent Expense	3,000	
Supplies Expense		200
General Expense	800	
	$44,500	$48,500

	Debit	Credit

SOLUTION

	Debit	Credit
Cash	$ 2,700	
Accounts Receivable	11,400	
Supplies	800	
Equipment	18,500	
Accounts Payable		$ 1,500
Notes Payable		
Greg Johnson, Capital		15,400
Greg Johnson, Drawing	500	
Fees Income		29,000
Salaries Expense	8,000	
Rent Expense	3,000	
Supplies Expense	200	
General Expense	800	
	$45,900	$45,900

3.12. Using the information of Prob. 1.16, record the entries in the accounts below for Dr. S. Braunstein, labeling each item by number as in Prob. 1.16. Then prepare a trial balance.

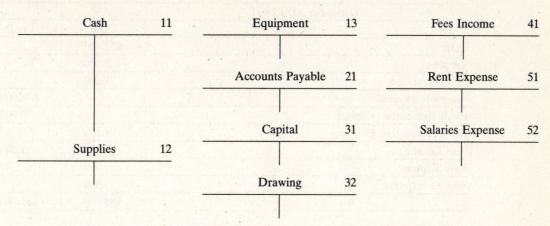

Dr. S. Braunstein		
Trial Balance		
December 31, 19X8		
	Debit	Credit
Cash		
Supplies		
Equipment		
Accounts Payable		
Dr. S. Braunstein, Capital		
Dr. S. Braunstein, Drawing		
Fees Income		
Rent Expense		
Salaries Expense		

SOLUTION

Cash 11

(1)	50,000	2,000	(3)
(4)	11,600	900	(5)
52,400	61,600	1,800	(6)
		3,000	(7)
		1,500	(8)
		9,200	

Supplies 12

| (3) | 2,000 | |

Equipment 13

| (2) | 27,000 | |

Accounts Payable 21

(7)	3,000	27,000	(2)
		24,000	

Capital 31

| | | 50,000 | (1) |

Drawing 32

| (8) | 1,500 | |

Fees Income 41

| | | 11,600 | (4) |

Rent Expense 51

| (5) | 900 | |

Salaries Expense 52

| (6) | 1,800 | |

Dr. S. Braunstein Trial Balance December 31, 19X8	Debit	Credit
Cash	$52,400	
Supplies	2,000	
Equipment	27,000	
Accounts Payable		$24,000
Dr. S. Braunstein, Capital		50,000
Dr. S. Braunstein, Drawing	1,500	
Fees Income		11,600
Rent Expense	900	
Salaries Expense	1,800	
	$85,600	$85,600

3.13. For the transactions below, record each entry in the T accounts furnished. (*Note*: The transactions are those of Prob. 1.17, which may be used in reference.)

(1) The Nu-Look Dry Cleaning Company opened a business bank account by depositing $12,000 on November 1.

(2) Purchased supplies for cash, $220.

(3) Purchased dry cleaning equipment from Hill Cleaning Equipment, Inc., for $3,500, paying $1,500 in cash with the balance on account.

(4) Paid rent for the month, $825.

(5) Cash sales for the month totaled $1,850.

(6) Paid salaries of $375.

(7) Paid $500 on account to Hill Cleaning Equipment, Inc.

(8) The cost of supplies used was determined to be $60.

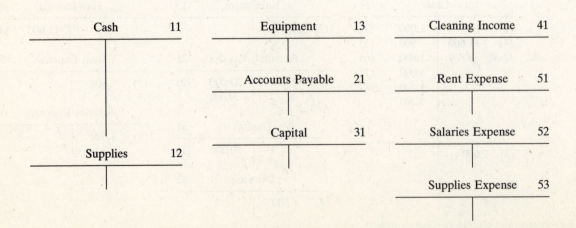

SOLUTION

	Cash		11		Equipment		13		Cleaning Income		41
(1)	12,000	220	(2)	(3)	3,500					1,850	(5)
(5)	1,850	1,500	(3)								
10,430	13,850	825	(4)		Accounts Payable		21		Rent Expense		51
		375	(6)					(4)	825		
		500	(7)	(7)	500	2,000	(3)				
		3,420				1,500			Salaries Expense		52
								(6)	375		
	Supplies		12		Capital		31				
						12,000	(1)		Supplies Expense		53
(2)	220	60	(8)					(8)	60		
	160										

3.14. Prepare a trial balance as of November 30 for the Nu-Look Dry Cleaning Company, using the account balances in Prob. 3.13.

Nu-Look Dry Cleaning Company		
Trial Balance		
November 30, 19X8		
	Debit	Credit
Cash		
Supplies		
Equipment		
Accounts Payable		
Nu-Look Dry Cleaning Company		
Cleaning Income		
Rent Expense		
Salaries Expense		
Supplies Expense		

SOLUTION

Nu-Look Dry Cleaning Company		
Trial Balance		
November 30, 19X8		
	Debit	Credit
Cash	$10,830	
Supplies	160	
Equipment	3,500	
Accounts Payable		$ 1,500
Nu-Look Dry Cleaning Company, Capital		12,000
Cleaning Income		1,850
Rent Expense	425	
Salaries Expense	375	
Supplies Expense	60	
	$15,350	$15,350

Examination I

Chapters 1–3

1. What is meant by the accounting cycle?

2. Define the following terms and give an example of each: (*a*) assets, (*b*) liabilities, (*c*) capital.

3. Define (*a*) revenue, (*b*) expense, (*c*) net income.

4. (*a*) What is an account?
   (*b*) What is a chart of accounts?

5. Distinguish between temporary and permanent accounts.

6. What is meant by the double-entry system of accounting?

7. What does the balance in the Supplies account at the end of the period represent?

8. Place a check mark in the appropriate box below to indicate the name of the account group in which each account belongs.

	Income Statement		Balance Sheet		
	Income	Expense	Assets	Liabilities	Owner's Equity
Accounts Payable					
Accounts Receivable					
Building					
Capital					
Cash					
Drawing					
Equipment					
Fees Income					
General Expense					
Interest Expense					
Interest Income					
Land					
Notes Payable					
Other Income					
Rent Expense					
Rent Income					
Salaries Expense					
Supplies					
Supplies Expense					
Tax Expense					

9. For each numbered transaction below, indicate the account to be debited and the account to be credited by placing the letter representing the account in the appropriate column. Accounts Payable (*a*); Capital (*b*); Cash (*c*); Drawing (*d*); Equipment (*e*); Fees Income (*f*); Notes Payable (*g*); Rent Expense (*h*); Salaries Expense (*i*); Supplies (*j*); Supplies Expense (*k*).

		Debit	Credit
(1)	Invested cash in the firm	(*c*)	(*b*)
(2)	Received cash for services rendered		
(3)	Paid salaries for the week		
(4)	Bought equipment on account		
(5)	Bought supplies on account		
(6)	Gave a note in settlement of the equipment on account		
(7)	Borrowed money from the bank		
(8)	Withdrew cash for personal use		
(9)	A count showed that approximately three-fourths of the supplies inventory had been used during the year		
(10)	Paid rent for the month		

10. Classify the following accounts by placing a check mark in the appropriate column.

		Current Assets	Fixed Assets	Current Liabilities	Long-Term Liabilities
(*a*)	Accounts Receivable				
(*b*)	Accounts Payable				
(*c*)	Notes Payable				
(*d*)	Mortgage Payable				
(*e*)	Cash				
(*f*)	Supplies				
(*g*)	Salaries Payable				
(*h*)	Bonds Payable				
(*i*)	Equipment				
(*j*)	Land				

11. Prepare the statement of owner's equity for the year ended December 31 of the Grant Company, given:

Capital, January 1	$72,400
Net income for period	27,600
Withdrawals by the proprietor	12,000

12. (*a*) Prepare the statement of owner's equity for the year ended December 31 for the Mary Tyler Company, given:

Capital, January 1	$86,240
Net income for period	12,000
Withdrawals by Ms. Tyler	18,000

(*b*) If there were a net loss of $12,000 instead of net income, find the new capital as of December 31.

13. On January 1, Anita Accord began business by investing $5,000 in her firm. Prepare the income statement for January, given the following income and expenditures:

Income from Services	$12,600	Supplies Expense	$ 75
Rent Expense	200	Utilities Expense	125
Salaries Expense	150	Repairs Expense	400
Commission Expense	100	Miscellaneous Expense	225

14. Below are the account balances of the State-Rite Cleaning Company as of December 31, 19X8. Prepare (*a*) an income statement, (*b*) a statement of owner's equity, (*c*) a balance sheet.

Accounts Payable	$11,600	Notes Payable	$ 2,800
Capital (beginning)	14,300	Rent Expense	12,600
Cash	9,300	Repairs Expense	2,400
Cleaning Income	39,500	Salaries Expense	9,200
Drawing	4,800	Supplies	5,300
Equipment	19,200	Supplies Expense	2,400
Miscellaneous Expense	3,000		

15. The Sullivan Residence Club was established on January 1, 19X8, and $15,000 cash and a $22,000 building were invested in the club. A summary of transactions for January follows. Record this information in the appropriate T accounts.

(1) Collected rents for the month of January, $2,400

(2) Wrote check for insurance, $850

(3) Paid the electric bill, $240

(4) Paid $350 to the maintenance person as January salary

(5) Bought supplies on account, $800

(6) Borrowed $15,000 from the bank for additions to the building

(7) Withdrew $300 for personal use

(8) Supplies worth $500 on hand at the end of the month

16. The following T accounts were taken from the ledger of the Utility Service Company. Prepare a trial balance from these accounts.

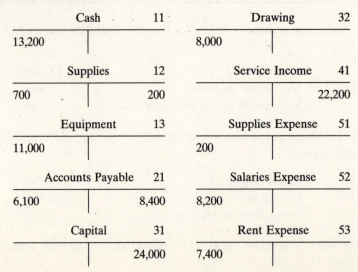

Cash	11		Drawing	32
13,200			8,000	

Supplies	12		Service Income	41
700	200			22,200

Equipment	13		Supplies Expense	51
11,000			200	

Accounts Payable	21		Salaries Expense	52
6,100	8,400		8,200	

Capital	31		Rent Expense	53
	24,000		7,400	

17. A. Levy Company's trial balance appears below. Certain accounts have been recorded improperly from the ledger to the trial balance, causing it not to balance. Present a corrected balance.

A. Levy Company
Trial Balance
January 31, 19X8

	Dr.	Cr.
Cash	$29,000	
Accounts Receivable		$ 4,000
Accounts Payable	3,000	
Capital		12,500
Drawing		500
Fees Income		22,000
Rent Income	11,000	
Rent Expense	1,000	
Salaries Expense	10,000	
General Expense		4,000
	$54,000	$43,000

Answers to Examination I

1. The accounting cycle is the sequence of procedures repeated each accounting period. The steps are (1) recording transactions in journals; (2) classifying data by posting to ledger; (3) summarizing data by classification; (4) adjusting and correcting recorded data; (5) preparing statements.

2. (*a*) Property of value owned by a business; Cash.

(*b*) Amounts owed by the business to outsiders; Accounts Payable.

(*c*) The investments by the owner(s) and the earnings retained in the business (also called *proprietorship* or *owner's equity*); J. Smith, Capital.

3. (*a*) The inflow of cash and receivables for an accounting period, resulting from the delivery of goods or the rendering of services.

(*b*) The cost of goods and services used up or consumed in the process of obtaining revenue.

(*c*) The increase in capital resulting from profitable operation of a business. Alternatively, the excess of revenues over expenses for the particular period.

4. (*a*) An account is a form used to record changes in a particular asset, liability, item of capital, revenue, or expense. It is used to classify and summarize transactions.

(*b*) A chart of accounts is a listing of the account titles showing the sequence of the accounts in the ledger and the number assigned to each account. It is a systematic method of identifying and locating each account.

5. Revenue and expense accounts are designated as temporary or nominal accounts because the increase in owner's equity resulting from the revenue is subject to reduction by expenses in the same period. These accounts are closed out at the end of the accounting period and the net balance transferred to the Capital

account. Permanent or real account balances—assets, liabilities, and capital—are not closed out at the end
of the accounting period.

6. In the double-entry system, each transaction must be recorded in such a way that the total debits equal the
total credits. In most cases, there will be only one debit and one credit account affected, and thus the dollar
amounts will be equal.

7. Amount on hand at the beginning of the period, plus purchases during the period, minus consumption during
the period.

8.

	Income Statement		Balance Sheet		
	Income	Expense	Assets	Liabilities	Owner's Equity
Accounts Payable				✓	
Accounts Receivable			✓		
Building			✓		
Capital					✓
Cash			✓		
Drawing					✓
Equipment			✓		
Fees Income	✓				
General Expense		✓			
Interest Expense		✓			
Interest Income	✓				
Land			✓		
Notes Payable				✓	
Other Income	✓				
Rent Expense		✓			
Rent Income	✓				
Salaries Expense		✓			
Supplies			✓		
Supplies Expense		✓			
Tax Expense		✓			

9.

		Debit	Credit
(1)	Invested cash in the firm	(c)	(b)
(2)	Received cash for services rendered	(c)	(f)
(3)	Paid salaries for the week	(i)	(c)
(4)	Bought equipment on account	(e)	(a)
(5)	Bought supplies on account	(j)	(a)
(6)	Gave a note in settlement of the equipment on account	(a)	(g)
(7)	Borrowed money from the bank	(c)	(g)
(8)	Withdrew cash for personal use	(d)	(c)
(9)	A count showed that approximately three-fourths of the supplies inventory had been used during the year	(k)	(j)
(10)	Paid rent for the month	(h)	(c)

10.

		Current Assets	Fixed Assets	Current Liabilities	Long-Term Liabilities
(a)	Accounts Receivable	✓			
(b)	Accounts Payable			✓	
(c)	Notes Payable			✓	
(d)	Mortgage Payable				✓
(e)	Cash	✓			
(f)	Supplies	✓			
(g)	Salaries Payable			✓	
(h)	Bonds Payable				✓
(i)	Equipment		✓		
(j)	Land		✓		

11.

Grant Company
Statement of Owner's Equity
Year Ended December 31, 19X8

Capital, January 1		$72,400
Net Income for Period	$27,600	
Less: Drawing	12,000	
Increase in Capital		15,600
Capital, December 31		$88,000

12.

Mary Tyler Company
Statement of Owner's Equity
Year Ended December 31, 19X8

(a)

Capital, January 1		$86,240
Net Income for Period	$12,000	
Less: Drawing	18,000	
Decrease in Capital		6,000
Capital, December 31		$80,240

(b)

Capital, January 1		$86,240
Net Loss for Period	$12,000	
Add: Drawing	18,000	
Decrease in Capital		30,000
Capital, December 31		$56,240

13.

Anita Accord
Income Statement
Month Ended January 31, 19X8

Income from Services		$12,600
Expenses		
Repairs Expense	$400	
Rent Expense	200	
Salaries Expense	150	
Utilities Expense	125	
Commission Expense	100	
Supplies Expense	75	
Miscellaneous Expense	225	
Total Expenses		1,275
Net Income		$11,325

Note: The investment of $5,000 has nothing to do with the income statement presentation.

14.   (*a*)

State-Rite Cleaning Company
Income Statement
Year Ended December 31, 19X8

Cleaning Income		$39,500
Expenses		
Rent Expense	$12,600	
Salaries Expense	9,200	
Repairs Expense	2,400	
Supplies Expense	2,400	
Miscellanous Expense	3,000	
Total Expenses		29,600
Net Income		$ 9,900

(*b*)

State-Rite Cleaning Company
Statement of Owner's Equity
Year Ended December 31, 19X8

Capital, January 1, 19X8		$14,300
Net Income for Period	$9,900	
Less: Drawing	4,800	
Increase in Capital		5,100
Capital, December 31, 19X8		$19,400

(*c*)

State-Rite Cleaning Company
Balance Sheet
December 31, 19X8

ASSETS

Cash	$ 9,300	
Supplies	5,300	
Equipment	19,200	
Total Assets		$33,800

LIABILITIES AND OWNER'S EQUITY

Accounts Payable	$11,600	
Notes Payable	2,800	
Total Liabilities		$14,400
Capital, December 31, 19X8		19,400
Total Liabilities and Owner's Equity		$33,800

15.

Cash			11
Bal.	15,000	850	(2)
(1)	2,400	240	(3)
(6)	15,000	350	(4)
		300	(7)

Supplies			12
(5)	800	300	(8)

Building		13
Bal.	22,000	

Accounts Payable		21
	800	(5)

Notes Payable		22
	15,000	(6)

Capital		31
	Bal.	37,000

Drawing		32
(7)	300	

Rent Income			41
		2,400	(1)

Salaries Expense		51
(4)	350	

Insurance Expense		52
(2)	850	

Utilities Expense		53
(3)	240	

Supplies Expense		54
(8)	300	

16.

Utility Service Company
Trial Balance

	Dr.	Cr.
Cash	$13,200	
Supplies	500	
Equipment	11,000	
Accounts Payable		$ 2,300
Capital		24,000
Drawing	8,000	
Service Income		22,200
Supplies Expense	200	
Salaries Expense	8,200	
Rent Expense	7,400	
	$48,500	$48,500

17.

A. Levy Company
Trial Balance
January 31, 19X8

	Dr.	Cr.
Cash	$29,000	
Accounts Receivable	4,000	
Accounts Payable		$ 3,000
Capital		12,500
Drawing	500	
Fees Income		22,000
Rent Income		11,000
Rent Expense	1,000	
Salaries Expense	10,000	
General Expense	4,000	
	$48,500	$48,500

CHAPTER 4

Recording Transactions

4.1 INTRODUCTION

In the preceding chapters we discussed the nature of business transactions and the manner in which they are analyzed and classified. The primary emphasis was the *why* rather than the *how* of accounting operations; we aimed at an understanding of the *reason* for making the entry in a particular way. We showed the effects of transactions by making entries in T accounts. However, these entries do not provide the necessary data for a particular transaction, nor do they provide a chronological record of transactions. The missing information is furnished by the use of an accounting form known as the journal.

4.2 THE JOURNAL

The journal, or day book, is the book of *original* entry for accounting data. Subsequently, the data is transferred or *posted* to the ledger, the book of subsequent or *secondary* entry. The various transactions are evidenced by sales tickets, purchase invoices, check stubs, etc. On the basis of this evidence, the transactions are entered in chronological order in the journal. The process is called *journalizing*.

There are a number of different journals that may be used in a business. For our purposes they may be grouped into (1) the general journal and (2) specialized journals. The latter type, which are used in businesses with a large number of repetitive transactions, are described in Chap. 10. To illustrate journalizing, we here use the general journal, whose standard form is shown below.

	General Journal			*Page J-1**
Date (1)	Description (2)	P.R. (3)	Dr. (4)	Cr. (5)
19X8 Oct. 7	Cash	11	10,000	
	John Hennessy, Capital	31		10,000
	Invested cash in the business (6)			

*Signifies General Journal, page 1.

73

4.3 JOURNALIZING

We describe the entries in the general journal according to the numbering on page 73.

(1) *Date*. The year, month, and day of the entry are written in the date column. The year and month do not have to be repeated for additional entries until a new month occurs or a new page is needed.

(2) *Description*. The account title to be debited is entered on the first line, next to the date column. The name of the account to be credited is entered on the line below and indented.

(3) *P.R. (Posting Reference)*. Nothing is entered in this column until the particular entry is posted, that is, until the amounts are transferred to the related ledger accounts. The posting process will be described in Sec. 4.4.

(4) *Debit*. The debit amount for each account is entered in this column adjacent to the left margin. Generally there is only one item, but there can be two or more separate items.

(5) *Credit*. The credit amount for each account is indented and entered in this column. Here again, there is generally only one account, but two or more accounts with different amounts can be involved. When there is more than one debit or credit in a single entry, the transaction is known as a compound entry.

(6) *Explanation*. A brief description of the transaction is usually made on the line below the credit. Some accountants feel that if the transaction is obvious, the explanation may be omitted. Generally a blank line is left between the explanation and the next entry.

EXAMPLE 1

To help in understanding the operation of the general journal, let us journalize the transactions previously described for Mr. Bagon's business (Example 2 in Chap. 3).

Jan. 4   Mr. Bagon invested $5,000 in his law practice
   4   Bought supplies for cash, $300
   4   Bought equipment from Altway Furniture Company on account, $2,500
 15   Received $2,000 in fees earned during the month
 30   Paid office rent for January, $500
 30   Paid salary for part-time help, $200
 31   Paid $1,000 to Altway Furniture Company, on account
 31   After taking an inventory, Mr. Bagon found that he had used $200 worth of supplies
 31   Withdrew $300 for personal use

Date	Description	P.R.	Dr.	Cr.
19X8				
Jan. 4	Cash		5,000	
	A. Bagon, Capital			5,000
	Investment in law practice.			
4	Supplies		300	
	Cash			300
	Bought supplies for cash.			
4	Equipment		2,500	
	Accounts Payable			2,500
	Bought equipment from Altway.			

Date	Description	P.R.	Dr.	Cr.
15	Cash		2,000	
	Fees Income			
	Received payment for services.			2,000
30	Rent Expense			
	Cash		500	
	Paid rent for month.			500
30	Salaries Expense			
	Cash		200	
	Paid salaries of part-time help.			200
31	Accounts Payable			
	Cash		1,000	
	Payment on account to Altway.			1,000
31	Supplies Expense			
	Supplies		200	
	Supplies used during the month.			200
31	A. Bagon, Drawing			
	Cash		300	
	Personal withdrawal.			300

4.4 POSTING

The process of transferring information from the journal to the ledger for the purpose of summarizing is called *posting*. Primarily a clerical task, posting is ordinarily carried out in the following steps:

1. ***Record the amount and date***. The date and the amounts of the debits and credits are entered in the appropriate accounts.

General Journal   *Page J-1*

Date	Description	P.R.	Dr.	Cr.
Jan. 4	Cash		5,000	
	A. Bagon, Capital			5,000

Cash		11		A. Bagon, Capital		31
Jan. 4	5,000				Jan. 4	5,000

2. *Record the posting reference in the account*. The number of the journal page is entered in the account.

3. *Record the posting in the journal*. For cross-referencing, the code number of the account is now entered in the P.R. column of the journal (solid line).

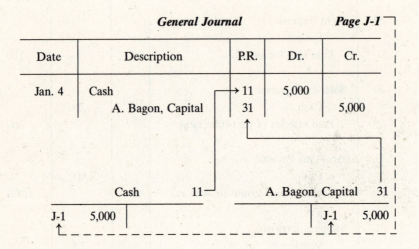

Date	Description	P.R.	Dr.	Cr.
Jan. 4	Cash	→ 11	5,000	
	A. Bagon, Capital	31		5,000

General Journal   *Page J-1*

Cash   11

| J-1 | 5,000 | |

A. Bagon, Capital   31

| | | J-1 | 5,000 |

EXAMPLE 2

The results of the posting from the journal of A. Bagon (see Example 1) appear below.

Assets = **Liabilities** + **Owner's Equity**

Cash   11

(1)	5,000	300	(2)
(4)	2,000	500	(5)
4,700	*7,000*	200	(6)
		1,000	(7)
		300	(9)
		2,300	

Supplies   12

| (2) | 300 | 200 | (8) |
| *100* | | | |

Equipment   13

| (3) | 2,500 | | |

Accounts Payable   21

| (7) | 1,000 | 2,500 | (3) |
| | | *1,500* | |

A. Bagon, Capital   31

| | | 5,000 | (1) |

A. Bagon, Drawing   32

| (9) | 300 | | |

Fees Income   41

| | | 2,000 | (4) |

Rent Expense   51

| (5) | 500 | | |

Salaries Expense   52

| (6) | 200 | | |

Supplies Expense   53

| (8) | 200 | | |

A. Bagon, Lawyer
Trial Balance
January 31, 19X8

	Debit	Credit
Cash	$4,700	
Supplies	100	
Equipment	2,500	
Accounts Payable		$1,500
A. Bagon, Capital		5,000
A. Bagon, Drawing	300	
Fees Income		2,000
Rent Expense	500	
Salaries Expense	200	
Supplies Expense	200	
	$8,500	$8,500

A. Bagon, Lawyer
Income Statement
Month Ended January 31, 19X8

Fees Income		$2,000
Expenses		
Rent Expense	$500	
Salaries Expense	200	
Supplies Expense	200	
Total Expenses		900
Net Income		$1,100

A. Bagon, Lawyer
Statement of Owner's Equity
Month Ended January 31, 19X8

Capital, January 1		$5,000
Add: Net Income	$1,100	
Less: Drawing	300	
Increase in Capital		800
Capital, January 31		$5,800

A. Bagon, Lawyer
Balance Sheet
January 31, 19X8

ASSETS

Current Assets		
Cash	$4,700	
Supplies	100	
Total Current Assets		$4,800
Fixed Assets		
Equipment		2,500
Total Assets		$7,300

LIABILITIES AND OWNER'S EQUITY

Accounts Payable	$1,500
Capital, January 31	5,800
Total Liabilities and Owner's Equity	$7,300

Summary

1. The initial book for recording all transactions is known as the _____ .

2. Another name for and description of the journal is the _____ .

3. The process of transferring information from the journal to the ledger is known as _____ .

4. The list of code numbers that identifies the entries in the journal is called the _____ .

5. The first digit of all asset accounts begins with _____ , whereas liabilities begin with _____ and capital begins with _____ .

6. All income account numbers begin with _____ , whereas expense account numbers begin with _____ .

7. The process of recording transactions in the journal is termed _____ .

8. The complete process of accounting is called the _____ .

Answers: 1. journal; 2. book of original entry; 3. posting; 4. chart of accounts; 5. 1, 2, 3; 6. 4, 5; 7. journalizing; 8. accounting cycle

Solved Problems

4.1.   What is a compound journal entry?

SOLUTION

An entry having more than one debit or more than one credit is called a compound entry. For example, land was bought (debit) for $10,000, with a down payment of cash (credit) of $1,000 and a mortgage (credit) of $9,000.

4.2.   How does the incorrect posting of a debit as a credit affect the trial balance?

SOLUTION

The trial balance will be out of balance by twice the amount incorrectly posted. For example, if a $200 debit to Cash is posted as a credit, there will be $400 in credits and 0 in debits, making a net difference of $400.

4.3.   In the shaded space below each entry, write a brief explanation of the transaction that might appear in the general journal.

(a)	Equipment	8,000	
	Cash		2,000
	Accounts Payable, William Smith		6,000
(b)	Accounts Payable, William Smith	2,000	
	Cash		2,000
(c)	Accounts Payable, William Smith	4,000	
	Notes Payable		4,000

SOLUTION

(a)	Equipment	8,000	
	Cash		2,000
	Accounts Payable, William Smith		6,000
	Purchase of equipment, 25% for cash, balance on account.		
(b)	Accounts Payable, William Smith	2,000	
	Cash		2,000
	Partial payment of the accounts payable.		
(c)	Accounts Payable, William Smith	4,000	
	Notes Payable		4,000
	Note payable in settlement of account payable.		

4.4. Dr. Stacey Kotin, Dentist, began her practice by investing the following assets:

Cash	$2,600
Supplies	1,400
Equipment	12,500
Furniture	3,000

Record the opening entry in the journal.

	Debit	Credit

SOLUTION

	Debit	Credit
Cash	2,600	
Supplies	1,400	
Equipment	12,500	
Furniture	3,000	
Stacey Kotin, Capital		19,500

4.5. If, in Prob. 4.4, Dr. Kotin owed a balance on the equipment of $3,500, what would be the opening entry then?

	Debit	Credit

SOLUTION

	Debit	Credit
Cash	2,600	
Supplies	1,400	
Equipment	12,500	
Furniture	3,000	
Accounts Payable		3,500
Stacey Kotin, Capital		16,000

4.6. Record the following entries in the general journal for the Sylvia Cleaning Company.

(a) Invested $12,000 cash in the business

(b) Paid $1,000 for office furniture

(c) Bought equipment costing $8,000 on account

(d) Received $2,200 in cleaning income

(e) Paid one-fifth of the amount owed on the equipment

		Debit	Credit
(a)			
(b)			
(c)			
(d)			
(e)			

SOLUTION

		Debit	Credit
(a)	Cash	12,000	
	Sylvia, Capital		12,000
(b)	Office Furniture	1,000	
	Cash		1,000
(c)	Equipment	8,000	
	Accounts Payable		8,000
(d)	Cash	2,200	
	Cleaning Income		2,200
(e)	Accounts Payable	1,600	
	Cash		1,600

4.7. Record the following entries in the general journal for the Leidner Medical Group.

(a) Invested $18,000 in cash, $4,800 in supplies, and $12,200 in equipment to begin the Leidner Medical Group.

(b) Received $2,400 in cash from patients for the week.

(c) Invested additional cash of $5,000 in the firm.

		Debit	Credit
(a)			
(b)			
(c)			

SOLUTION

		Debit	Credit
(a)	Cash	18,000	
	Supplies	4,800	
	Equipment	12,200	
	Leidner, Capital		35,000
(b)	Cash	2,400	
	Fees Income		2,400
(c)	Cash	5,000	
	Leidner, Capital		5,000

4.8. If, in Prob. 4.7, the Leidner Medical Group billed patients for the month for $1,600, present the necessary journal entry.

SOLUTION

Accounts Receivable	1,600	
Fees Income		1,600
To record services rendered on account.		

4.9. If the Leidner Medical Group (see Probs. 4.7 and 4.8) received $545 from patients who were billed last month, what entry would be necessary to record this information?

SOLUTION

Cash	545	
Accounts Receivable		545
Received cash on account		

4.10. Refer to Probs. 4.8 and 4.9. When payment is received from billed patients (accounts receivable), why isn't the income account credited?

SOLUTION

Fees Income was recorded in the previous month, when the service was rendered. Under the accrual basis, income and expense are recorded in the period of service or use, not in the period of payment.

4.11. Listed below are the January transactions for Big Ben Clock Repair Store, owned by David McDonald. Record them in general journal form.

Jan.   1   Invested $7,000 cash and equipment with a book value of $2,800
     3   Paid first month's rent, $700
     5   Cash repairs, $1,400
     7   Purchased supplies on account, $325
     8   Repaired a grandfather clock on account, $900
     8   Paid wages, $275
   11   Purchased equipment, $550 cash
   12   Cash repairs, $2,700
   15   Purchased equipment on account, $400
   17   Paid for advertising, $325
   19   Withdrew $500 for personal expenses
   21   Received $500 on account from Jan. 8 transaction
   22   Paid wages, $325
   25   Cash repairs, $3,400
   26   Paid $400 on account from Jan. 15 transaction
   29   Repaired a clock on account, $345

General Journal

Date		Debit	Credit

SOLUTION

General Journal

Date		Debit	Credit
Jan. 1	Cash	7,000	
	Equipment	2,800	
	David McDonald, Capital		9,800
3	Rent Expense	700	
	Cash		700
5	Cash	1,400	
	Repair Income		1,400
7	Supplies	325	
	Accounts Payable		325
8	Accounts receivable	900	
	Repair Income		900
8	Wage Expense	275	
	Cash		275
11	Equipment	550	
	Cash		550
12	Cash	2,700	
	Repair Income		2,700
15	Equipment	400	
	Accounts Payable		400
17	Advertising Expense	325	
	Cash		325
19	David McDonald, Drawing	500	
	Cash		500
21	Cash	500	
	Accounts Receivable		500
22	Wage Expense	325	
	Cash		325
25	Cash	3,400	
	Repair Income		3,400
26	Accounts Payable	400	
	Cash		400
29	Accounts Receivable	345	
	Repair Income		345

4.12. Norm Egglund owns and operates a toy repair store and had the following transactions. Record the entries in general journal form.

July 1   Invested $8,000 in business
     3   Purchased supplies on account, $175
     5   Purchased equipment for $9,000, paying $6,000 cash and issuing a 30-day note for the remainder
     7   Received $1,500 cash for repairs
     9   Purchased supplies on account, $255
   11   Paid rent for month, $350
   15   Paid electric bill, $155
   17   Paid $100 on account from July 9 transaction
   19   Withdrew $500 for personal use
   23   Received $200 up front on a $500 repair
   25   Paid $155 on account
   30   Record cash repairs, $2,150
   30   Paid wages, $1,000

General Journal

Date		Debit	Credit

General Journal

Date		Debit	Credit

SOLUTION

General Journal

Date		Debit	Credit
July 1	Cash	8,000	
	Norm Egglund, Capital		8,000
3	Supplies	175	
	Accounts Payable		175
5	Equipment	9,000	
	Cash		6,000
	Notes Payable		3,000
7	Cash	1,500	
	Repair Income		1,500
9	Supplies	255	
	Accounts Payable		255
11	Rent Expense	350	
	Cash		350
15	Utilities Expense	155	
	Cash		155
17	Accounts Payable	100	
	Cash		100
19	Norm Egglund, Drawing	500	
	Cash		500

General Journal

Date		Debit	Credit
23	Cash	200	
	Accounts Receivable	300	
	Repair Income		500
25	Accounts Payable	155	
	Cash		155
30	Cash	2,150	
	Repair Income		2,150
30	Wage Expense	1,000	
	Cash		1,000

4.13. Post the following journal entries for the Canny Taxi Company to the T accounts below. Disregard posting references at this time.

		Debit	Credit
(a)	Cash	6,000	
	Canny, Capital		6,000
(b)	Equipment	4,000	
	Accounts Payable		3,000
	Cash		1,000
(c)	Accounts Payable	3,000	
	Cash		3,000
(d)	Cash	1,500	
	Fares Income		1,500
(e)	Salaries Expense	600	
	Cash		600

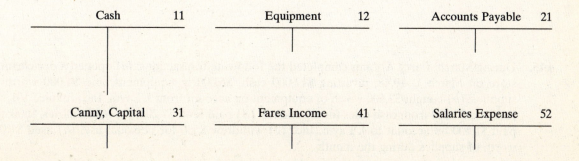

SOLUTION

Cash			11		Equipment		12		Accounts Payable		21
(a)	6,000	(b)	1,000	(b)	4,000			(c)	3,000	(b)	3,000
(d)	1,500	(c)	3,000								
2,900	7,500	(e)	600								
			4,600								

Canny, Capital			31		Fares Income		41		Salaries Expense		52
		(a)	6,000			(d)	1,500	(e)	600		

4.14. Use the balances of the T accounts in Prob. 4.13 to prepare a trial balance for the Canny Taxi Company.

Canny Taxi Company		
Trial Balance		
Cash		
Equipment		
Accounts Payable		
Canny, Capital		
Fares Income		
Salaries Expense		

SOLUTION

Canny Taxi Company		
Trial Balance		
Cash	$2,900	
Equipment	4,000	
Accounts Payable		
Canny, Capital		$6,000
Fares Income		1,500
Salaries Expense	600	
	$7,500	$7,500

4.15. During March, Larry Abrams completed the following transactions: (a) opened a dry cleaning store on March 1, 19X8, investing $12,000 cash, $6,000 in equipment, and $4,000 worth of supplies; (b) bought $2,600 worth of equipment on account from J. Laym, Inc., Invoice 101; (c) received $2,800 from cash sales for the month; (d) paid rent, $1,200; (e) paid salaries, $600; (f) paid $1,600 on account to J. Laym, Inc.; (g) withdrew $500 for personal use; (h) used $1,000 worth of supplies during the month.

(1) Journalize each of the transactions.

(2) Post each of them to their appropriate accounts.

General Journal   J-1

	P.R.	Debit	Credit
(a)			
(b)			
(c)			
(d)			
(e)			
(f)			
(g)			
(h)			

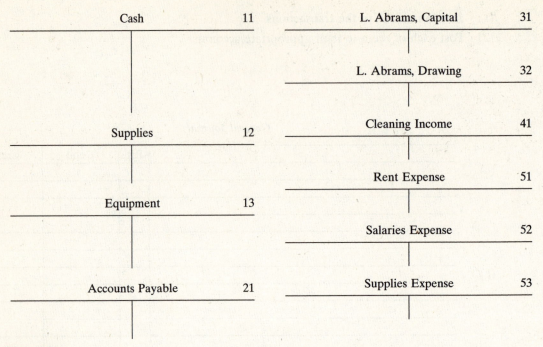

Cash	11	L. Abrams, Capital	31
Supplies	12	L. Abrams, Drawing	32
Equipment	13	Cleaning Income	41
		Rent Expense	51
Accounts Payable	21	Salaries Expense	52
		Supplies Expense	53

SOLUTION

General Journal J-1

		P.R.	Debit	Credit
(a)	Cash	11	12,000	
	Supplies	12	4,000	
	Equipment	13	6,000	
	L. Abrams, Capital	31		22,000
	Investment in business.			
(b)	Equipment	13	2,600	
	Accounts Payable	21		2,600
	J. Laym, Inc., Invoice 101.			
(c)	Cash	11	2,800	
	Cleaning Income	41		2,800
	Sales for month.			
(d)	Rent Expense	51	1,200	
	Cash	11		1,200
	Rent for month.			
(e)	Salaries Expense	52	600	
	Cash	11		600
	Salaries for month.			
(f)	Accounts Payable	21	1,600	
	Cash	11		1,600
	Paid J. Laym, Inc., on account.			

General Journal   J-1

		P.R.	Debit	Credit
(g)	L. Abrams, Drawing	32	500	
	Cash	11		500
	Personal withdrawal.			
(h)	Supplies Expense	53	1,000	
	Supplies	12		1,000
	Supplies used during month.			

Cash				11
(a)	J-1	12,000	(d)	J-1	1,200
(c)	J-1	2,800	(e)	J-1	600
	10,900	14,800	(f)	J-1	1,600
			(g)	J-1	500
					3,900

Supplies				12
(a)	J-1	4,000	(h)	J-1	1,000
	3,000				

Equipment			13
(a)	J-1	6,000	
(b)	J-1	2,600	
		8,600	

Accounts Payable				21
(f)	J-1	1,600	(b)	J-1	2,600
				1,000	

L. Abrams, Capital			31
	(a)	J-1	22,000

L. Abrams, Drawing			32
(g)	J-1	500	

Cleaning Income			41
	(c)	J-1	2,800

Rent Expense			51
(d)	J-1	1,200	

Salaries Expense			52
(e)	J-1	600	

Supplies Expense			53
(h)	J-1	1,000	

4.16. From the answer to Prob. 4.15, prepare a trial balance for Abrams Dry Cleaning Company.

Abrams Dry Cleaning Company		
Trial Balance		
Cash		
Supplies		
Equipment		
Accounts Payable		
L. Abrams, Capital		
L. Abrams, Drawing		
Cleaning Income		
Rent Expense		
Salaries Expense		
Supplies Expense		

SOLUTION

Abrams Dry Cleaning Company		
Trial Balance		
Cash	$10,900	
Supplies	3,000	
Equipment	8,600	
Accounts Payable		$ 1,000
L. Abrams, Capital		22,000
L. Abrams, Drawing	500	
Cleaning Income		2,800
Rent Expense	1,200	
Salaries Expense	600	
Supplies Expense	1,000	
	$25,800	$25,800

4.17. The trial balance for Vanguard Playhouse on October 31, 19X8, was as follows:

Vanguard Playhouse
Trial Balance
October 31, 19X8

Cash	$ 2,400	
Accounts Receivable	1,500	
Supplies	350	
Equipment	11,200	
Building	10,000	
Accounts Payable		$ 9,450
Notes Payable		12,000
Vanguard Playhouse, Capital		4,000
	$25,450	$25,450

Selected transactions for November were as follows:

(*a*) Nov. 2 Paid $1,000 due on the notes payable
(*b*)   8 Paid $3,000 on account
(*c*)   15 Receipts for the 2-week period totaled $8,400
(*d*)   22 Bought an additional projector at a cost of $15,500 with a cash
                 down payment of $5,000, the balance to be paid within 1 year
(*e*)   30 Paid salaries of $1,600

Using these data, transfer the October 31 balances to the ledger accounts below, prepare journal
entries for the month of November, and post to the ledger accounts.

Journal   *Page J-6*

Date	Description	P.R.	Debit	Credit

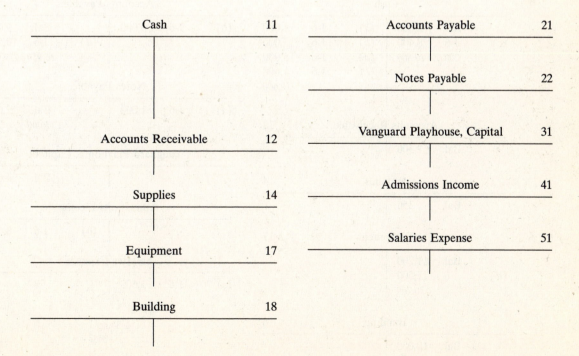

| Cash | 11 | Accounts Payable | 21 |

| Accounts Receivable | 12 | Notes Payable | 22 |

| Supplies | 14 | Vanguard Playhouse, Capital | 31 |

| Equipment | 17 | Admissions Income | 41 |

| Building | 18 | Salaries Expense | 51 |

SOLUTION

Journal   *Page J-6*

	Date	Description	P.R.	Debit	Credit
	19X8				
(a)	Nov. 2	Notes Payable	22	1,000	
		Cash	11		1,000
		Payment of installment note.			
(b)	8	Accounts Payable	21	3,000	
		Cash	11		3,000
		Payment on outstanding accounts.			
(c)	15	Cash	11	8,400	
		Admissions Income	41		8,400
		Receipts for the 2-week period to date.			
(d)	22	Equipment	17	15,500	
		Cash	11		5,000
		Accounts Payable	21		10,500
		Purchased projector with balance			
		due in 1 year.			
(e)	30	Salaries Expense	51	1,600	
		Cash	11		1,600
		Salaries paid to employees.			

	Cash				11
	Bal.	2,400	(a)	J-6	1,000
(c)	J-6	8,400	(b)	J-6	3,000
	200	*10,800*	(d)	J-6	5,000
			(e)	J-6	1,600
					10,600

	Accounts Receivable		12
Bal.	1,500		

	Supplies		14
Bal.	350		

	Equipment		17
	Bal.	11,200	
(d)	J-6	15,500	
	26,700		

	Building		18
Bal.	10,000		

	Accounts Payable		21
(b)	J-6	3,000	Bal.	9,450
			(d)	J-6	10,500
		16,950		*19,950*

	Notes Payable		22
(a)	J-6	1,000	Bal.	12,000
		11,000		

	Vanguard Playhouse, Capital		31
		Bal.	4,000

	Admissions Income		41
	(c)	J-6	8,400

	Salaries Expense		51
(e)	J-6	1,600	

4.18. For Vanguard Playhouse (Prob. 4.17), prepare (*a*) a trial balance and (*b*) a balance sheet as of November 30, 19X8.

(*a*)

Vanguard Playhouse		
Trial Balance		
November 30, 19X8		
Cash		
Accounts Receivable		
Supplies		
Equipment		
Building		
Accounts Payable		
Notes Payable		
Vanguard Playhouse, Capital		
Admissions Income		
Salaries Expense		

(*b*)

Vanguard Playhouse		
Balance Sheet		
November 30, 19X8		
ASSETS		
Current Assets		
Total Current Assets		
Fixed Assets		
Total Fixed Assets		
Total Assets		
LIABILITIES AND OWNER'S EQUITY		
Current Liabilities		
Total Current Liabilities		
*Vanguard Playhouse, Capital, November 30, 19X8		
Total Liabilities and Owner's Equity		
*(Additional space to compute capital)		

SOLUTION

(a)

Vanguard Playhouse		
Trial Balance		
November 30, 19X8		
Cash	$ 200	
Accounts Receivable	1,500	
Supplies	350	
Equipment	26,700	
Building	10,000	
Accounts Payable		$16,950
Notes Payable		11,000
Vanguard Playhouse, Capital		4,000
Admissions Income		8,400
Salaries Expense	1,600	
	$40,350	$40,350

(b)

Vanguard Playhouse		
Balance Sheet		
November 30, 19X8		
ASSETS		
Current Assets		
Cash	$ 200	
Accounts Receivable	1,500	
Supplies	350	
Total Current Assets		$ 2,050
Fixed Assets		
Equipment	$26,700	
Building	10,000	
Total Fixed Assets		36,700
Total Assets		$38,750

LIABILITIES AND OWNER'S EQUITY

Current Liabilities		
Accounts Payable	$16,950	
Notes Payable	11,000	
Total Current Liabilities		$27,950
*Vanguard Playhouse, Capital, November 30, 19X8		10,800
Total Liabilities and Owner's Equity		$38,750
*To obtain the capital balance as of		
November 30, first determine the net income for		
the period (income statement):		
Admissions Income	$ 8,400	
Less: Salaries Expense	1,600	
Net Income	$ 6,800	
Since there is no drawing involved, add the		
net income to the beginning capital:		
Capital, November 1	$ 4,000	
Add: Net Income	6,800	
Capital, November 30	$10,800	

CHAPTER 5

Adjusting and Closing Procedures

5.1 INTRODUCTION: THE ACCRUAL BASIS OF ACCOUNTING

As mentioned in Chap. 2, accounting records are kept on the *accrual* basis, except in the case of very small businesses. This means that *revenue is recognized when earned, regardless of when cash is actually collected; and expense is matched to the revenue, regardless of when cash is paid out.* Most revenue is earned when goods or services are delivered. At this time, title to the goods or services is transferred and a legal obligation to pay for such goods or services is created. Some revenue, such as rental income, is recognized on a time basis, and is earned when the specified period of time has passed. The accrual concept demands that expenses be kept in step with revenue, so that each month sees only that month's expenses applied against the revenue for that month. The necessary matching is brought about through a type of journal entry. In this chapter we shall discuss these *adjusting entries*, and also the *closing entries* through which the adjusted balances are ultimately transferred to balance sheet accounts at the end of the fiscal year.

5.2 ADJUSTING ENTRIES

(A) Covering Recorded Data

To adjust expense or income items that have already been recorded, a reclassification is required; that is, amounts have to be transferred from an asset, one of the prepaid expenses accounts (e.g., Prepaid Insurance), to an expense account (Insurance Expense). The following eight examples will show how adjusting entries are made for the principal types of *recorded expenses*.

EXAMPLE 1 Prepaid Insurance

Assume that on April 1, a business paid a $1,200 premium for 1 year's insurance in advance. This represents an increase in one asset (prepaid expense) and a decrease in another asset (cash). Thus, the entry would be

April 1	Prepaid Insurance	1,200	
	Cash		1,200

At the end of April, one-twelfth of the $1,200, or $100, has expired (been used up). Therefore, an adjustment has to be made, decreasing or crediting Prepaid Insurance and increasing or debiting Insurance Expense. The entry would be

April 30   Insurance Expense   100
         Prepaid Insurance   100

Thus, $100 would be shown as Insurance Expense in the income statement for April and the balance of $1,100 would be shown as part of Prepaid Insurance in the balance sheet.

EXAMPLE 2   Prepaid Taxes

Assume that on April 1 a business made the quarterly property tax payment of $600. At that time the transaction would be recorded with a debit to Prepaid Taxes and a credit to Cash for $600. Since the payment covers 3 months, the tax expense will be $200 per month. The entries would be as follows:

Apr. 1   Prepaid Property Taxes   600
        Cash   600

30   Property Tax Expense   200
      Prepaid Property Taxes   200

The balance to be shown on the balance sheet of April 30 for Prepaid Property Taxes would be $400.

EXAMPLE 3   Prepaid Rent

Assume that on April 1 a business paid $1,800 to cover rent for the next three months. The full amount would have been recorded as a prepaid expense in April. Since there is a 3-month period involved, the rent expense each month is $600. The balance of Prepaid Rent would be $1,200 at the beginning of May. The adjusting entry for April would be

Rent Expense   600
    Prepaid Rent   600

EXAMPLE 4   Prepaid Interest

Assume that the business found it necessary to take out a loan of $5,000 from the local bank on April 1. The period of the loan was 2 months, with interest of 12 percent a year. When interest is deducted in advance (discount), there is prepaid interest involved. On April 1 the entry would be

Cash   4,900
Prepaid Interest   100
    Notes Payable   5,000

*The prepaid interest, an asset, was computed as follows:

$$\$5,000 \times 12\% \text{ per year} \times 1/6 \text{ year} = \$100$$

At the end of April the adjusting entry would be

Interest Expense   50
    Prepaid Interest   50

EXAMPLE 5   Supplies

A type of prepayment that is somewhat different from those previously described is the payment for office or factory supplies. Assume that on April 1, $400 worth of supplies were purchased. There were none on hand before. This would increase the asset Supplies and decrease the asset Cash. At the end of April, when expense and revenue are to be matched and statements prepared, a count of the amount of supplies on hand will be made. Assume that the inventory count shows that $250 of supplies are still on hand. Then the amount consumed (used up) during April was $150 ($400 − $250). The two entries would be as follows:

Apr. 1	Supplies	400	
	Cash		400
30	Supplies Expense	150	
	Supplies		150

Supplies Expense of $150 will be included in the April income statement; Supplies of $250 will be included as an asset on the balance sheet of April 30.

In each of the above examples, the net effect of the adjusting entry is to credit the same account as was originally debited.

EXAMPLE 6   Accumulated Depreciation

In the previous five adjusting entries, the balances of the assets mentioned (Prepaid Insurance, Prepaid Taxes, Prepaid Rent, Prepaid Interest, and Supplies) were all reduced. These assets usually lose their value in a relatively short period of time. However, assets that have a longer life expectancy (such as a building, equipment, etc.) are treated differently because the accounting profession wants to keep a balance sheet record of the equipment's original (historical) cost. Thus, the adjusting entry needed to reflect the true value of the long-term asset each year must allocate (spread) its original cost. This spreading concept is known as depreciation. In order to accomplish the objectives of keeping original cost of the equipment and also maintaining a running total of the depreciation allocated, we must create a new account entitled Accumulated Depreciation. This account, known as a contra asset (an account that has the opposite balance to its asset), summarizes and accumulates the amount of depreciation over the equipment's total useful life. Assume that machinery costing $15,000 was purchased on February 1 of the current year and was expected to last 10 years. With the straight-line method of accounting (i.e., equal charges each period), the depreciation would be $1,500 a year, or $125 a month. The adjusting entry would be as follows:

Depreciation Expense	125	
Accumulated Depreciation		125

At the end of April, Accumulated Depreciation would have a balance of $375, representing 3 months' accumulated depreciation. The account would be shown in the balance sheet as follows:

Machinery	$15,000	
Less: Accumulated Depreciation	375	$14,625

EXAMPLE 7   Unearned Rent

In the following two examples, a new type of account is introduced. Known as Unearned Rent (Example 7) and Unearned Commission (Example 8), these accounts are liabilities and represent income that was received before the service was completed. In other words, the income was not earned. After a period of time, when the income is actually earned, an adjusting entry is made to reduce the liability account, and the earned income account is then recorded.

Assume that a landlord received $1,800 rent in advance ($600 per month) on April 1. The following entry would be made:

April 1	Cash	1,800	
	Unearned Rent		1,800

At the end of April, one month's rent has been earned, and Unearned Rent would be debited:

Apr. 30	Unearned Rent	600*	
	Rent Income		600

*($1,800 ÷ 3 months)

EXAMPLE 8   Unearned Commissions

Assume that $300 was received and recorded on April 1, for commissions for 3 months. At the end of April, Unearned Commissions would be debited, and Earned Commissions Income would be credited, for $100. The entries would be as follows:

Apr. 1	Cash	300	
	Unearned Commissions		300
30	Unearned Commissions	100	
	Earned Commissions Income		100

(B) Covering Unrecorded Data

In the previous section we discussed various kinds of adjustments to accounts to which entries had already been made. Now we consider those instances in which an expense has been incurred or an income earned but the applicable amount has not been recorded during the month. For example, if salaries are paid on a weekly basis, the last week of the month may run into the next month. If April ends on a Tuesday, then the first 2 days of the week will apply to April and will be an April expense, whereas the last 3 days will be a May expense.

To arrive at the proper total for salaries for the month of April, we must include, along with the April payrolls that were paid in April, the 2 days' salary that was not paid until May. Thus, we make an entry to *accrue* the 2 days' salary. To accrue means to collect or accumulate.

The following two examples show adjusting entries for the most important types of *unrecorded expenses* (accrued expenses).

EXAMPLE 9   Accrued Salaries

Assume that April 30 falls on Tuesday. Then, 2 days of that week will apply to April and 3 days to May. The payroll is $500 per day, $2,500 per week. For this example, $1,000 would thus apply to April (Monday and Tuesday) and $1,500 to May (Wednesday, Thursday, and Friday). The entry would be as follows:

Apr. 30	Salaries Expense	1,000	
	Salaries Payable		1,000

When the payment of the payroll is made—say, on May 8—the entry would be as follows:

May 8	Salaries Expense	1,500	
	Salaries Payable	1,000	
	Cash		2,500

As can be seen above, $1,000 was charged to expense in April and $1,500 in May. The debit to Accrued Salaries Payable of $1,000 in May merely canceled the credit entry made in April, when the liability was set up for the April salaries expense.

EXAMPLE 10   Interest Payable

At the end of the accounting period, the interest accrued on any business liability should be recognized in the accounts. Assume that instead of interest on the $5,000 loan described in Example 4 being prepaid, the interest is due when the loan is due. In that case, there would be accrued interest for April of $50, and the following adjusting entries would be required for April:

April 1	Cash	5,000	
	Notes Payable		5,000
30	Interest Expense	50	
	Interest Payable		50

Most businesses will have some *unrecorded revenue* (accrued income), that is, income earned but not yet received. Generally, this will be interest earned on notes from customers, rent earned on premises rented to a tenant, or various other items for which income has been earned but has not yet been collected.

EXAMPLE 11   Interest Receivable

A business holds a note receivable from a customer for $10,000. The note, due in 3 months, bears interest at 12 percent and was issued on March 1. The total interest would be $300 ($10,000 × 12% per year × 1/4 year). By the end of April, interest for 2 months has been earned. The following adjusting entry would be required for April:

Apr. 30	Interest Receivable	100	
	Interest Income		100

When the note is settled by the customer in May, he would pay the principal plus the interest, as shown below:

May 31	Cash	10,300	
	Note Receivable		10,000
	Interest Receivable		200
	Interest Income		100

As can be seen, the interest earned was $100 a month. Therefore, Interest Receivable was debited $100 for March and $100 for April. The same entry was not necessary for May, since the note was settled at the end of May.

5.3   CLOSING ENTRIES

The information for the month-to-month adjusting entries and the related financial statements can be obtained from the work sheet, whose use will be fully described in Chap. 6. After the income statement and balance sheet have been prepared from the work sheet for the last month in the fiscal year, a summary account—known as Income Summary—is set up. Then, by means of *closing entries*, each income account is debited so as to produce a zero balance, and the total amount for the closed-out accounts is credited to Income Summary. Similarly, the individual expense accounts are closed out by crediting them and their total amount is debited to the summary account. Thus, the new fiscal year starts with zero balances in the income and expense accounts, whereas the Income Summary balance gives the net income or the net loss for the old year.

EXAMPLE 12

To illustrate the closing procedure, we refer to the accounts of Alan Bagon.

Alan Bagon, Lawyer
Trial Balance
April 30, 19X8

Cash	$4,700	
Supplies	100	
Equipment	2,500	
Accounts Payable		$1,500
Alan Bagon, Capital		5,000
Alan Bagon, Drawing	300	
Fees Income		2,000
Rent Expense	500	
Salaries Expense	200	
Supplies Expense	200	
	$8,500	$8,500

The closing entries are as follows.

(1) *Close out revenue accounts.* Debit the individual revenue accounts and credit their total to Income Summary. Here, there is only one income account.

Apr. 30	Fees Income	2,000	
	Income Summary		2,000

(2) *Close out expense accounts.* Credit the individual expense accounts and debit their total to Income Summary.

Apr. 30	Income Summary	900	
	Rent Expense		500
	Salaries Expense		200
	Supplies Expense		200

(3) *Close out the Income Summary account.* If there is a profit, the credit made for total income in **(1)** above will exceed the debit made for total expense in **(2)** above. Therefore, to close out the balance to zero, a debit entry will be made to Income Summary. A credit will be made to the Capital account to transfer the net income for the period. If expenses exceed income, then a loss has been sustained and a credit will be made to Income Summary and a debit to the Capital account. Based on the information given above, the entry is

Apr. 30	Income Summary	1,100	
	Alan Bagon, Capital		1,100

(4) *Close out the Drawing account.* The Drawing account is credited for the total amount of the drawings for the period, and the Capital account is debited for that amount. The difference between net income and drawing for the period represents the net change in the Capital account for the period. The net income of $1,100 less drawings of $300 results in a net increase of $800 in the Capital account. The closing entry for the Drawing account is

Apr. 30	Alan Bagon, Capital	300	
	Alan Bagon, Drawing		300

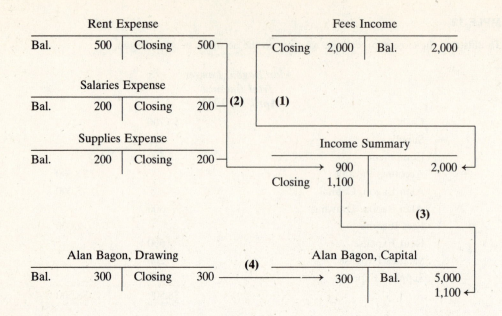

Notes:

(1) Close Fees Income account to Income Summary.

(2) Close all expense accounts to Income Summary.

(3) Close Income Summary to Capital.

(4) Close the Drawing account to Capital.

After the closing entries **(1)** through **(4)** are made, the various accounts will appear as below. The income account, the expense accounts, and the Drawing account are ruled off (closed out), thus showing no balance. The net profit for the period and the Drawing account balance were transferred to Alan Bagon, Capital, a balance sheet account.

Cash		Equipment		Alan Bagon, Capital	
Bal. 4,700		Bal. 2,500		(4) 300	5,000 Bal.
					1,100 (3)

Supplies		Accounts Payable		Alan Bagon, Drawing	
Bal. 100			1,500 Bal.	Bal. 300	300 (4)

Fees Income			Salaries Expense		Income Summary	
(1) 2,000	2,000 Bal.	Bal. 200	200 (2)	(2) 900	2,000 (1)
				(3) 1,100	
				2,000	2,000

Rent Expense			Supplies Expense	
Bal. 500	500 (2)	Bal. 200	200 (2)

The above transactions are based on the sole proprietorship form of business. If this business were a corporation (see p. 263), the Capital account would be replaced by a new account known as "Retained Earnings."

5.4 POST-CLOSING TRIAL BALANCE

After the closing entries are made, only balance sheet accounts—assets, liabilities, and capital—remain open. A trial balance of these accounts, known as a *post-closing trial balance*, is then taken.

EXAMPLE 13

Alan Bagon
Post-Closing Trial Balance
April 30, 19X8

Cash	$4,700	
Supplies	100	
Equipment	2,500	
Accounts Payable		$1,500
Alan Bagon, Capital		5,800
	$7,300	$7,300

5.5 REVERSING ENTRIES

The *reversing entry* (which is optional) is an accounting method that reverses a specific adjusting entry that was made at the end of the previous period (not all adjusting entries need to be reversed). The reversing entry is made at the beginning of a period and, as a result, transactions for the remainder of the current year are routine. The amounts used in the reversing entry are identical to those used in the adjusting entry. The rule to determine whether or not to reverse is as follows: "Any adjusting entry that creates (not there before) an asset or a liability has to be reversed."

EXAMPLE 14

Assume that Larry Pile receives a $500 weekly ($100 daily) salary. The entry to record the salary for the week ending Friday, December 27, 19X8, would be

(1)	Salary Expense	500	
	Cash		500

However, on December 31, 19X8, the accrual of salaries payable must be made for Monday and Tuesday, December 30 and 31.

(2)	Salary Expense	200	
	Salaries Payable		200

Since Salaries Payable is a liability and was created by an adjusting entry, a reversing entry would be needed at the beginning of January, 19X9:

(3)	Salaries Payable	200	
	Salary Expense		200

Salaries Expense

	Payments (Jan.–Dec. 26, 19X8)	24,000		
(1)	Dec. 27 payment	500		
(2)	Adjusting entry 12/31/X8	200	Closing entry 12/31/X8	24,700
			Reversing entry 1/1/X9	200 (3)

Salaries Payable

			Adjusting entry 12/31/X8	200	(2)
(3)	1/1/X9 Reversing entry	200	Balance 1/1/X9	200	(3)

Note that Salaries Payable had been recorded as a liability on the balance sheet (12/31/X8) and has been canceled as of 1/1/X9. The expense account shows a credit of $200, which will be reduced when the salaries of $500 are paid on Friday, January 3, 19X9.

Summary

1. The basis of accounting that recognizes revenue when earned, regardless of when cash is received, and matches the expenses to the revenue, regardless of when cash is paid out, is known as the _____ .

2. An adjusting entry that records the expired amount of prepaid insurance would debit the _____ account.

3. Supplies on hand is classified as a(n) _____ and appears in the _____ , while supplies expense is a(n) _____ and appears in the _____ .

4. Accumulated Depreciation appears in the balance sheet as a(n) _____ from the related asset.

5. Accrued Salaries is treated in the balance sheet as a(n) _____ , whereas Salaries Expense appears in the income statement as a(n) _____ .

6. Income that has been earned but not yet received is known as _____ .

7. Expenses that have been incurred but not yet paid for are known as _____ .

8. The revenue and expense accounts are closed out to the summary account known as _____ .

9. For a sole proprietorship, all income, expense, drawing, and summary accounts will be netted and closed into the _____ account.

10. The post-closing trial balance will involve only _____ , _____ , and _____ accounts.

Answers: 1. accrual basis; 2. Insurance Expense; 3. asset, balance sheet, expense, income statement; 4. deduction; 5. liability account, expense account; 6. unrecorded revenue or accrued income; 7. unrecorded expenses or accrued expenses; 8. Income Summary; 9. Capital; 10. asset, liability, capital

Solved Problems

5.1. An insurance policy covering a 2-year period was purchased on November 1 for $600. The amount was debited to Prepaid Insurance. Show the adjusting entry for the 2-month period ending December 31.

SOLUTION

Insurance Expense	50*	
Prepaid Insurance		50

$$*\frac{\$600}{2 \text{ years}} \times \frac{2 \text{ months}}{12 \text{ months}} = \$50$$

5.2. Taxes of $900 were debited to Prepaid Taxes representing payment made for a 6-month period beginning December 1. What adjustment is needed on December 31?

SOLUTION

Tax Expense	150*	
Prepaid Taxes		150

*$900 × 1/6

5.3. Based on Prob. 5.2, explain the balances of each of the two accounts.

SOLUTION

Tax Expense: The balance of $150 represents the amount of the expense for 1 month and would appear in the income statement as a general expense.

Prepaid Taxes: The balance of $750 represents future payments for the next 5 months and would appear as a current asset in the balance sheet.

5.4. On December 1, 19X8, Big John Construction Company issued a $10,000, ninety-day, 12 percent note. Big John's year ends December 31. What is the year-end adjusting entry for Interest Expense?

SOLUTION

Dec. 31
Dec. <u>1</u>
30 days accrued interest

Interest Expense	100	
Interest Payable		100

5.5. On January 1, 19X8, Hill Top Farm purchased a 3-year fire insurance policy for $3,600, paying cash. The entry made on January 1, 19X8, was a debit to Prepaid Insurance and a credit to Cash. What is the year-end adjusting entry?

SOLUTION

Insurance Expense	1,200*	
Prepaid Insurance		1,200

*$3,600 \times 1/3 = $1,200$

5.6. Hill Top Apartments rented an apartment on November 1, 19X8, for 6 months, receiving $3,000 in advance. The entry made on November 1 was

Cash   3,000
    Rental Income   3,000

What would the year-end adjusting entry be?

SOLUTION

Rental Income	2,000	
Unearned Rent		2,000*

*Four months' rent had not yet been earned from January to April 30, 19X9 ($500 \times 4 = $2,000$).

5.7. On April 1, 19X8, Luckey Printing Company purchased a new printing press for $7,000, paying cash. The printing press is being depreciated by the straight-line method over a 5-year period with no salvage value. Show the year-end adjusting entry.

SOLUTION

Depreciation Expense	1,050*	
Accumulated Depreciation (Printing Press)		1,050

$$*\frac{\$7,000}{5} = \$1,400 \qquad \$1,400 \times \frac{9}{12} = \underline{\underline{\$1,050}}$$

5.8. On September 1, $2,400 was paid; this represented an advance payment for 6 months' rent of a new factory office. The account Prepaid Rent was debited for this transaction. (*a*) What adjusting entry is necessary in order to show the true value of the accounts at the end of the year? (*b*) What amount will appear as an asset in the balance sheet as of the end of the year?

SOLUTION

(*a*)

Rental Expense	1,600*	
Prepaid Rent		1,600

*$2,400 ÷ 6 × 4 months

(*b*) The amount of Prepaid Rent appearing in the current asset section of the balance sheet will be $800 ($2,400–$1,600), representing future payments for 2 months, January and February of the following year.

5.9. A purchase of $900 was debited to Office Supplies. A count of the supplies at the end of the period showed $500 still on hand. Make the adjusting entry at the end of the period.

SOLUTION

Office Supplies Expense	400	
Office Supplies		400

5.10. Below is the opening balance of the Store Supplies account at the beginning of the year. After taking an inventory count of the remaining supplies, it was discovered that $750 had been used during the year. (*a*) Post the adjusting entry. (*b*) In what statements will the account balances be reflected?

	Stores Supplies		Store Supplies Expense
Bal.	2,250		

SOLUTION

(*a*)

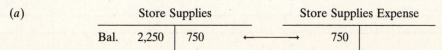

	Store Supplies		Store Supplies Expense
Bal.	2,250	750	750

(*b*) Store Supplies: Appears in the balance sheet as a current asset with a balance of $1,500. Store Supplies Expense: Appears in the income statement as an operating expense of $750.

5.11. Machinery costing $12,000, purchased November 30, is being depreciated at the rate of 10 percent per year. Show the adjusting entry for December 31.

SOLUTION

Depreciation Expense, Machinery	100*	
Accumulated Depreciation, Machinery		100

*$12,000 × 10% per year × $\frac{1}{12}$ year = $100

5.12. How would the information in Prob. 5.11 be presented in the balance sheet?

SOLUTION

Fixed Assets:

Machinery	12,000	
Less: Accumulated Depreciation, Machinery	100	11,900

5.13. The business received $6,000 as an advance payment for work to be done for a customer. At the end of the year, $4,000 of the services had been performed. (*a*) Prepare the adjusting entry if the original amount had been credited to Unearned Income. (*b*) What type of account is Unearned Income?

SOLUTION

(*a*)	Unearned Income	4,000	
	Service Income		4,000

(*b*) It is unrealized income and therefore a liability.

5.14. A business pays weekly salaries of $10,000 on Friday for a 5-day week. Show the adjusting entry when the fiscal period ends on (*a*) Tuesday; (*b*) Thursday.

(*a*)			
(*b*)			

SOLUTION

(a)	Salaries Expense	4,000*	
	Salaries Payable		4,000
(b)	Salaries Expense	8,000*	
	Salaries Payable		8,000

*($10,000 ÷ 5 days) = $2,000 per day. Tuesday = $2,000 × 2.
Thursday = $2,000 × 4.

5.15. On September 1, Mary Sudol borrowed $8,000 for 6 months at 15 percent interest from the First National Bank. What is the necessary adjusting entry to record the accrued interest as of December 31, the end of the fiscal year?

SOLUTION

Interest Expense	400*	
Interest Payable		400

*Interest is calculated for 4 months, September 1–December 31.

$$\$8,000 \times \frac{15}{100} \times \frac{4 \text{ months}}{12 \text{ months}} = \$400$$

5.16. The Willet Wilkinson Company's before-closing trial balance shows service revenue of $10,000 and interest income of $2,000. The expenses are salaries, $6,000; rent, $2,000; depreciation, $1,500; and interest, $500. Give the closing entries to be made to Income Summary for (a) income and (b) expense.

(a)		
(b)		

SOLUTION

(a)	Service Income	10,000	
	Interest Income	2,000	
	Income Summary		12,000
(b)	Income Summary	10,000	
	Salaries Expense		6,000
	Rent Expense		2,000
	Depreciation Expense		1,500
	Interest Expense		500

5.17. Using Prob. 5.16(a) and (b), prepare the closing entry for net income, and (c) post the transactions to the Income Summary and to the Capital account. Finally, close out the applicable account.

Income Summary		Willet Wilkinson, Capital
(b) 10,000	(a) 12,000	Bal. 20,000
(c) ?		

SOLUTION

Income Summary	2,000	
Willet Wilkinson, Capital		2,000

Income Summary		Willet Wilkinson, Capital
(b) 10,000	(a) 12,000	Bal. 20,000
(c) 2,000		(c) 2,000
12,000	12,000	

5.18. If all the revenue and expense accounts have been closed at the end of the fiscal year, what do the debit and credit figures in the account below indicate? What is the net profit or loss?

Income Summary	
98,000	102,000

SOLUTION

The debit amount represents $98,000 of expenses, whereas the credit amount of $102,000 depicts income for the period. The net balance of the account, $4,000 ($102,000 − $98,000), shows the net income for the period and will be closed out to the Capital account.

5.19. Listed below in various selected T accounts are the account balances. Prepare the closing entries. Remember, not all accounts are to be closed out.

Cash	Supplies	Supplies Expense
7,700	1,500	700

Rent Expense		John King, Drawing		Wage Expense	
1,200		12,000		22,000	

Fees Earned		Interest Expense		Equipment	
	47,550	450		11,700	

Depreciation Expense		Miscellaneous Expense		John King, Capital	
950		215			25,000

SOLUTION

Dec. 31	Fees Earned	47,550	
	Income Summary		47,550
31	Income Summary	25,515	
	Wage Expense		22,000
	Rent Expense		1,200
	Depreciation Expense		950
	Interest Expense		450
	Miscellaneous Expense		215
	Supplies Expense		700
31	Income Summary	22,035	
	John King, Capital		22,035
31	John King, Capital	12,000	
	John King, Drawing		12,000

Note: The Supplies account and the Equipment account do not affect the closing entries.

5.20. After all revenue and expense accounts were closed at the end of the fiscal year, the Income Summary account had a debit total of $100,000 and a credit total of $150,000. The Drawing account for William Whyte had a debit balance of $35,000. Journalize the closing entries.

SOLUTION

Income Summary	50,000	
William Whyte, Capital		50,000
William Whyte, Capital	35,000	
William Whyte, Drawing		35,000

5.21. Listed below are the ending balances of Chin Ling Dry Cleaners.

(*a*) Prepare the end-of-year closing entries. The beginning balance in Chin Ling's Capital account is $11,500. Ending balances are as follows:

Dry Cleaning Sales	$27,000	Supplies Expense	4,000
Wages Expense	12,000	Depreciation Expense	2,000
Rent Expense	7,000	Chin Ling, Drawing	4,000

(*b*) What would Chin Ling's, Capital account balance be after the closing entries?

(*a*)

(*b*)
                Chin Ling, Capital

SOLUTION

(a)

Dec. 31	Dry Cleaning Sales		27,000	
	Income Summary			27,000
31	Income Summary		25,000	
	Wages Expense			12,000
	Rent Expense			7,000
	Supplies Expense			4,000
	Depreciation Expense			2,000
31	Income Summary		2,000	
	Chin Ling, Capital			2,000
31	Chin Ling, Capital		4,000	
	Chin Ling, Drawing			4,000

(b)

Chin Ling, Capital

4,000	11,500
	2,000
	Bal. 9,500

5.22. Based on the balances below, prepare entries to close out (a) revenue accounts, (b) expense accounts, (c) the Income Summary account, (d) the Drawing account.

P. Silver, Capital		$22,000
P. Silver, Drawing	$6,000	
Service Income		12,000
Interest Income		1,500
Salaries Expense	8,000	
Rent Expense	4,000	
Depreciation Expense	3,000	
Interest Expense	2,000	

(a)

(b)

(c)

(d)

SOLUTION

(a)	Service Income	12,000	
	Interest Income	1,500	
	Income Summary		13,500
(b)	Income Summary	17,000	
	Salaries Expense		8,000
	Rent Expense		4,000
	Depreciation Expense		3,000
	Interest Expense		2,000
(c)	P. Silver, Capital	3,500*	
	Income Summary		3,500
(d)	P. Silver, Capital	6,000	
	P. Silver, Drawing		6,000

*3,500 represents a net loss and is debited to the Capital account.

5.23. Post the transactions shown in Prob. 5.22.

Capital			Salaries Expense	
	Bal.	22,000	Bal.	8,000

Drawing			Rent Expense	
Bal.	6,000		Bal.	4,000

Service Income			Depreciation Expense	
	Bal.	12,000	Bal.	3,000

Interest Income			Interest Expense	
	Bal.	1,500	Bal.	2,000

Income Summary

SOLUTION

Capital					Salaries Expense			
(c)	3,500	Bal.	22,000		Bal.	8,000	(b)	8,000
(d)	6,000							

Drawing					Rent Expense			
Bal	6,000	(d)	6,000		Bal.	4,000	(b)	4,000

Service Income					Depreciation Expense			
(a)	12,000	Bal.	12,000		Bal.	3,000	(b)	3,000

Interest Income					Interest Expense			
(a)	1,500	Bal.	1,500		Bal.	2,000	(b)	2,000

Income Summary			
(b)	17,000	(a)	13,500
		(c)	3,500
	17,000		17,000

Note that all income and expense accounts have been closed out. No balances exist in any of the above accounts except Capital, which now has a balance of $12,500.

5.24. Listed below are T accounts of the Kapela Realty Co. with the balances before adjusting. Make the necessary adjusting entries. (The year ends December 31, 19X8.)

Supplies		Prepaid Advertising		Prepaid Insurance	
1,250		975		2,400	

Unearned Rent Income		Accumulated Depreciation	
	6,000		1,600

Adjustments at year end:

(a) Depreciation Expense, $800.

(b) Inventory of store supplies on December 31, $300.

(c) Insurance was for 2 years, starting July 1, 19X8.

(d) Rent income received was for 3 months, starting on December 1, 19X8.

(e) Advertising was for 3 months, starting November 1, 19X8.

Adjusting Entries

(a)			
(b)			
(c)			
(d)			
(e)			

SOLUTION

Adjusting Entries

	Dec. 31			
(a)		Depreciation Expense	800	
		Accumulated Depreciation		800
(b)		Supplies Expense	950	
		Supplies		950
(c)		Insurance Expense	600	
		Prepaid Insurance		600
(d)		Unearned Rent Income	2,000	
		Rent Income		2,000
(e)		Advertising Expense	650	
		Prepaid Advertising		650

Examination II

Chapters 4–5

1. Compare the journal and the ledger.

2. What effect does the incorrect posting of a debit as a credit have on the trial balance?

3. Distinguish between prepaid expenses and accrued expenses.

4. What are adjusting entries? Closing entries?

5. Interpret the balance in the Supplies account at the end of the accounting period (*a*) before adjustment; (*b*) after adjustment.

6. The balances of the accounts of the Judith Playhouse, as of November 30, were as follows:

Judith Playhouse
Trial Balance
November 30

Cash	$10,000	
Accounts Receivable	2,100	
Supplies	600	
Equipment	12,000	
Building	9,000	
Accounts Payable		$ 6,500
Notes Payable		12,000
Judith Playhouse, Capital		15,200
	$33,700	$33,700

Selected transactions for the month of December were

(*a*) Bought new theatrical equipment for $3,000, paying half in cash and giving our note for the balance
(*b*) Paid $1,000 due on the notes payable
(*c*) Receipts for the 2-week period (admissions income) totaled $9,600
(*d*) Paid utilities, $150
(*e*) Paid $1,000 for 5-year insurance policy on the theater
(*f*) Paid monthly salaries, $1,250

Journalize the transactions.

7. The Eugene Don Company's trial balance shows Fees Income of $30,000 and the following expenses: salaries, $8,000; rent, $16,000; and depreciation, $1,500. If the Capital account balance is $30,000 and the Drawing account balance is $1,000, what closing entries are needed?

8. (*a*) Weekly salaries of $8,000 are payable on Friday, for a 5-day week. What is the adjusting entry if the fiscal period ends on Wednesday?

(b) An insurance policy covering a 4-year period was purchased on February 1, for $1,200. What is the adjusting entry on December 31?

(c) Office supplies of $700 were debited to Office Supplies. At the end of the month, the account shows $300 worth still on hand. Prepare the adjusting entry.

9. In the following, assume a fiscal year extending from January 1 through December 31.

(a) A machine costing $8,000 was purchased on October 31 and is being depreciated at the rate of 10 percent per year. What amount will appear as the adjusting entry on December 31?

(b) An insurance policy covering a 6-year period was purchased on March 1 for $1,800. What amount will appear as an expense on the income statement at the end of the year? What amount will appear on the balance sheet as an asset?

10. After all revenue and expense accounts of the Gold Silver Company were closed at the end of the year, the Income Summary had a debit balance of $125,000 and a credit balance of $190,000. The Capital account had a credit balance of $72,000, and the Drawing account had a debit balance of $12,000. Journalize the closing entries.

11. Listed below are the T accounts and the necessary adjustments for the year ending June 30, 19X8. Make the adjusting and reversing entries when appropriate. Year-end balances before adjustments:

Supplies		Accumulated Depreciation		Prepaid Rent	
2,100			2,000	5,000	

Salaries Expense	
24,000	

(a) Supplies on hand, June 30, 19X8, $700

(b) Depreciation Expense, $500

(c) Rent was for a 5-month period starting April 1, 19X8

(d) Salaries accrued (owed, not yet paid), $1,200

12. Prepare an income statement, statement of owner's equity, and balance sheet based on the following data: On January 1, 19X8, the Mary Moore Co. had capital of $15,200. On December 31, the end of the fiscal year, the balances after adjustments of assets, liabilities, revenue, and expenses were as follows:

Accounts Payable	$3,100
Accumulated Depreciation	500
Cash	14,800
Depreciation Expense	500
Drawing	2,600
Equipment	14,400
Fees Income	37,700
Insurance Expense	800
Miscellaneous Expense	1,850
Prepaid Insurance	830

Prepaid Rent	500
Rent Expense	3,000
Salaries Expense	16,500
Salaries Payable	200
Supplies	570
Supplies Expense	350

Answers to Examination II

1. The journal is a book of original entry that contains a *chronological* record of transactions. Each transaction is recorded first in the journal, which specifies the accounts to be debited and credited, along with a brief explanation of the transaction. The ledger is the complete set of accounts. It takes various physical forms, depending on whether the accounting system is manual or computerized.

2. The trial balance will be out of balance by twice the amount of the incorrect posting.

3. Prepaid expenses are those paid in advance of consumption; accrued expenses are those for which the consumption precedes the payment.

4. *Adjusting entries* are the entries required at the end of the accounting period to make the accounts properly reflect the results of operations for the period and the financial position at the end of the period. *Closing entries* are the entries that summarize the activities of the period, matching the inflow of income with the outflow of expenses to arrive at the net increase or decrease in owner's equity for the period. They separate the operations of one period from those of another. The accounts that are closed are the nominal or temporary accounts, which are really only extensions of the capital accounts.

5. (a) The balance before adjustment is the balance at the beginning of the period plus the amount purchased during the period. It includes both the amount on hand and the amount used.

   (b) The balance after adjustment includes only the inventory of supplies on hand at the end of the period. The amount used has been transferred to the Supplies Expense account.

6. (a)

	Equipment	3,000	
	Cash		1,500
	Notes Payable		1,500

   (b)

	Notes Payable	1,000	
	Cash		1,000

   (c)

	Cash	9,600	
	Admissions Income		9,600

   (d)

	Utilities Expense	150	
	Cash		150

   (e)

	Prepaid Insurance	1,000	
	Cash		1,000

   (f)

	Salaries Expense	1,250	
	Cash		1,250

7. (*a*)

Fees Income	30,000	
Income Summary		30,000

(*b*)

Income Summary	25,500	
Salaries Expense		8,000
Rent Expense		16,000
Depreciation Expense		1,500

(*c*)

Income Summary	4,500	
Don, Capital		4,500

(*d*)

Don, Capital	1,000	
Don, Drawing		1,000

8. (*a*)

Salaries Expense	4,800	
Salaries Payble		4,800
$[3 \times (8,000/5) = 4,800]$		

(*b*)

Insurance Expense	275	
Prepaid Insurance		275
$(1,200 \div 4 = 300; 11/12 \times 300 = 275)$		

(*c*)

Supplies Expense	400	
Supplies		400

9. (*a*) $133.33 ($8,000 \times 10\% = $800; 1/6 \times $800 = $133.33)$

   (*b*) Expense: $250 ($1,800 \div 6 = $300; 5/6 \times $300 = $250)$
      Asset: $1,550 ($1,800 - $250 = $1,550)$

10.

Income Summary	65,000	
Capital		65,000
Capital	12,000	
Drawing		12,000

11.   ***Adjusting Entries***

(*a*)

June 30	Supplies Expense	1,400	
	Supplies		1,400

(*b*)

Depreciation Expense	500	
Accumulated Depreciation		500

(*c*)

Rent Expense	3,000	
Prepaid Rent		3,000

(*d*)

Salaries Expense	1,200	
Salaries Payable		1,200

Reversing Entries

(*a*) None

(*b*) None

(*c*) None

(*d*) July 1   Salaries Payable   1,200
                                     Salaries Expense   1,200

12.

Mary Moore Company
Income Statement
Year Ended December 31, 19X8

Fees Income		$37,700
Operating Expenses		
Salaries Expense	$16,500	
Rent Expense	3,000	
Insurance Expense	800	
Depreciation Expense	500	
Supplies Expense	350	
Miscellaneous Expense	1,850	
Total Operating Expense		23,000
Net Income		$14,700

Mary Moore Company
Statement of Owner's Equity
Year Ended December 31, 19X8

Capital, January 1		$15,200
Net Income for the year	$14,700	
Less: Withdrawals	2,600	
Increase in Capital		12,100
Capital, December 31		$27,300

Mary Moore Company
Balance Sheet
December 31, 19X8

ASSETS

Current Assets		
Cash	$14,800	
Supplies	570	
Prepaid Insurance	830	
Prepaid Rent	500	
Total Current Assets		$16,700
Fixed Assets		
Equipment	$14,400	
Less: Accumulated Depreciation	500	13,900
Total Assets		$30,600

LIABILITIES AND OWNER'S EQUITY

Current Liabilities

Accounts Payable	$ 3,100	
Salaries Payable	200	
Total Current Liabilities		$ 3,300
Capital, December 31		27,300
Total Liabilities and Owner's Equity		$30,600

CHAPTER 6

Summarizing and Reporting via the Service Business Work Sheet

6.1 INTRODUCTION

The recording of transactions and the adjusting and closing procedures have been discussed in previous chapters. It is reasonable to expect that among the hundreds of computations and clerical tasks involved, some errors will occur, such as posting a debit as a credit. Today many financial records are maintained on the computer or on mechanical bookkeeping systems. The use of machine time to correct errors can be very costly and can bring painful questions from high financial executives.

One of the best ways yet developed of avoiding errors in the permanent accounting records, and also of simplifying the work at the end of the period, is to make use of an informal record called the *work sheet*.

6.2 WORK SHEET PROCEDURES FOR A SERVICE BUSINESS

We are already familiar with the types of accounts found in a service business—i.e., a business in which revenue comes from services rendered—so we shall first discuss the work sheet for such a business.

The work sheet is usually prepared in pencil on a large sheet of accounting stationery called analysis paper. On the work sheet, the ledger accounts are adjusted, balanced, and arranged in proper form for preparing the financial statements. All procedures can be reviewed quickly, and the adjusting and closing entries can be made in the formal records with less chance of error. Moreover, with the data for the income statement and balance sheet already proved out on the work sheet, these statements can be prepared more quickly.

For a typical service business we may suppose the work sheet to have eight money columns, namely, a debit and a credit column for each of four groups of figures: (1) trial balance, (2) adjustments, (3) income statement, and (4) balance sheet. A ten-column work sheet also is used, consisting of (1) trial balance, (2) adjustments, (3) adjusted trial balance, (4) income statement, and (5) balance sheet. The adjusted trial balance columns simplify the extension to the financial statement columns, but for the illustrations in this chapter, the eight-column work sheet will be used. The steps in completing the work sheet are then:

1. Enter the trial balance figures from the ledger.
2. Enter the adjustments.
3. Extend the adjusted figures to either the income statement or balance sheet columns.
4. Total the income statement columns and the balance sheet columns.
5. Enter the net income or net loss.

EXAMPLE 1

Prepare the work sheet for the Thomas Company, whose ledger balances follow.

Thomas Company
Trial Balance
December 31, 19X8

Cash	$ 3,510	
Accounts Receivable	4,010	
Supplies	1,050	
Prepaid Rent	400	
Equipment	18,000	
Accumulated Depreciation		$ 3,000
Notes Payable		4,000
Accounts Payable		2,380
Taxes Payable		400
Jane Thomas, Capital		13,690
Jane Thomas, Drawing	2,000	
Service Fees Income		10,500
Salaries Expense	4,600	
Miscellaneous Expense	400	
	$33,970	$33,970

1. **Enter the trial balance figures.** The balance of each general ledger account is entered in the appropriate trial balance column of the work sheet (see Fig. 6-1). The balances summarize all the transactions for the year ending December 31 before any adjusting entries have been applied.

2. **Enter the adjustments.** After the trial balance figures have been entered and the totals are in agreement, the adjusting entries should be entered in the second pair of columns. The related debits and credits are keyed by letters so that they may be rechecked quickly for any errors. The letters should be in proper sequence, beginning with asset accounts at the top of the page.

   (a) *Supplies.* In order to determine the amount of supplies used, it is necessary to make a count of the amount on hand on December 31. The amount was found to be $550. The balance at the beginning of the year plus supplies bought amounted to $1,050. Therefore,

Thomas Company
Work Sheet
Year Ended December 31, 19X8

Account Title	Trial Balance Debit	Trial Balance Credit	Adjustments Debit	Adjustments Credit	Income Statement Debit	Income Statement Credit	Balance Sheet Debit	Balance Sheet Credit
Cash	3,510						3,510	
Accounts Receivable	4,010						4,010	
Supplies	1,050			(a) 500			550	
Prepaid Rent	400			(b) 100			300	
Equipment	18,000						18,000	
Accumulated Deprec.		3,000		(c) 1,800				4,800
Notes Payable		4,000						4,000
Accounts Payable		2,380						2,380
Taxes Payable		400						400
Jane Thomas, Capital		13,690						13,690
Jane Thomas, Drawing	2,000						2,000	
Service Fees Income		10,500				10,500		
Salaries Expense	4,600		(d) 200		4,800			
Misc. Expense	400				400			
	33,970	33,970						
Supplies Expense			(a) 500		500			
Rent Expense			(b) 100		100			
Depreciation Expense			(c) 1,800		1,800			
Salaries Payable				(d) 200				200
Interest Expense			(e) 40		40			
Interest Payable				(e) 40				40
			2,640	2,640	7,640	10,500	28,370	25,510
Net Income					2,860			2,860
					10,500	10,500	28,370	28,370

Fig. 6-1

$1,050 − $550 = $500 worth of supplies have been used. There is no account for supplies expense, so the account name must be listed at the bottom of the work sheet. The adjusting entry is

Supplies Expense	500	
Supplies		500

(b) *Rent.* Rent of $400 for 4 months was paid in advance on December 1. Therefore, the original amount charged to Prepaid Rent must be reduced by $100, the amount of rent for December. The account name Rent Expense should be listed at the bottom of the work sheet. The adjusting entry for December is

Rent Expense	100	
Prepaid Rent		100

(c) *Depreciation*. The equipment is being written off over a 10-year period using the straight-line method. Thus, $1,800 a year ($18,000 ÷ 10) is being charged to expense. The title Depreciation Expense will also have to be written in at the bottom of the work sheet. The entry will be

Depreciation Expense	1,800	
Accumulated Depreciation		1,800

(d) *Salaries*. The salaries amount in the trial balance column would include only the payments that have been recorded and paid during the year. The portion that was earned in December 19X8 but paid in January 19X9, because the weekly pay period ended in January, would not be included. If the amount is $200, the accrued entry would be

Salaries Expense	200	
Salaries Payable		200

The account title Salaries Payable will also have to be listed on the work sheet.

(e) *Interest*. On the notes payable, there is accrued interest for 1 month. Assuming that the note bears 12 percent interest, the accrued interest would be $40 ($4,000 × 12% × 1/12). The entry will be

Interest Expense	40	
Interest Payable		40

3. ***Extend the adjusted figures to either the income statement or balance sheet columns***. The process of extending the balances horizontally should begin with the account at the top of the sheet. The revenue and expense accounts should be extended to the income statement columns; the assets, liabilities, and capital to the balance sheet columns. Each figure is extended to only one of the columns.

4. ***Total the income statement columns and the balance sheet columns***. The difference between the debit and credit totals in both sets of columns should be the same amount, which represents net income or net loss for the period.

	Income Statement		Balance Sheet	
	Dr.	Cr.	Dr.	Cr.
Total	7,640	10,500	28,370	25,510
Net Income	2,860			2,860
	10,500	10,500	28,370	28,370

5. ***Enter the net income or net loss***. The credit column total in the income statement is $10,500; the debit column total is $7,640. The credit column, or income side, is the larger, representing a net income of $2,860. Since net income increases capital, the net income figure should go on the credit side of the balance sheet. The balance sheet credit column total of $25,510 plus net income of $2,860 totals $28,370, which equals the debit column total. Since both the income statement columns and balance sheet columns are in agreement, it is a simple matter to prepare the formal income statement and balance sheet.

If there had been a loss, the debit or expense column in the income statement would have been the larger and the loss amount would have been entered in the credit column in order to balance the two columns. As a loss would decrease the capital, it would be entered in the balance sheet debit column.

After the work sheet has been completed, financial statements should be prepared. Based on the work sheet in Fig. 6-1 (page 127), the following statements are prepared:

Thomas Company
Income Statement
Year Ended December 31, 19X8

Service Fees Income		$10,500
Expenses		
Salaries Expense	$4,800	
Miscellaneous Expense	400	
Supplies Expense	500	
Rent Expense	100	
Depreciation Expense	1,800	
Interest Expense	40	
Total Expenses		7,640
Net Income		$ 2,860

Thomas Company
Statement of Owner's Equity
Year Ended December 31, 19X8

Capital, January 1		$13,690
Net Income, 19X8	$2,860	
Less: Withdrawals	2,000	
Increase in Capital		860
Capital, December 31		$14,550

Thomas Company
Balance Sheet
December 31, 19X8

ASSETS

Current Assets		
Cash	$ 3,510	
Accounts Receivable	4,010	
Supplies	550	
Prepaid Rent	300	
Total Current Assets		$ 8,370
Fixed Assets		
Equipment	$18,000	
Less Accumulated Depreciation	4,800	13,200
Total Assets		$21,570

LIABILITIES AND OWNER'S EQUITY

Liabilities

Notes Payable	$ 4,000	
Accounts Payable	2,380	
Taxes Payable	400	
Salaries Payable	200	
Interest Payable	40	
Total Liabilities		$ 7,020
Capital, December 31		14,550
Total Liabilities and Owner's Equity		$21,570

Summary

1. One of the best accounting methods for avoiding errors in the permanent accounting records and also simplifying the work at the end of the period is to make use of the _____ .

2. The work sheet is a(n) _____ accounting record, usually prepared in _____ .

3. On the work sheet, the ledger accounts are _____ , _____ , and _____ in proper form for preparing the financial statements.

4. The balances of the accounts appearing in the work sheet in the first two columns are obtained from the _____ .

5. If the total of the debit column of the income statement in the work sheet is larger than the total of the credit column of the income statement, the balance is said to be a(n) _____ for the period.

6. The account that is used to show the amount of depreciation for the fiscal year is titled _____ , whereas the account that gives the total depreciation to date is called _____ .

7. The amount of salaries in the trial balance column includes payments that have been recorded and paid _____ .

Answers: 1. work sheet; 2. informal, pencil; 3. adjusted, balanced, arranged; 4. ledger; 5. net loss; 6. Depreciation Expense, Accumulated Depreciation; 7. during the year

Solved Problems

6.1.   Prepare adjusting entries for the two separate situations below.

(*a*)   P. Jones had supplies at the beginning of the month of $745. At the end of the month, there remained a balance of $325. Prepare the adjusting entry needed to reflect the above data.

(b) The Bernie Hirsh Co. had supplies at the beginning of the month of $745. At the end of the month, it was determined that $325 had been used. Prepare the adjusting entry needed to reflect the above data.

		Dr.	Cr.
(a)			

		Dr.	Cr.
(b)			

SOLUTION

		Dr.	Cr.
(a)	Supplies Expense	420	
	Supplies		420

		Dr.	Cr.
(b)	Supplies Expense	325	
	Supplies		325

6.2. A truck bought on January 5, 19X8, for $14,000 has an estimated life of 7 years.

(a) What is the entry to record the depreciation expense as of December 31, 19X8?

(b) How would this information be presented on the balance sheet at the end of the year?

		Dr.	Cr.
(a)			

	Balance Sheet		
(b)			

SOLUTION

		Dr.	Cr.
(a)	Depreciation Expense	2,000	
	Accumulated Depreciation ($14,000 ÷ 7)		2,000

	Balance Sheet		
(b)	Truck	14,000	
	Less: Accumulated Depreciation	2,000	12,000

Note: The book value of the truck on December 31 would be $12,000.

6.3. Assume the same information as in Prob. 6.2, except that the truck was purchased on October 1, 19X8.

(a) Present the adjusting entry needed to record the information.

(b) Based on part (a), how would this information be presented on the balance sheet as of December 31, 19X9, fifteen months later?

	Dr.	Cr.
(a)		

Balance Sheet		
(b)		

SOLUTION

	Dr.	Cr.
(a) Depreciation Expense	500*	
Accumulated Depreciation		500

*$14,000 \div 7 \text{ years} = \$2,000: \dfrac{3 \text{ months}}{12 \text{ months}} \times \$2,000 = \$500$

Balance Sheet		
(b) Truck	14,000	
Less: Accumulated Depreciation	2,500*	11,500

*   500 for 19X8
  2,000 for 19X9
$\overline{\$2,500}$ Accumulated Depreciation

6.4. An $8,000 note payable written on November 1 for 180 days bears interest at 12 percent. What is the adjusting entry as of December 31?

SOLUTION

Interest Expense	160	
Interest Payable		160

Note: The amount of interest expense in 19X8 from November 1 to December 31 (60 days) is computed as follows:

$$\$8,000 \times 12\% \times 60/360$$

or

$$\frac{\$8,000}{1} \times \frac{12}{100} \times \frac{1}{6} = \$160$$

6.5. Journalize the following adjusting entries at December 31:

(a) Supplies on hand: January 1, $950; December 31, $460.

(b) The Prepaid Rent account has a balance of $3,000, representing rent for 1 year paid in advance on March 1.

(c)   Depreciation on equipment during the year, $450.

(d)   Salaries accrued but not paid at December 31, $280.

		Dr.	Cr.
(a)			
(b)			
(c)			
(d)			

SOLUTION

		Dr.	Cr.
(a)	Supplies Expense	490	
	Supplies		490
(b)	Rent Expense	2,500*	
	Prepaid Rent		2,500
(c)	Depreciation Expense	450	
	Accumulated Depreciation		450
(d)	Salaries Expense	280	
	Salaries Payable		280

*Rent expense for expired 10 months of the year, $10/12 \times \$3,000 = \$2,500$

6.6.   The following selected accounts are taken from the ledger of C. Gold Co. Place check marks in the appropriate columns to which the accounts will be extended in the work sheet.

Title	Income Statement		Balance Sheet	
	Dr.	Cr.	Dr.	Cr.
1. Cash				
2. Accounts Receivable				
3. Notes Receivable				
4. Accounts Payable				
5. C. Gold, Drawing				
6. C. Gold, Capital				
7. Fees Income				
8. Depreciation Expense				
9. Salaries Payable				

SOLUTION

	Income Statement		Balance Sheet	
Title	Dr.	Cr.	Dr.	Cr.
1. Cash			✓	
2. Accounts Receivable			✓	
3. Notes Receivable		?	✓	
4. Accounts Payable				✓
5. C. Gold, Drawing			✓	
6. C. Gold, Capital				✓
7. Fees Income		✓		
8. Depreciation Expense	✓			
9. Salaries Payable				✓

6.7.   From the partial view of the work sheet below, determine the net income or loss.

Income Statement		Balance Sheet	
Dr.	Cr.	Dr.	Cr.
29,500	36,200	52,400	45,700

SOLUTION

$$\begin{array}{r}36,200 \\ -29,500 \\ \hline 6,700\end{array}\quad\begin{array}{l}\text{(total credits of income statement)} \\ \text{(total debits of income statement)} \\ \text{(net income)}\end{array}$$

	Income Statement		Balance Sheet	
	Dr.	Cr.	Dr.	Cr.
	29,500	36,200	52,400	45,700
Net Income	6,700			6,700
	36,200	36,200	52,400	52,400

6.8.   Complete the work sheet below. What do the figures tell the reader?

Income Statement		Balance Sheet	
Dr.	Cr.	Dr.	Cr.
46,200	42,000	65,600	69,800
	?	?	
?	?	?	?

SOLUTION

	Income Statement		Balance Sheet	
	Dr.	Cr.	Dr.	Cr.
	46,200	42,000	65,600	69,800
Net Loss		4,200	4,200	
	46,200	46,200	69,800	69,800

The above figures show that the firm has experienced a net loss of $4,200. This is because more expenses ($46,200) have been reported than income ($42,000). As a loss decreases capital, it would be entered in the balance sheet debit column.

6.9. Below is the work sheet for the Juaz Company. Prepare adjusting entries on the work sheet based on the following year-end data:

(a) Supplies on hand, $3,000

(b) Insurance expired during the year, $600

(c) Depreciation on equipment, $1,500

(d) Salaries accrued, $1,000

Juaz Company
Work Sheet
Year Ended December 31, 19X8

Account Title	Trial Balance		Adjustments	
	Dr.	Cr.	Dr.	Cr.
Cash	18,000			
Supplies	4,000			
Prepaid Insurance	900			
Equipment	11,000			
Accumulated Depreciation		2,000		
Accounts Payable		7,000		
Juaz, Capital		20,000		
Juaz, Drawing	1,000			
Service Income		22,900		
Rent Expense	2,000			
Salaries Expense	9,000			
General Expense	6,000			
	51,900	51,900		

SOLUTION

Juaz Company
Work Sheet
Year Ended December 31, 19X8

Account Title	Trial Balance Dr.	Trial Balance Cr.	Adjustments Dr.	Adjustments Cr.
Cash	18,000			
Supplies	4,000			(a) 1,000
Prepaid Insurance	900			(b) 600
Equipment	11,000			
Accumulated Depreciation		2,000		(c) 1,500
Accounts Payable		7,000		
Juaz, Capital		20,900		
Juaz, Drawing	1,000			
Service Income		22,000		
Rent Expense	2,000			
Salaries Expense	9,000		(d) 1,000	
General Expense	6,000			
	51,900	51,900		
Supplies Expense			(a) 1,000	
Insurance Expense			(b) 600	
Depreciation Expense			(c) 1,500	
Salaries Payable				(d) 1,000
			4,100	4,100

6.10. Based on the data in Prob. 6.9, extend the work sheet figures to the income statement and balance sheet columns.

Juaz Company
Work Sheet
Year Ended December 31, 19X8

Account Title	Trial Balance Dr.	Trial Balance Cr.	Adjustments Dr.	Adjustments Cr.	Income Statement Dr.	Income Statement Cr.	Balance Sheet Dr.	Balance Sheet Cr.
Cash	18,000							
Supplies	4,000			(a) 1,000				
Prepaid Insurance	900			(b) 600				
Equipment	11,000							
Accumulated Deprec.		2,000		(c) 1,500				
Accounts Payable		7,000						
Juaz, Capital		20,900						
Juaz, Drawing	1,000							
Service Income		22,000						
Rent Expense	2,000							
Salaries Expense	9,000		(d) 1,000					
General Expense	6,000							
	51,900	51,900						

Account Title	Trial Balance Dr.	Trial Balance Cr.	Adjustments Dr.	Adjustments Cr.	Income Statement Dr.	Income Statement Cr.	Balance Sheet Dr.	Balance Sheet Cr.
Supplies Expense			(a) 1,000					
Insurance Expense			(b) 600					
Depreciation Expense			(c) 1,500					
Salaries Payable				(d) 1,000				
			4,100	4,100				
Net Income								

SOLUTION

Juaz Company
Work Sheet
Year Ended December 31, 19X8

Account Title	Trial Balance Dr.	Trial Balance Cr.	Adjustments Dr.	Adjustments Cr.	Income Statement Dr.	Income Statement Cr.	Balance Sheet Dr.	Balance Sheet Cr.
Cash	18,000						18,000	
Supplies	4,000			(a) 1,000			3,000	
Prepaid Insurance	900			(b) 600			300	
Equipment	11,000						11,000	
Accumulated Deprec.		2,000		(c) 1,500				3,500
Accounts Payable		7,000						7,000
Juaz, Capital		20,900						20,900
Juaz, Drawing	1,000						1,000	
Service Income		22,000				22,000		
Rent Expense	2,000				2,000			
Salaries Expense	9,000		(d) 1,000		10,000			
General Expense	6,000				6,000			
	51,900	51,900						
Supplies Expense			(a) 1,000		1,000			
Insurance Expense			(b) 600		600			
Depreciation Expense			(c) 1,500		1,500			
Salaries Payable				(d) 1,000				1,000
			4,100	4,100	21,100	22,000	33,300	32,400
Net Income					900			900
					22,000	22,000	33,300	33,300

6.11. Prepare an eight-column work sheet using the following adjustments: (*a*) rent expired for year, $1,200; (*b*) supplies on hand, $200; (*c*) salaries accrued, $400.

P. C. Silver Company
Work Sheet
Year Ended December 31, 19X8

Account Title	Trial Balance Dr.	Trial Balance Cr.	Adjustments Dr.	Adjustments Cr.	Income Statement Dr.	Income Statement Cr.	Balance Sheet Dr.	Balance Sheet Cr.
Cash	7,000							
Accounts Receivable	3,500							
Prepaid Rent	3,000							
Supplies	800							
Equipment	6,200							
Accounts Payable		4,500						
P. C. Silver, Capital		12,000						
Fees Income		10,000						
Salaries Expense	4,600							
General Expense	1,400							
	26,500	26,500						

SOLUTION

P. C. Silver Company
Work Sheet
Year Ended December 31, 19X8

Account Title	Trial Balance Dr.	Trial Balance Cr.	Adjustments Dr.	Adjustments Cr.	Income Statement Dr.	Income Statement Cr.	Balance Sheet Dr.	Balance Sheet Cr.
Cash	7,000						7,000	
Accounts Receivable	3,500						3,500	
Prepaid Rent	3,000			(a) 1,200			1,800	
Supplies	800			(b) 600			200	
Equipment	6,200						6,200	
Accounts Payable		4,500						4,500
P. C. Silver, Capital		12,000						12,000
Fees Income		10,000				10,000		
Salaries Expense	4,600		(c) 400		5,000			
General Expense	1,400				1,400			
	26,500	26,500						
Rent Expense			(a) 1,200		1,200			
Supplies Expense			(b) 600		600			
Salaries Expense								
Salaries Payable				(c) 400				400
			2,200	2,200	8,200	10,000	18,700	16,900
Net Income					1,800			1,800
					10,000	10,000	18,700	18,700

6.12.   From the information in Prob. 6.11, prepare all adjusting and closing entries.

Adjusting Entries

(a)			
(b)			
(c)			

Closing Entries

(a)			
(b)			
(c)			

SOLUTION

Adjusting Entries

(a)	Rent Expense	1,200	
	Prepaid Rent		1,200
(b)	Supplies Expense	600	
	Supplies		600
(c)	Salaries Expense	400	
	Salaries Payable		400

Closing Entries

(a)	Fees Income	10,000	
	Income Summary		10,000
(b)	Income Summary	8,200	
	Salaries Expense		5,000
	General Expense		1,400
	Rent Expense		1,200
	Supplies Expense		600
(c)	Income Summary	1,800	
	P. C. Silver, Capital		1,800

6.13. From the data of Prob. 6.11, prepare the income statement and balance sheet. A statement of owner's equity is not needed, as no withdrawals have taken place during the period.

P. C. Silver Company		
Income Statement		
Year Ended December 31, 19X8		
Fees Income		
Expenses		
Salaries Expense		
General Expense		
Rent Expense		
Supplies Expense		
Total Expenses		
Net Income		

P. C. Silver Company			
Balance Sheet			
December 31, 19X8			
ASSETS		**LIABILITIES AND OWNER'S EQUITY**	
Current Assets		Liabilities	
Cash		Accounts Payable	
Accounts Receivable		Salaries Payable	
Prepaid Rent		Total Liabilities	
Supplies		Owner's Equity	
Total Current Assets		Capital, January 1, 19X8	
Fixed Assets		Add: Net Income	
Equipment		Capital, December 31, 19X8	
Total Assets		Total Liabilities and Owner's Equity	

SOLUTION

P. C. Silver Company		
Income Statement		
Year Ended December 31, 19X8		
Fees Income		$10,000
Expenses		
Salaries Expense	$5,000	
General Expense	1,400	
Rent Expense	1,200	
Supplies Expense	600	
Total Expenses		8,200
Net Income		$ 1,800

P. C. Silver Company			
Balance Sheet			
December 31, 19X8			

ASSETS		LIABILITIES AND OWNER'S EQUITY	
Current Assets		Liabilities	
Cash	$ 7,000	Accounts Payable	$ 4,500
Accounts Receivable	3,500	Salaries Payable	400
Prepaid Rent	1,800	Total Liabilities	$ 4,900
Supplies	200	Owner's Equity	
Total Current Assets	$12,500	Capital, January 1, 19X8 $12,000	
Fixed Assets		Add: Net Income 1,800	
Equipment	6,200	Capital, December 31, 19X8	13,800
Total Assets	$18,700	Total Liabilities and Owner's Equity	$18,700

6.14. Based on the following information, complete the work sheet on the next page.

(*a*)   Rent expired, $2,100

(*b*)   Insurance expired, $700

(*c*)   Supplies on hand, December 31, $300

(*d*)   Depreciation on equipment, $900

(*e*)   Salaries accrued, $100

Perez Company
Work Sheet
Year Ended December 31, 19X8

Account Title	Trial Balance Dr.	Trial Balance Cr.	Adjustments Dr.	Adjustments Cr.	Income Statement Dr.	Income Statement Cr.	Balance Sheet Dr.	Balance Sheet Cr.
Cash	12,000							
Accounts Receivable	11,300							
Prepaid Rent	3,100							
Prepaid Insurance	1,600							
Supplies	800							
Equipment	11,500							
Accumulated Deprec.		900						
Accounts Payable		6,400						
J. Perez, Capital		15,200						
J. Perez, Drawing	8,000							
Fees Income		42,500						
Salaries Expense	14,000							
Misc. Expense	2,700							
	65,000	65,000						
Rent Expense								
Insurance Expense								
Supplies Expense								
Depreciation Expense								
Salaries Payable								

SOLUTION

Perez Company
Work Sheet
Year Ended December 31, 19X8

Account Title	Trial Balance Dr.	Trial Balance Cr.	Adjustments Dr.	Adjustments Cr.	Income Statement Dr.	Income Statement Cr.	Balance Sheet Dr.	Balance Sheet Cr.
Cash	12,000						12,000	
Accounts Receivable	11,300						11,300	
Prepaid Rent	3,100			(a) 2,100			1,000	
Prepaid Insurance	1,600			(b) 700			900	
Supplies	800			(c) 500			300	
Equipment	11,500						11,500	
Accumulated Deprec.		900		(d) 900				1,800
Accounts Payable		6,400						6,400
J. Perez, Capital		15,200						15,200
J. Perez, Drawing	8,000						8,000	
Fees Income		42,500				42,500		
Salaries Expense	14,400		(e) 100		14,100			
Misc. Expense	2,700				2,700			
	65,000	65,000						

Account Title	Trial Balance Dr.	Trial Balance Cr.	Adjustments Dr.	Adjustments Cr.	Income Statement Dr.	Income Statement Cr.	Balance Sheet Dr.	Balance Sheet Cr.
Rent Expense			(a) 2,100		2,100			
Insurance Expense			(b) 700		700			
Supplies Expense			(c) 500		500			
Depreciation Expense			(d) 900		900			
Salaries Payable				(e) 100				100
			4,300	4,300	21,000	42,500	45,000	23,500
Net Income					21,500			21,500
					42,500	42,500	45,000	45,000

6.15. Based on the information in Prob. 6.14, prepare the adjusting and closing entries.

Adjusting Entries

(a)

(b)

(c)

(d)

(e)

Closing Entries

(a)

(b)

(c)

(d)

SOLUTION

Adjusting Entries

(a)	Rent Expense	2,100	
	Prepaid Rent		2,100
(b)	Insurance Expense	700	
	Prepaid Insurance		700
(c)	Supplies Expense	500	
	Supplies		500
(d)	Depreciation Expense	900	
	Accumulated Depreciation		900
(e)	Salaries Expense	100	
	Salaries Payable		100

Closing Entries

(a)	Fees Income	42,500	
	Income Summary		42,500
(b)	Income Summary	21,000	
	Salaries Expense		14,100
	Miscellaneous Expense		2,700
	Rent Expense		2,100
	Insurance Expense		700
	Supplies Expense		500
	Depreciation Expense		900
(c)	Income Summary	21,500	
	J. Perez, Capital		21,500
(d)	J. Perez, Capital	8,000	
	J. Perez, Drawing		8,000

6.16. Prepare an income statement, statement of owner's equity, and balance sheet based on the information in Prob. 6.14.

Perez Company		
Income Statement		
Year Ended December 31, 19X8		

Perez Company		
Statement of Owner's Equity		
Year Ended December 31, 19X8		

Perez Company		
Balance Sheet		
December 31, 19X8		

SOLUTION

Perez Company		
Income Statement		
Year Ended December 31, 19X8		
Revenue		
Fees Income		$42,500
Expenses		
Salaries Expense	$14,100	
Rent Expense	2,100	
Depreciation Expense	900	
Insurance Expense	700	
Supplies Expense	500	
Miscellaneous Expense	2,700	
Total Expenses		21,000
Net Income		$21,500

Perez Company		
Statement of Owner's Equity		
Year Ended December 31, 19X8		
Capital, January 1		$15,200
Net Income for the Year	$21,500	
Less: Withdrawals	8,000	
Increase in Capital		13,500
Capital, December 31		$28,700

Perez Company		
Balance Sheet		
December 31, 19X8		
ASSETS		
Current Assets		
Cash	$12,000	
Accounts Receivable	11,300	
Prepaid Rent	1,000	
Prepaid Insurance	900	
Supplies	300	
Total Current Assets		$25,500
Fixed Assets		
Equipment	$11,500	
Less: Accumulated Depreciation	1,800	
Net Fixed Assets		9,700
Total Assets		$35,200
LIABILITIES AND OWNER'S EQUITY		
Current Liabilities		
Accounts Payable	$ 6,400	
Salaries Payable	100	
Total Liabilities		$ 6,500
J. Perez, Capital		28,700
Total Liabilities and Owner's Equity		$35,200

6.17. Based on the data below, prepare an income statement, a statement of owner's equity, and a balance sheet. On January 1, 19X8, the High Jack Company's Capital account was $34,750. At the end of the fiscal year, the balance of the asset, liability, revenue, and expense accounts was as follows:

Service Income	$109,550	Salaries Expense	$24,275
Supplies Expense	3,750	Accounts Receivable	4,100
Drawing	25,000	Equipment	28,000
Miscellaneous Expense	4,110	Accumulated Depreciation,	
Accounts Payable	1,770	Equipment	15,200
Cash	12,200	Building	28,600
Supplies	2,400	Accumulated Depreciation, Building	12,085
Mortgage Note Payable (12/04)	16,000	Salaries Payable	1,430
Prepaid Rent	1,800	Insurance Expense	7,350
Interest Expense	12,950	Rent Expense	36,250

High Jack Company		
Income Statement		
Year Ended December 31, 19X8		

High Jack Company		
Statement of Owner's Equity		
Year Ended December 31, 19X8		

High Jack Company		
Balance Sheet		
Year Ended December 31, 19X8		
ASSETS		
LIABILITIES AND OWNER'S EQUITY		

SOLUTION

High Jack Company		
Income Statement		
Year Ended December 31, 19X8		
Service Income		$109,550
Operating Expenses		
Rent Expense	$36,250	
Salaries Expense	24,275	
Interest Expense	12,950	
Insurance Expense	7,350	
Supplies Expense	3,750	
Miscellaneous Expense	4,110	
Total Operating Expense		88,685
Net Income		$ 20,865

High Jack Company		
Statement of Owner's Equity		
Year Ended December 31, 19X8		
Capital, January 1, 19X8		$34,750
Net Income for Year	$20,865	
Less: Withdrawals	25,000	
Decrease in Capital		4,135
Capital, December 31, 19X8		$30,615

High Jack Company		
Balance Sheet		
December 31, 19X8		
ASSETS		
Current Assets		
Cash	$12,200	
Accounts Receivable	4,100	
Supplies	2,400	
Prepaid Rent	1,800	
Total Current Assets		$20,500
Fixed Assets		
Equipment	$28,000	
Less: Accumulated Depreciation	15,200	$12,800
Building	$28,600	
Less: Accumulated Depreciation	12,085	16,515
Total Fixed Assets		29,315
Total Assets		$49,815
LIABILITIES AND OWNER'S EQUITY		
Current Liabilities		
Accounts Payable	$ 1,770	
Salaries Payable	1,430	
Total Current Liabilities		$ 3,200
Long-Term Liabilities		
Mortgage Note Payable (due 12/04)		16,000
Total Liabilities		$19,200
Capital, December 31, 19X8		30,615
Total Liabilities and Owner's Equity		$49,815

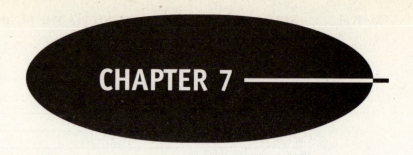

CHAPTER 7

Summarizing and Reporting via the Merchandising Business Work Sheet

7.1 WORK SHEET PROCEDURES FOR A MERCHANDISING BUSINESS

Merchandising (trading) businesses are those whose income derives largely from buying or selling goods rather than from rendering services. In addition to the accounts discussed in Chap. 6, the work sheet for a merchandising business will carry new accounts, and headings such as Inventory, Cost of Goods Sold, and Purchases. Let us discuss these new accounts separately, and then illustrate their handling on the work sheet.

7.2 INVENTORY AND PURCHASES TREATMENT

Inventory represents the value of goods on hand at either the beginning or the end of the accounting period. The beginning balance would be the same amount as the ending balance of the previous period. Generally, not all merchandise purchased is sold in the same period; so unsold merchandise must be counted and priced, and the total recorded in the ledger as Ending Inventory. The amount of this inventory will be shown as an asset in the balance sheet. The dollar amount of goods sold during the period will be shown as a classified heading known as Cost of Goods Sold in the income statement. (See Sec. 7.4.)

EXAMPLE 1

Assume that the January 1 (beginning) inventory is $20,000 and the December 31 (ending) inventory is $26,000. Two adjusting entries are required to show the replacement of the old by the new inventory:

Entry 1   Income Summary   20,000
                    Merchandise Inventory   20,000

Entry 2   Merchandise Inventory   26,000
                    Income Summary   26,000

The effect on the inventory and the income summary balances is as follows:

Merchandise Inventory				Income Summary			
Jan. 1	20,000	Dec. 31	20,000	Dec. 31	20,000	Dec. 31	26,000
Dec. 31	26,000						

On the work sheet (Fig. 7-1), the $20,000 balance of the Inventory account that appears in the trial balance represents the inventory at the beginning of the year. This amount will be transferred to Income Summary.

(*a*)   Income Summary   20,000
            Merchandise Inventory   20,000

The inventory at the end of the current year, $26,000, is an asset and will be adjusted on the work sheet.

(*a*)   Merchandise Inventory   26,000
            Income Summary   26,000

Unlike the procedure for other accounts, both the debit and the credit amounts for Income Summary are extended to the income statement in Fig. 7-1. This is done because the amounts of the debit adjustment (which represents the beginning inventory of $20,000) and of the credit adjustment (which represents the ending inventory of $26,000) are needed to prepare the income statement. It would not be practical to net the two items, as the single figure would not give enough information regarding the beginning and ending inventories. The merchandise inventory of $26,000 (ending) is extended to the debit column of the balance sheet.

Purchases

It is preferable for managerial purposes to maintain a separate account for purchases (under the periodic system—see Chap. 8) rather than including them in the Inventory account. This account includes only merchandise purchased for retail and appears in the income statement; purchases of machinery, trucks, etc., to be used in the business are debited to the particular asset account.

The journal entry to record a merchandise purchase is as follows:

Purchases   7,000
    Accounts Payable (or Cash)   7,000

At the end of the period, the total in the Purchases account is closed to the Income Summary account.

7.3   OTHER MERCHANDISING ACCOUNTS

(A)   Transportation-In

The cost of transportation-in, such as freight or trucking, is part of the cost of merchandise. Where the purchaser pays the transportation-in, a separate account should be maintained. The entry to record the payment of transportation-in is as follows:

Transportation-In   1,000
    Accounts Payable (or Cash)   1,000

(B) Purchase Returns

Sometimes goods purchased may be found to be unsatisfactory. The entire shipment may be returned to the vendor, or the vendor may allow a reduction in price without the return of the goods. A return of $600 of goods to the vendor is shown as follows:

Accounts Payable	600	
Purchase Returns		600

7.4   COST OF GOODS SOLD

Since we do not reflect purchases or sales of goods in the Inventory account during the year (periodic method), we must determine the cost of the inventory remaining on hand at the end of the accounting period and make any adjustments necessary. Ending inventory, or merchandise that has not been sold and is on hand at the end of the period, is an asset that appears on the balance sheet. Cost of Goods Sold appears in the income statement as a deduction from Sales. This cost may be calculated by the following procedure:

(a) **Inventory (beginning).** The amount to be used will be the same as the ending inventory of 19X7 (determined by counting and applying one of the methods discussed in Chaps. 8 and 9).

(b) **Purchases.** This is the total amount of goods bought for resale during 19X8, minus any purchases returned to the seller and any discounts given (*net* purchases), plus transportation.

(c) **Goods Available for Sale.** This is computed by adding the inventory at the beginning of the year to the net purchases during 19X8.

(d) **Inventory (ending).** This is determined by taking a physical count of all goods remaining in the business on December 31, 19X8, and applying one of the methods discussed in Chaps. 8 and 9.

(e) **Cost of Goods Sold.** This is the difference between what was available for sale and what is left at the end of the year. The cost of goods sold will then be deducted from net sales to determine the gross profit.

EXAMPLE 2

In the income statement, the Cost of Goods Sold section might appear as

	Sales			$45,000
	Cost of Goods Sold			
(a)	Inventory, January 1		$10,000	
	Purchases	$25,000		
	Less: Purchase Returns	600		
(b)	Net Purchases	$24,400		
	Transportation-In	1,000	25,400	
(c)	Goods Available for Sale		$35,400	
(d)	Inventory, December 31		12,000	
(e)	Total Cost of Goods Sold			23,400
	Gross Profit on Sales			$21,600

7.5 THE CLASSIFIED INCOME STATEMENT

The classified income statement sets out the amount of each function and enables management, stockholders, analysts, and others to study the changes in function costs over successive accounting periods. There are four functional classifications of the income statement.

1. **Revenue.** This includes gross income from the sale of products or services. It may be designated as Sales, Income from Fees, etc., to indicate gross income. The gross amount is reduced by Sales Returns and by Sales Discounts (see Chap. 10) to arrive at Net Sales.

2. **Cost of goods sold.** This includes the costs related to the products or services sold. It would be relatively simple to compute for a firm that retails furniture; it would be more complex for a manufacturing firm that changes raw materials into finished products.

3. **Operating expenses.** This includes all expenses or resources consumed in obtaining revenue. Operating expenses are further divided into two groups. *Selling expenses* are those related to the promotion and sale of the company's product or service. Generally, one individual is held accountable for this function, and his or her performance is measured by the results in increasing sales and maintaining selling expenses at an established level. *General and Administrative expenses* are those related to the overall activities of the business, such as the salaries of the president and other officers.

4. **Other expenses (net).** This includes nonoperating and incidental expenses, such as interest expense. Often any incidental income, such as interest income, is offset against the expense and a net amount shown.

EXAMPLE 3

J. Ales
Classified Income Statement

(*a*) Gross Sales

Sales of Goods or Services		$25,000	
Less: Sales Returns	$1,250		
Sales Discounts	750	2,000	
Net Sales			$23,000

(*b*) Cost of Goods Sold

Inventory, January 1	$ 2,500	
Purchases	16,500	
Goods Available for Sale	$19,000	
Inventory, December 31	3,000	
Cost of Goods Sold		16,000

(*c*) Gross Profit

Gross Profit	$ 7,000

(d)   Operating Expenses

Selling Expenses				
Sales Salaries Expense	$1,200			
Travel Expense	200			
Advertising Expense	600	$ 2,000		
General Expenses				
Officers' Salaries Expense	$1,000			
Insurance Expense	600	1,600		
Total Operating Expenses			3,600	

(e)   Operating Income

Net Income from Operations	$ 3,400

(f)   Other Expenses (net)

Interest Expense	$ 500	
Less: Interest Income	100	
Other Expenses (net)		400

(g)   Net Income

Net Income	$ 3,000

In this form of income statement, a number of subcategories of cost and expense are used. The key items are labeled with letters, and we will describe them briefly.

(a)   This is the total of all charges to customers for merchandise sold, both for cash and on account.

(b)   This is one of the most important sections of the income statement. It shows the cost of the goods delivered to customers during the period and the relationship of this cost to sales. This relationship can be conveniently compared with the figures for other periods.

(c)   The amount of gross profit (gross margin) must be sufficient to pay all expenses (other than those in Cost of Goods Sold) and to yield a reasonable return or profit. The gross profit ratio is a key control figure in managing a business. The selling price must be kept in such a relationship to cost as to yield a desired gross profit. To improve the gross profit ratio, sales prices may be increased or costs decreased. Favorable or unfavorable trends can be easily seen by comparing the gross profit ratio with the ratios for other periods.

(d)   These are the expenses necessary for carrying on the operations of the business. They do not include unusual expenses or financial expenses not of an operating nature, which are classed separately.

(e)   This is the amount by which the gross profit exceeds total operating expenses. It measures the degree of profitability from operations, before nonoperating items are considered.

(f)   This nonoperating item is offset and the net amount is shown in the summary column of the income statement.

(g)   This represents the net income for the period. Had there been more expenses than income, the figure would have been called *net loss*.

7.6 · THE MERCHANDISING WORK SHEET

For simplicity, the Thomas Company's work sheet (Fig. 7-1) and trial balance will be used with the addition of the Merchandise Inventory and Purchases accounts. This will have the effect of making the Thomas Company service industry (Chap. 6) a merchandising company.

Thomas Company
Trial Balance
December 31, 19X8

Cash	$ 3,510	
Accounts Receivable	4,010	
*Merchandise Inventory	20,000	
Supplies	1,050	
Prepaid Rent	400	
Equipment	18,000	
Accumulated Depreciation		$ 3,000
Notes Payable		4,000
Accounts Payable		2,380
Taxes Payable		400
*Jane Thomas, Capital		38,690
Jane Thomas, Drawing	2,000	
*Sales		30,500
*Purchases	25,000	
Salaries Expense	4,600	
Misc. Expense	400	
	$78,970	$78,970

*New accounts or amounts.

Additional data:

(a) Merchandise Inventory, end of year, $26,000
(b) Supplies on hand, $550
(c) Rent expired, $100
(d) Depreciation for year, $1,800
(e) Accrued salaries, $200
(f) Accrued interest on notes payable, $40

Note that with the exception of Merchandise Inventory and related accounts, all adjustments are identical to the work sheet (see Fig. 6-1) in Chap. 6.

Thomas Company
Work Sheet
Year Ended December 31, 19X8

Account Title	Trial Balance Dr.	Trial Balance Cr.	Adjustments Dr.	Adjustments Cr.	Income Statement Dr.	Income Statement Cr.	Balance Sheet Dr.	Balance Sheet Cr.
Cash	3,510						3,510	
Accounts Receivable	4,010						4,010	
Merchandise Inventory	**20,000**		(a) **26,000**	(a) **20,000**			**26,000**	
Supplies	1,050			(b) 500			550	
Prepaid Rent	400			(c) 100			300	
Equipment	18,000						18,000	
Accumulated Deprec.		3,000		(d) 1,800				4,800
Notes Payable		4,000						4,000
Accounts Payable		2,380						2,380
Taxes Payable		400						400
Jane Thomas, Capital		38,690						38,690
Jane Thomas, Drawing	2,000						2,000	
Sales		30,500				30,500		
Purchases	**25,000**				**25,000**			
Salaries Expense	4,600		(e) 200		4,800			
Misc. Expense	400				400			
	78,970	78,970						
Income Summary			(a) **20,000**	(a) **26,000**	20,000	26,000		
Supplies Expense			(b) 500		500			
Rent Expense			(c) 100		100			
Depreciation Expense			(d) 1,800		1,800			
Salaries Payable				(e) 200				200
Interest Expense			(f) 40					
Interest Payable				(f) 40	40			40
			48,640	48,640	52,640	56,500	54,370	50,510
Net Income					3,860			3,860
					56,500	56,500	54,370	54,370

Fig. 7-1

Based on the work sheet (see Fig. 7-1), the Cost of Goods Sold section of the income statement would appear as

Cost of Goods Sold		
Merchandise Inventory (beginning)	$20,000	
Purchases	25,000	
Goods Available for Sales	$45,000	
Less: Merchandise Inventory		
(ending)	26,000	
Total Cost of Goods Sold		$19,000

The income statement for the merchandising business of Thomas Company would then be

Sales		$30,500
Cost of Goods Sold		19,000
Gross Profit		$11,500
Operating Expenses		
Salaries Expense	$4,800	
Miscellaneous Expense	400	
Supplies Expense	500	
Rent Expense	100	
Depreciation Expense	1,800	
Interest Expense	40	
Total Expenses		7,640
Net Income		$ 3,860

Summary

1. A business whose income is derived largely from buying or selling goods, rather than rendering services, is known as a(n) _____ firm.

2. The goods on hand at the beginning or the end of the accounting period are called _____.

3. The merchandise inventory on hand at the end of the period will appear both in the _____ section of the income statement and in the _____ of the balance sheet.

4. The Purchases account is used only for goods for _____. Purchases of trucks and equipment are debited to _____ accounts.

5. Beginning inventory plus net purchases will equal _____.

6. In recording both beginning inventory and ending inventory as an adjusting entry, the _____ account is used.

7. The difference between what was available for sale and what is left at the end of the year is known as the _____.

Answers: 1. merchandising; 2. inventory; 3. Cost of Goods Sold, Asset; 4. resale, asset; 5. Goods Available for Sale; 6. Income Summary; 7. Cost of Goods Sold

Solved Problems

7.1. The Folk Company purchased merchandise costing $150,000. What is the cost of goods sold under each assumption below?

	Beginning Inventory	Ending Inventory
(a)	100,000	60,000
(b)	75,000	50,000
(c)	50,000	30,000
(d)	0	10,000

SOLUTION

Beginning Inventory + Purchases − Ending Inventory = Cost of Goods Sold

	Beginning Inventory	Purchases	Ending Inventory	Cost of Goods Sold
(a)	100,000	150,000	60,000	190,000
(b)	75,000	150,000	50,000	175,000
(c)	50,000	150,000	30,000	170,000
(d)	0	150,000	10,000	140,000

7.2. Compute the cost of goods sold from the following information: Beginning Inventory, $20,000; Purchases, $70,000; Ending Inventory, $34,000.

SOLUTION

Beginning Inventory	$20,000
Purchases	70,000
Goods Available for Sale	$90,000
Less: Ending Inventory	34,000
Cost of Goods Sold	$56,000

7.3. For each situation below, determine the missing figures.

	Beginning Inventory	Purchases During Period	Ending Inventory	Cost of Goods Sold
(a)	18,000	40,000	_____	35,000
(b)	_____	41,000	15,000	42,000
(c)	21,000	37,000	20,000	_____
(d)	27,000	_____	25,000	38,000

SOLUTION

(a) 23,000; (b) 16,000; (c) 38,000; (d) 36,000

7.4. Following are various accounts from the Cost of Goods Sold section of the income statement. Each has an account figure missing. Find the missing figure. *Hint*: Make up a blank income statement and fill in the information already supplied.

	Sales	Beginning Inventory	Purchases	Ending Inventory	Cost of Goods Sold	Gross Income
(a)	_____	28,000	74,000	36,000	66,000	117,500
(b)	212,000	54,000	_____	62,500	88,500	123,500
(c)	157,000	37,500	67,000	47,500	57,000	_____
(d)	247,000	_____	97,000	61,000	100,000	147,000
(e)	224,000	74,000	104,000	72,000	_____	118,000

SOLUTION

(a) 183,500; (b) 97,000; (c) 100,000; (d) 64,000; (e) 106,000

7.5. Journalize the following data as of December 31:

(a) Merchandise inventory, January 1, $31,800; December 31, $38,500.

(b) Prepaid insurance before adjustment, $1,540. It was found that $460 had expired during the year.

(c) Office supplies physically counted on December 31 were worth $120. The original balance of Supplies was $750.

(d) Office salaries for a 5-day week ending on Friday average $2,500. The last payday was Friday, December 27.

	Dr.	Cr.
(a)		
(b)		
(c)		
(d)		

SOLUTION

		Dr.	Cr.
(a)	Income Summary	31,800	
	Merchandise Inventory		31,800
	Merchandise Inventory	38,500	
	Income Summary		38,500
(b)	Insurance Expense	460	
	Prepaid Insurance		460

		Dr.	Cr.
(c)	Office Supplies Expense	630	
	Office Supplies		630
(d)	Office Salaries Expense	1,000	
	Salaries Payable*		1,000

*December 30 and 31.

7.6. Journalize the adjusting entries, based on the following data:

(a) Merchandise inventory: January 1, $31,700; December 31, $37,500.

(b) Office supplies inventory on January 1, $1,200; office supplies on hand, December 31, $780.

(c) Sales salaries average $3,000 for a 5-day workweek ending on Friday. The last payday of the year was Friday, December 26.

(d) Prepaid insurance before adjustments has a balance of $1,230. Analysis of the account shows that $750 has expired during the year.

(a)		
(b)		
(c)		
(d)		

SOLUTION

(a)	Income Summary	31,700	
	Merchandise Inventory		31,700
	Merchandise Inventory	37,500	
	Income Summary		37,500
(b)	Office Supplies Expense	420	
	Office Supplies		420
(c)	Sales Salaries Expense	1,800	
	Sales Salaries Payable*		1,800
(d)	Insurance Expense	750	
	Prepaid Insurance		750

*December 29, 30, and 31.

7.7. The trial balance below includes the Merchandise Inventory balance of $12,400. At the end of the year, it was found that the Merchandise Inventory balance was $16,200. Post the needed entry directly to the work sheet columns below.

Trial Balance

	Adjustments	
	Dr.	Cr.
Merchandise Inventory, 12,400		
Income Summary		

SOLUTION

Trial Balance

	Adjustments	
	Dr.	Cr.
Merchandise Inventory, 12,400	16,200	12,400
Income Summary	12,400	16,200

7.8. Based on the above solution, extend the figures to the appropriate columns.

	Income Statement		Balance Sheet	
	Dr.	Cr.	Dr.	Cr.
Merchandise Inventory				
Income Summary				

SOLUTION

	Income Statement		Balance Sheet	
	Dr.	Cr.	Dr.	Cr.
Merchandise Inventory			16,200	
Income Summary	12,400	16,200		

7.9. A section of the work sheet is presented below. Enter the adjustment required for Inventory, if it is assumed that Ending Inventory was $38,000.

Title	Trial Balance		Adjustments	
	Dr.	Cr.	Dr.	Cr.
Merchandise Inventory	32,400			
Income Summary				

SOLUTION

Title	Trial Balance		Adjustments	
	Dr.	Cr.	Dr.	Cr.
Merchandise Inventory	32,400		38,000	32,400
Income Summary			32,400	38,000

7.10. Using the information in Prob. 7.9, extend the accounts in the work sheet. What does the debit balance in the balance sheet represent?

Title	Income Statement		Balance Sheet	
	Dr.	Cr.	Dr.	Cr.
Merchandise Inventory	32,400			
Income Summary				

SOLUTION

Title	Income Statement		Balance Sheet	
	Dr.	Cr.	Dr.	Cr.
Merchandise Inventory			38,000	
Income Summary	32,400	38,000		

The $38,000 represents inventory on hand at the end of the year.

7.11. Based on the work sheet's income statement columns below, prepare an income statement.

Income Summary	26,400	28,200
Sales		62,500
Purchases	31,400	
Rent Expense	6,000	
Salaries Expense	18,300	
Depreciation Expense	500	
	82,600	90,700

SOLUTION

Sales		$62,500
Cost of Goods Sold		
Merchandise Inventory (beginning)	$26,400	
Purchases	31,400	
Goods Available for Sale	$57,800	
Merchandise Inventory (ending)	28,200	
Cost of Goods Sold		29,600
Gross Profit		$32,900
Operating Expenses		
Rent Expense	$ 6,000	
Salaries Expense	18,300	
Depreciation Expense	500	
Total Expenses		24,800
Net Income		$ 8,100

7.12. From the trial balance of the J. J. Company below, prepare an eight-column work sheet. Use the following data for adjustments: (*a*) Merchandise Inventory, June 30, 19X8, $1,900; (*b*) supplies on hand, $150; (*c*) expired insurance, $200.

J. J. Company
Trial Balance
June 30, 19X8

	Debit	Credit
Cash	$12,300	
Accounts Receivable	16,000	
Merchandise Inventory	2,700	
Supplies	450	
Prepaid Insurance	500	
Accounts Payable		$ 3,200
Notes Payable		7,100
J. J., Capital		14,750
Sales		39,800
Purchases	17,200	
Salaries Expense	11,400	
Advertising Expense	2,300	
General Expense	2,000	
	$64,850	$64,850

J. J. Company
Work Sheet
Year Ended June 30, 19X8

Account Title	Trial Balance Dr.	Trial Balance Cr.	Adjustments Dr.	Adjustments Cr.	Income Statement Dr.	Income Statement Cr.	Balance Sheet Dr.	Balance Sheet Cr.
Cash	12,300							
Accounts Receivable	16,000							
Merchandise Inventory	2,700							
Supplies	450							
Prepaid Insurance	500							
Accounts Payable		3,200						
Notes Payable		7,100						
J. J., Capital		14,750						
Sales		39,800						
Purchases	17,200							
Salaries Expense	11,400							
Advertising Expense	2,300							
General Expense	2,000							
	64,850	64,850						
Income Summary								
Supplies Expense								
Insurance Expense								
Net Income								

SOLUTION

J. J. Company
Work Sheet
Year Ended June 30, 19X8

Account Title	Trial Balance Dr.	Trial Balance Cr.	Adjustments Dr.	Adjustments Cr.	Income Statement Dr.	Income Statement Cr.	Balance Sheet Dr.	Balance Sheet Cr.
Cash	12,300						12,300	
Accounts Receivable	16,000						16,000	
Merchandise Inventory	2,700		(a) 1,900	(a) 2,700			1,900	
Supplies	450			(b) 300			150	
Prepaid Insurance	500			(c) 200			300	
Accounts Payable		3,200						3,200
Notes Payable		7,100						7,100
J. J., Capital		14,750						14,750
Sales		39,800				39,800		
Purchases	17,200				17,200			
Salaries Expense	11,400				11,400			
Advertising Expense	2,300				2,300			
General Expense	2,000				2,000			
	64,850	64,850						
Income Summary			(a) 2,700	(a) 1,900	2,700	1,900		
Supplies Expense			(b) 300		300			
Insurance Expense			(c) 200		200			
			5,100	5,100	36,100	41,700	30,650	25,050
Net Income					5,600			5,600
					41,700	41,700	30,650	30,650

7.13.   The accounts and their balances in the M. Rothfeld Company ledger on December 31, the end of the fiscal year, are as follows:

Cash	$ 4,600
Accounts Receivable	6,900
Merchandise Inventory	28,300
Supplies	750
Prepaid Rent	1,800
Equipment	16,000
Accumulated Depreciation, Equipment	1,900
Accounts Payable	6,110
M. Rothfeld, Capital	48,200
M. Rothfeld, Drawing	12,900
Sales	128,000
Purchases	91,000
Advertising Expense	3,200
Salaries Expense	16,600
Miscellaneous Expense	2,160

Prepare an eight-column work sheet, with the following adjustments:

(*a*)   Merchandise inventory as of December 31, $33,400

(*b*)   Supplies on hand, $250

(*c*)   Depreciation for the period, $600

(*d*)   Accrued salaries, $1,250

Account Title	Trial Balance		Adjustments		Income Statement		Balance Sheet	
	Dr.	Cr.	Dr.	Cr.	Dr.	Cr.	Dr.	Cr.
Cash	4,600							
Accounts Receivable	6,900							
Merchandise Inventory	28,300							
Supplies	750							
Prepaid Rent	1,800							
Equipment	16,000							
Accumulated Deprec.		1,900						
Accounts Payable		6,110						
M. Rothfeld, Capital		48,200						
M. Rothfeld, Drawing	12,900							
Sales		128,000						
Purchases	91,000							
Advertising Expense	3,200							
Salaries Expense	16,600							
Miscellaneous Expense	2,160							
	184,210	184,210						
Income Summary								
Supplies Expense								
Depreciation Expense								
Salaries Payable								
Net Income								

SOLUTION

Account Title	Trial Balance		Adjustments		Income Statement		Balance Sheet	
	Dr.	Cr.	Dr.	Cr.	Dr.	Cr.	Dr.	Cr.
Cash	4,600						4,600	
Accounts Receivable	6,900						6,900	
Merchandise Inventory	28,300		(*a*) 33,400	(*a*) 28,300			33,400	
Supplies	750			(*b*) 500			250	
Prepaid Rent	1,800						1,800	
Equipment	16,000						16,000	
Accumulated Deprec.		1,900		(*c*) 600				2,500
Accounts Payable		6,110						6,110
M. Rothfeld, Capital		48,200						48,200
M. Rothfeld, Drawing	12,900						12,900	
Sales		128,000				128,000		

Account Title	Trial Balance		Adjustments		Income Statement		Balance Sheet	
	Dr.	Cr.	Dr.	Cr.	Dr.	Cr.	Dr.	Cr.
Purchases	91,000				91,000			
Advertising Expense	3,200				3,200			
Salaries Expense	16,600		(d) 1,250		17,850			
Miscellaneous Expense	2,160				2,160			
	184,210	184,210						
Income Summary			(a) 28,300	(a) 33,400	28,300	33,400		
Supplies Expense			(b) 500		500			
Depreciation Expense			(c) 600		600			
Salaries Payable				(d) 1,250				1,250
			64,050	64,050	143,610	161,400	75,850	58,060
Net Income					17,790			17,790
					161,400	161,400	75,850	75,850

7.14. Based on the data in Prob. 7.13, prepare (a) an income statement, (b) a statement of owner's equity, and (c) a balance sheet.

M. Rothfeld Company
Income Statement

Statement of Owner's Equity

Balance Sheet

ASSETS		
LIABILITIES AND OWNER'S EQUITY		

SOLUTION

M. Rothfeld Company
Income Statement

Sales		$128,000
Cost of Goods Sold		
Merchandise Inventory, January 1, 19X8	$ 28,300	
Purchases	91,000	
Goods Available for Sale	$119,300	
Merchandise Inventory, December 31, 19X8	33,400	
Cost of Goods Sold		85,900
Gross Profit		$ 42,100
Expenses		
Advertising Expense	$ 3,200	
Salaries Expense	17,850	
Supplies Expense	500	
Depreciation Expense	600	
Miscellaneous Expense	2,160	
Total Expenses		24,310
Net Income		$ 17,790

Statement of Owner's Equity

Capital, January 1, 19X8		$48,200
Net Income for Year 19X8	$17,790	
Drawing for Year 19X8	12,900	
Increase in Capital		4,890
Capital, December 31, 19X8		$53,090

Balance Sheet

ASSETS		
Current Assets		
Cash	$ 4,600	
Accounts Receivable	6,900	
Merchandise Inventory	33,400	
Supplies	250	
Prepaid Rent	1,800	
Total Current Assets		$46,950
Fixed Assets		
Equipment	$16,000	
Less: Accumulated Depreciation	2,500	13,500
Total Assets		$60,450

LIABILITIES AND OWNER'S EQUITY		
Current Liabilities		
Accounts Payable	$ 6,110	
Salaries Payable	1,250	
Total Liabilities		$ 7,360
Capital, December 31, 19X8		53,090
Total Liabilities and Owner's Equity		$60,450

7.15. Shown are the balances for P. Widmann Company on December 31, before adjustments.

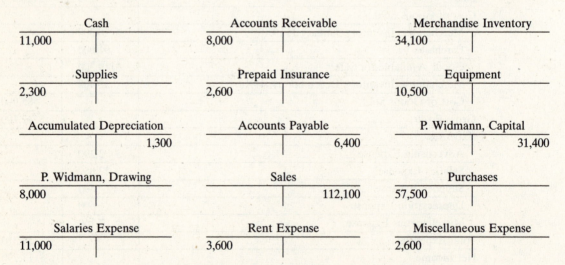

Cash		Accounts Receivable		Merchandise Inventory	
11,000		8,000		34,100	

Supplies		Prepaid Insurance		Equipment	
2,300		2,600		10,500	

Accumulated Depreciation		Accounts Payable		P. Widmann, Capital	
	1,300		6,400		31,400

P. Widmann, Drawing		Sales		Purchases	
8,000			112,100	57,500	

Salaries Expense		Rent Expense		Miscellaneous Expense	
11,000		3,600		2,600	

Using the additional data below, prepare an eight-column work sheet.

(*a*) Merchandise inventory, December 31, $32,800

(*b*) Supplies inventory, December 31, $800

(*c*) Insurance expired during the year, $1,400

(*d*) Depreciation for the year, $900

(*e*) Accrued salaries, December 31, $200

P. Widmann Company
Work Sheet
Year Ended December 31, 19X8

Account Title	Trial Balance Dr.	Trial Balance Cr.	Adjustments Dr.	Adjustments Cr.	Income Statement Dr.	Income Statement Cr.	Balance Sheet Dr.	Balance Sheet Cr.
Cash	11,000							
Accounts Receivable	8,000							
Merchandise Inventory	34,100							
Supplies	2,300							
Prepaid Insurance	2,600							
Equipment	10,500							
Accumulated Depreciation		1,300						
Accounts Payable		6,400						
P. Widmann, Capital		31,400						
P. Widmann, Drawing	8,000							
Sales		112,100						
Purchases	57,500							
Salaries Expense	11,000							
Rent Expense	3,600							
Miscellaneous Expense	2,600							
	151,200	151,200						
Income Summary								
Supplies Expense								
Insurance Expense								
Depreciation Expense								
Salaries Payable								
Net Income								

SOLUTION

P. Widmann Company
Work Sheet
Year Ended December 31, 19X8

Account Title	Trial Balance Dr.	Trial Balance Cr.	Adjustments Dr.	Adjustments Cr.	Income Statement Dr.	Income Statement Cr.	Balance Sheet Dr.	Balance Sheet Cr.
Cash	11,000						11,000	
Accounts Receivable	8,000						8,000	
Merchandise Inventory	34,100		(a) 32,800	(a) 34,100			32,800	
Supplies	2,300			(b) 1,500			800	
Prepaid Insurance	2,600			(c) 1,400			1,200	
Equipment	10,500						10,500	
Accumulated Depreciation		1,300		(d) 900				2,200
Accounts Payable		6,400						6,400
P. Widmann, Capital		31,400						31,400
P. Widmann, Drawing	8,000						8,000	

Account Title	Trial Balance		Adjustments		Income Statement		Balance Sheet	
	Dr.	Cr.	Dr.	Cr.	Dr.	Cr.	Dr.	Cr.
Sales		112,100				112,100		
Purchases	57,500				57,500			
Salaries Expense	11,000		(e) 200		11,200			
Rent Expense	3,600				3,600			
Miscellaneous Expense	2,600				2,600			
	151,200	151,200						
Income Summary			(a) 34,100	(a) 32,800	34,100	32,800		
Supplies Expense			(b) 1,500		1,500			
Insurance Expense			(c) 1,400		1,400			
Depreciation Expense			(d) 900		900			
Salaries Payable				(e) 200				200
			70,900	70,900	112,800	144,900	72,300	40,200
Net Income					32,100			32,100
					144,900	144,900	72,300	72,300

7.16. Based on the information in Prob. 7.15, journalize the adjusting and closing entries.

Adjusting Entries

(a)

(b)

(c)

(d)

Closing Entries

(a)

(b)

(c)			
(d)			

SOLUTION

Adjusting Entries

(a)	Income Summary	34,100	
	Merchandise Inventory		34,100
	Merchandise Inventory	32,800	
	Income Summary		32,800
(b)	Supplies Expense	1,500	
	Supplies		1,500
(c)	Insurance Expense	1,400	
	Prepaid Insurance		1,400
(d)	Depreciation Expense	900	
	Accumulated Depreciation		900
(e)	Salaries Expense	200	
	Salaries Payable		200

Closing Entries

(a)	Sales	112,100	
	Income Summary		112,100
(b)	Income Summary	78,700	
	Purchases		57,500
	Salaries Expense		11,200
	Rent Expense		3,600
	Supplies Expense		1,500
	Insurance Expense		1,400
	Depreciation Expense		900
	Miscellaneous Expense		2,600
(c)	Income Summary	32,100	
	P. Widmann, Capital		32,100
(d)	P. Widmann, Capital	8,000	
	P. Widmann, Drawing		8,000

7.17. Based on the information in Prob. 7.15, prepare an income statement, a statement of owner's equity, and a balance sheet for 19X8.

P. Widmann Company		
Income Statement		
Year Ended December 31, 19X8		

P. Widmann Company		
Statement of Owner's Equity		
Year Ended December 31, 19X8		

P. Widmann Company		
Balance Sheet		
December 31, 19X8		
ASSETS		

LIABILITIES AND OWNER'S EQUITY		

SOLUTION

P. Widmann Company		
Income Statement		
Year Ended December 31, 19X8		
Sales		$112,100
Cost of Goods Sold		
Merchandise Inventory, January 1	$34,100	
Purchases	57,500	
Goods Available for Sale	$91,600	
Less: Merchandise Inventory, December 31	32,800	
Cost of Goods Sold		58,800
Gross Profit		$ 53,300
Operating Expenses:	$11,200	
Salaries Expenses	3,600	
Rent Expense	1,500	
Supplies Expense	1,400	
Insurance Expense	900	
Depreciation Expense	2,600	
Miscellaneous Expense		
Total Expenses		21,200
Net Income		$ 32,100

P. Widmann Company		
Statement of Owner's Equity		
Year Ended December 31, 19X8		
Capital, January 1, 19X8		$ 31,400
Net Income	$32,100	
Less: Withdrawals	8,000	
Increase in Capital		24,100
Capital, December 31, 19X8		$ 55,500

P. Widmann Company		
Balance Sheet		
December 31, 19X8		
ASSETS		
Current Assets		
Cash	$11,000	
Accounts Receivable	8,000	
Merchandise Inventory	32,800	
Supplies	800	
Prepaid Insurance	1,200	
Total Current Assets		$ 53,800
Fixed Assets		
Equipment	$10,500	
Less: Accumulated Depreciation	2,200	8,300
Total Assets		$ 62,100
LIABILITIES AND OWNER'S EQUITY		
Current Liabilities		
Accounts Payable	$ 6,400	
Salaries Payable	200	
Total Current Liabilities		$ 6,600
Capital, December 31		55,500
Total Liabilities and Owner's Equity		$ 62,100

7.18. Given the accounts below, prepare the income statement for the Blasberg Company as of December 31, 19X8.

Sales	$86,400
Sales Returns	1,200
Purchases	59,700
Purchase Returns	650
Sales Salaries	14,700
Advertising Expense	2,100
Depreciation Expense, Delivery Equipment	900
Store Supplies Expense	650
Insurance Expense	3,200
Miscellaneous Selling Expense	590
Tax Expense	2,440
Office Supplies Expense	750
Inventory, Jan. 1, 19X8	36,240
Inventory, Dec. 31, 19X8	41,630

Blasberg Company		
Income Statement		
Year Ended December 31, 19X8		
Sales		
Cost of Goods Sold		
Gross Profit		
Operating Expenses		
Selling Expenses		
General Expenses		

SOLUTION

Blasberg Company		
Income Statement		
Year Ended December 31, 19X8		
Sales Income	$86,400	
Sales Returns	1,200	
Net Sales		$85,200
Cost of Goods Sold		
Merchandise Inventory, Jan. 1	$36,240	
Purchases	$59,700	
Purchase Returns	650	59,050
Goods Available for Sale		$95,290
Merchandise Inventory, Dec. 31		41,630
Total Cost of Goods Sold		53,660
Gross Profit		$31,540

Operating Expenses			
Selling Expenses			
Sales Salaries	$14,700		
Advertising Expense	2,100		
Depreciation Expense, Delivery Equipment	900		
Store Supplies Expense	650		
Insurance Expense	3,200		
Miscellaneous Selling Expense	590		
Total Selling Expenses		22,140	
General Expenses			
Tax Expense	$ 2,440		
Office Supplies Expense	750		
Total General Expenses		3,190	
Total Operating Expenses			25,330
Net Profit			$ 6,210

7.19. The trial balance of the Altman Sales Company, as of December 31, 19X8, is as follows:

Cash	$14,200	
Accounts Receivable	6,500	
Merchandise Inventory	38,100	
Supplies	4,200	
Prepaid Insurance	8,000	
Equipment	15,100	
Accumulated Depreciation		$ 3,400
Accounts Payable		11,200
J. Altman, Capital		37,200
J. Altman, Drawing	2,400	
Sales		98,200
Purchases	42,100	
Purchase Returns		300
Salaries Expense	11,200	
Transportation-In	4,500	
Misc. Gen. Expense	4,000	

1. Prepare an eight-column work sheet, using the following additional information for year-end adjustments: (*a*) Merchandise inventory on December 31, $42,500; (*b*) supplies inventory, December 31, $4,000; (*c*) insurance expired during this year, $2,000; (*d*) depreciation for the current year, $800; (*e*) salaries accrued on December 31, $400.

2. Prepare all necessary adjusting and closing entries.

1.

Account Title	Trial Balance		Adjustments		Income Statement		Balance Sheet	
	Dr.	Cr.	Dr.	Cr.	Dr.	Cr.	Dr.	Cr.

2.

Adjusting Entries

(a)

(b)

(c)

(d)

(e)

Closing Entries

(a)			
(b)			
(c)			
(d)			

SOLUTION

1.

Accounts Title	Trial Balance Dr.	Trial Balance Cr.	Adjustments Dr.	Adjustments Cr.	Income Statement Dr.	Income Statement Cr.	Balance Sheet Dr.	Balance Sheet Cr.
Cash	14,200						14,200	
Accounts Receivable	6,500						6,500	
Merchandise Inventory	38,100		(a) 42,500	(a) 38,100			42,500	
Supplies	4,200			(b) 200			4,000	
Prepaid Insurance	8,000			(c) 2,000			6,000	
Equipment	15,100						15,100	
Accumulated Depreciation		3,400		(d) 800				4,200
Accounts Payable		11,200						11,200
J. Altman, Capital		37,200						37,200
J. Altman Drawing	2,400						2,400	
Sales		98,200				98,200		
Purchases	42,100				42,100			
Purchase Returns		300				300		
Salaries Expense	11,200		(e) 400		11,600			
Transportation-In	4,500				4,500			
Misc. Gen. Expense	4,000				4,000			
	150,300	150,300						
Income Summary			(a) 38,100	(a) 42,500	38,100	42,500		
Supplies Expense			(b) 200		200			
Insurance Expense			(c) 2,000		2,000			
Depreciation Expense			(d) 800		800			
Salaries Payable				(e) 400				400
			84,000	84,000	103,300	141,000	90,700	53,000
Net Income					37,700			37,700
					141,000	141,000	90,700	90,700

2. | | | **Adjusting Entries** | | |
|---|---|---|---|---|
| (a) | Income Summary | | 38,100 | |
| | | Merchandise Inventory | | 38,100 |
| | Merchandise Inventory | | 42,500 | |
| | | Income Summary | | 42,500 |
| | | | | |
| (b) | Supplies Expense | | 200 | |
| | | Supplies | | 200 |
| | | | | |
| (c) | Insurance Expense | | 2,000 | |
| | | Prepaid Insurance | | 2,000 |
| | | | | |
| (d) | Depreciation Expense | | 800 | |
| | | Accumulated Depreciation | | 800 |
| | | | | |
| (e) | Salaries Expense | | 400 | |
| | | Salaries Payable | | 400 |

		Closing Entries		
(a)	Sales		98,200	
	Purchase Returns		300	
		Income Summary		98,500
(b)	Income Summary		65,200	
		Purchases		42,100
		Salaries Expense		11,600
		Transportation-In		4,500
		Misc. General Expense		4,000
		Supplies Expense		200
		Insurance Expense		2,000
		Depreciation Expense		800
(c)	Income Summary		37,700	
		J. Altman, Capital		37,700
(d)	J. Altman, Capital		2,400	
		J. Altman, Drawing		2,400

7.20. From the information in Prob. 7.19, prepare all financial statements.

Altman Sales Company		
Income Statement		
Year Ended December 31, 19X8		

Altman Sales Company		
Statement of Owner's Equity		
Year Ended December 31, 19X8		

Altman Sales Company		
Balance Sheet		
December 31, 19X8		

SOLUTION

Altman Sales Company		
Income Statement		
Year Ended December 31, 19X8		
Sales		$98,200
Cost of Goods Sold		
Merchandise Inventory, Jan. 1	$38,100	
Purchases	$42,100	
Add: Transportation-In	4,500	
	$46,600	
Less: Purchase Returns	300	46,300
Goods Available for Sale	$84,400	
Less: Merchandise Inventory, Dec. 31	42,500	
Total Cost of Goods Sold		41,900
Gross Profit		$56,300
Operating Expenses		
Salaries Expense	$11,600	
Insurance Expense	2,000	
Supplies Expense	200	
Depreciation Expense	800	
Miscellaneous General Expense	4,000	
Total Expenses		18,600
Net Income		$37,700

Altman Sales Company		
Statement of Owner's Equity		
Year Ended December 31, 19X8		
Capital, January 1, 19X8		$37,200
Net Income 19X8	$37,700	
Less: Drawing 19X8	2,400	
Increase in Capital		35,300
Capital, December 31, 19X8		$72,500

Altman Sales Company		
Balance Sheet		
December 31, 19X8		
ASSETS		
Current Assets		
Cash	$14,200	
Accounts Receivable	6,500	
Merchandise Inventory	42,500	
Supplies	4,000	
Prepaid Insurance	6,000	
Total Current Assets		$73,200
Fixed Assets		
Equipment	$15,100	
Less: Accumulated Depreciation	4,200	10,900
Total Assets		$84,100
LIABILITIES AND OWNER'S EQUITY		
Current Liabilities		
Accounts Payable	$11,200	
Salaries Payable	400	
Total Current Liabilities		$11,600
Capital, December 31, 19X8		72,500
Total Liabilities and Owner's Equity		$84,100

7.21. Listed below are the account balances for the Jim Small Clothing Company. Prepare the year-end financial statements.

Income Statement Accounts

Sales	$210,000
Sales Returns	1,050
Purchases	78,100
Supplies Expense	3,450
Insurance Expense	2,900
Purchases Discounts	900
Sales Discount	350
Depreciation Expense—Equipment	10,200
Depreciation Expense—Building	9,800
Miscellaneous Expense	1,100
Salaries Expense	54,600
Merchandise Inventory, January 1, 19X8	64,500
Merchandise Inventory, December 31, 19X8	72,400
Purchases Returns	1,150

Statement of Owner's Equity Accounts

Jim Small, Capital, January 1, 19X8	$22,500
Jim Small, Withdrawals for Year	19,500
Net Income from Income Statement	?
Increase in Capital	?
Jim Small, Capital, December 31, 19X8	?

Balance Sheet Accounts

Cash	$22,900
Prepaid Rent	4,700
Accounts Receivable	7,600
Supplies	6,000
Merchandise Inventory	72,400
Notes Payable	77,500
Accounts Payable	11,200
Salaries Payable	9,600
Capital from Statement of Owner's Equity	?
Equipment	64,500
Accumulated Depreciation—Equipment	54,400
Accumulated Depreciation—Building	76,000
Building	90,000
Land	22,000

Jim Small Clothing Company		
Income Statement		
Year Ended December 31, 19X8		

Jim Small Clothing Company		
Statement of Owner's Equity		
Year Ended December 31, 19X8		

Jim Small Clothing Company		
Balance Sheet		
December 31, 19X8		
ASSETS		
LIABILITIES		
OWNER'S EQUITY		

SOLUTION

Jim Small Clothing Company Income Statement Year Ended December 31, 19X8			
Revenue from Sales			
Sales		$210,000	
Less: Sales Returns	$1,050		
Sales Discount	350	1,400	
Net Sales			$208,600
Cost of Merchandise Sold			
Merchandise Inventory, January 1, 19X8		$ 64,500	
Purchases	$78,100		
Less: Purchases Returns	$1,150		
Purchases Discounts	900	2,050	
Net Purchases		76,050	
Merchandise Available for Sale		$140,550	
Less: Ending Inventory, December 31, 19X8		72,400	
Cost of Merchandise Sold			68,150
Gross Profit			$140,450
Operating Expenses		$ 54,600	
Salaries Expense		10,200	
Depreciation Expense—Equipment		9,800	
Depreciation Expense—Building		3,450	
Supplies Expense		2,900	
Insurance Expense		1,100	
Miscellaneous Expense			
Total Operating Expenses			82,050
Net Income from Operations			$ 58,400

Jim Small Clothing Company Statement of Owner's Equity Year Ended December 31, 19X8		
Jim Small, Capital, January 1, 19X8		$ 22,500
Net Income for Year	$ 58,400	
Less: Withdrawals for Year	19,500	
Increase in Capital		38,900
Jim Small, Capital, December 31, 19X8		$ 61,400

Jim Small Clothing Company		
Balance Sheet		
December 31, 19X8		
ASSETS		
Current Assets		
Cash		$ 22,900	
Accounts Receivable		7,600	
Merchandise Inventory		72,400	
Supplies		6,000	
Prepaid Rent		4,700	
Total Current Assets			$113,600
Plant and Equipment			
Equipment	$64,500		
Less: Accumulated Depreciation	54,400	$ 10,100	
Building	$90,000		
Less: Accumulated Depreciation	76,000	14,000	
Land		22,000	
Total Plant and Equipment			46,100
Total Assets			$159,700
LIABILITIES			
Current Liabilities			
Notes Payable		$ 77,500	
Accounts Payable		11,200	
Salaries Payable		9,600	
Total Liabilities			$ 98,300
OWNER'S EQUITY			
Jim Small, Capital			61,400
Total Liabilities and Owner's Equity			$159,700

CHAPTER 8

Costing Merchandise Inventory

8.1 INTRODUCTION

In a mercantile business, inventory is merchandise that is held for resale. As such, it will ordinarily be converted into cash in less than a year and is thus a current asset. In a manufacturing business, there will usually be inventories of raw materials and goods in process in addition to an inventory of finished goods. Since we have discussed the Merchandise Inventory account as it relates to the work sheet (Chap. 7), let us now examine how the merchandise inventory amount is calculated.

8.2 PERIODIC AND PERPETUAL METHODS OF INVENTORY

Under the *periodic method*, inventory is physically counted at regular intervals (annually, quarterly, or monthly). When this system is used, credits are made to the Inventory account or to Purchases not as each sale is made, but rather in total at the end of the inventory period.

The *perpetual method* is generally used when units are of relatively high value. Running balances by unit and by cost are maintained for units purchased and sold. Individual receipts of goods are debited to the Inventory account, and individual sales are credited to this account. At the end of the accounting period, the cost of goods sold can be determined by adding the costs of the individual items sold.

EXAMPLE 1

If goods were purchased for $10,000 under the periodic system, the account *Purchases* would be debited. However, under the perpetual system, everything would be debited to *Merchandise Inventory*.

Conversely, every time a sale is made, the account is credited.

EXAMPLE 2

If goods costing $6,000 were sold for $10,000, under the periodic system Sales Income would be credited for the sale of $10,000.

Accounts Receivable	10,000	
Sales Income		10,000

However, under the perpetual system of valuation, even though the sale is recognized and treated in the same manner, a second entry is required to show the reduction in the value of Merchandise Inventory.

Accounts Receivable	10,000	
Sales Income		10,000
Cost of Goods Sold	6,000	
Merchandise Inventory		6,000

Thus, the inventory account shows a running balance that always reflects the amount on hand.

Since all inventory transactions under the perpetual inventory system are charged to Merchandise Inventory, any purchase returns or freight charges would not be recognized as separate accounts, but would also fall under the Merchandise Inventory account.

EXAMPLE 3

Present the entries in the following four situations for both the periodic and perpetual systems.

Situation A. Purchased $1,600 of merchandise on account.
Solution.

Periodic:	Purchases	1,600	
	Accounts Payable		1,600
Perpetual:	Merchandise Inventory	1,600	
	Accounts Payable		1,600

Situation B. Sold merchandise costing $1,000 on account for $3,000.
Solution.

Periodic:	Accounts Receivable	3,000	
	Sales Income		3,000
Perpetual:	Accounts Receivable	3,000	
	Sales Income		3,000
	Cost of Goods Sold	1,000	
	Merchandise Inventory		1,000

Situation C. Paid freight charge of $25 on merchandise purchased.
Solution.

Periodic:	Freight-In	25	
	Cash		25
Perpetual:	Merchandise Inventory	25	
	Cash		25

Situation D. Returned $500 of merchandise previously bought.
Solution.

Periodic:	Accounts Payable	500	
	Purchase Returns		500
Perpetual:	Accounts Payable	500	
	Merchandise Inventory		500

Note that under the perpetual system, Purchases, Freight-In, and Purchase Returns are nonexistent as accounts. Under this system, everything involving merchandise is charged immediately to Merchandise Inventory.

Because of the increasing use of bar codes, the perpetual inventory method should eliminate the need to physically count each item in the inventory at the end of the period as in the periodic method. However, some firms still take a physical inventory at the end of the year in case of theft, spoilage, or clerical error. Therefore, because of this double checking, the periodic inventory system is generally used and will be assumed in future discussions on inventory.

8.3 DETERMINING INVENTORY

Firms that use the periodic system do not keep records that show a continuous count for each product; or rather, the amounts are determined through a physical inventory. A physical inventory is the process of actually counting each item on hand. This laborious task is usually done when the business is closed, either after business hours or by actually closing the store for a short period of time. A typical "hands on" count would involve two people, one counting and the other recording the data on an inventory sheet.

(A) Goods in Transit

Any goods in transit that have been ordered by the firm should be included in the inventory if the title to the goods has already passed, even if they are not physically on the premises for the inventory count. The term *FOB* (Free On Board) is used to show the passing of title from the seller to the buyer. FOB shipping point means that title passed when the goods left the seller. FOB destination means that title will pass when the goods are received by the purchaser. Therefore, for inventory determination, goods in transit that are FOB shipping point should become part of the inventory, whereas those that are FOB destination should not.

EXAMPLE 4

At the end of the year, $66,000 appears as inventory of Drew Corp. On order is another $14,000 ($10,000 FOB shipping point and $4,000 FOB destination). The inventory to be recorded is determined as:

$66,000	Inventory on hand
10,000	Ordered FOB shipping point
$76,000	Total inventory to be recorded

The $4,000 of goods ordered FOB destination will not become part of the inventory until the goods are received, as title does not pass to Drew Corp. until receipt of the inventory.

(B) Sales

Merchandise that has already been sold (sales revenue) but has not as yet been shipped should not be considered part of the inventory figure. The same rules for goods in transit apply for sales as for purchases.

EXAMPLE 5

A physical count of merchandise shows that $46,000 is on hand. However, $16,000 of the inventory has already been sold by Acme but has not as yet been shipped. Since inventory is an asset, Acme does not own and cannot record $46,000 of merchandise inventory, but only $30,000, the amount that is actually owned.

(C) Consignment

Only inventory that is owned by the firm should be recorded. For example, merchandise on consignment (sold on a commission basis) would not be counted, as it is not owned by the business (consignee), but rather by the firm that shipped it (consignor).

EXAMPLE 6

If Ferdic Co. has an inventory count showing a cost of $24,000 that consists of $18,000 of goods purchased and the balance ($6,000) of goods received on consignment, only the $18,000 would be considered as inventory. Since inventory is an asset, the balance sheet of Ferdic Co. would reflect only the asset $18,000 and not the $6,000 loaned for resale.

8.4 INVENTORY MEASUREMENT

To approach the problem of inventory measurement, in order to assign the business cost to each item, three methods of valuation (FIFO, LIFO, and weighted average) have been developed and approved by GAAP (General Accepted Accounting Principles). To compare these three methods, the same identical data (Chart I) will be used in the following inventory examples.

Chart I

Date	Type	Units	Unit Cost	Totals
Jan. 1	Inventory	100	$ 6	$ 600
Mar. 10	Purchase	150	$ 8	1,200
June 6	Purchase	200	$ 9	1,800
Oct. 4	Purchase	250	$10	2,500
Available for sale		700		$6,100

It is to be assumed that a physical count of inventory as of the last day of the accounting period (December 31) showed 320 units on hand. Therefore, 380 units (700 − 320) were sold during the year.

(A) Costing Inventory: First-In–First-Out (FIFO)

This method of costing inventory makes the assumption that goods are sold in the order in which they are purchased. Therefore, the goods that were bought first (first-in) are the first goods to be sold (first-out), and the goods that remain on hand (ending inventory) are assumed to be made up of the latest costs. Therefore, for income determination, earlier costs are matched with revenue and the most recent costs are used for balance sheet valuation.

This method is consistent with the actual flow of costs, since merchandisers attempt to sell their old stock first. (Perishable items and high fashion items are examples.) FIFO is the most widely used inventory method of those that will be discussed.

EXAMPLE 7

Under FIFO, those goods left at the end of the period are considered to be those received last. Therefore, the 320 units on hand on Dec. 31 would be costed as follows:

Most recent purchase (Oct. 4)	250 units @ $10 =	$2,500
Next most recent purchase (June 6)	70 units @ $ 9 =	630
Ending inventory	320 units	$3,130

The latest cost of the inventory consists of 250 units at $10. However, since the ending inventory consists of 320 units, we must refer to the next most recent purchase and include 70 units at $9. Therefore, you could say that the process for determining the cost of the units on hand involves working backward through the purchases until there is a sufficient quantity to cover the ending inventory count. Thus the ending inventory under the FIFO method would be valued and recorded at $3,130.

The cost of goods sold can be determined by subtracting the value of the ending inventory from the total value of the inventory available for sale ($6,100 − $3,130 = $2,970). Since 320 units remain as ending inventory, the number of units sold is 380 (700 − 320).

EXAMPLE 8

This can also be computed as

100 units of inventory	@ $6 =	$ 600
150 units purchased (Mar. 10)	@ $8 =	1,200
130 units purchased (June 6)	@ $9 =	1,170
380	Total cost of goods sold	$2,970

It should be noted that as a method of assigning costs, FIFO may be used regardless of the actual physical flow of merchandise. Indeed, we might say that FIFO really stands for first-price-in–first-price-out. In a period of rising prices—inflation, for example—the FIFO method will yield the largest inventory value, thus resulting in a greater net income. This situation occurs because this method assigns an inventory cost based on the most recent higher costs. Conversely, the FIFO method would produce a smaller cost of goods sold because the earlier lower costs are assigned to the cost of goods sold. Because FIFO assigns the most recent charges to inventory, the value of the ending inventory is closer to its replacement cost than any other method.

EXAMPLE 9

Two years of determining the value of the same number of units in the inventory are shown below.

(a)   First year

19X8 (Rising Costs)

Inventory	10 units @ $5 =	$ 50
First purchase	10 units @ 6 =	60
Second purchase	10 units @ 7 =	70
Third purchase	10 units @ 8 =	80
40 units		$260

If 10 units are on hand, the value under FIFO would be computed as

Third purchase	10 units @ $8 = $80

Thus, the ending inventory of 10 units is $80.

The cost of goods sold would be calculated as $260 − $80 = $180.

(b)   Second year

19X9 (Declining Costs)

Inventory	10 units @ $8 =	$ 80
First purchase	10 units @ 7 =	70
Second purchase	10 units @ 6 =	60
Third purchase	10 units @ 5 =	50
40 units		$260

If 10 units are on hand, its value under FIFO would be computed as

Third purchase   10 units @ $5 = $50

Thus, the ending inventory of 10 units is $50.
The cost of goods sold would be calculated as $260 − $50 = $210.

Note that even though there are 10 units left in both years, under FIFO, the year 19X8 produces a higher ending inventory in a period of rising costs, thus producing a higher net income. This is because the cost of goods sold is lower when costs are rising ($260 − $80 = $180) than when they are declining ($260 − $50 = $210), and the lower the cost, the higher the profit.

(B) Costing Inventory: Last-In–First-Out (LIFO)

The last-in–first-out (LIFO) method of inventory measurement assumes that the most recently purchased items are to be the first ones sold and that the remaining inventory will consist of the earliest items purchased. In other words, the order in which the goods are sold is the reverse of the order in which they are bought. Unlike FIFO, the LIFO method specifies that the cost of inventory on hand (ending inventory) is determined by working forward from the beginning inventory through purchases until sufficient units are obtained to cover the ending inventory. This is the opposite of the FIFO system.

Remember that FIFO assumes that costs flow in the order in which they are incurred, whereas LIFO assumes that costs flow in the reverse of the order in which they are incurred.

EXAMPLE 10

Under LIFO, the inventory at the end of the period is considered to be merchandise purchased in the first part of the period. What is the cost of the 320 units on hand (see Chart I)?

Earliest purchase (Jan. 1)	100 units @ $6 =	$ 600
Next purchase (Mar. 10)	150 units @ $8 =	1,200
Next purchase (June 6)	70 units @ $9 =	630
Ending inventory	320 units	$2,430

Thus, ending inventory under the LIFO method would be valued at $2,430.

EXAMPLE 11

Determine the cost of goods sold for Example 10.
The cost of goods sold is determined by subtracting the value of the ending inventory from the total value of the inventory available for sale ($6,100 − $2,430 = $3,670). This cost may also be computed as

Oct. 4	250 units @ $10 =	$2,500
June 6	130 units @ $ 9 =	1,170
Cost of goods sold	380 units	$3,670

A disadvantage of the LIFO method is that it does not reflect the actual physical movement of goods in the business, as most businesses do not move out their most recent purchases. Yet firms favor this method because it matches the most recent costs against the current revenue, thereby keeping earnings from being greatly distorted by any fluctuating increases or decreases in prices. Yet it sometimes allows managers to do too much maneuvering to change net income. For example, if prices are rising rapidly, and a company wishes to pay less in taxes (lower net income) for that year, management can buy large amounts of inventory near the end of that period. Under LIFO, these higher inventory costs, because of rising prices, immediately become an expense (cost of goods sold), and thus result in the financial statement's showing a lower net income. Conversely, if the firm is having a bad year, management may want to increase net income to garner favor from its stockholders. This can be done by delaying any large purchase of high-cost inventory until the following period, thus keeping the purchase out of the Cost of Goods Sold section for the current year and avoiding any decrease in net income.

When prices are rising, certain tax advantages are gained through LIFO because it yields a lower profit because of the higher cost of goods sold.

EXAMPLE 12

Use Chart I.

	FIFO		**LIFO**	
Sales (assumed)		$20,000		$20,000
Cost of Goods Sold:				
Goods Avail. for Sale	$6,100		$6,100	
Less: Ending Inventory	3,130		2,430	
Cost of Goods Sold		2,970		3,670
Gross Profit		$17,030		$16,330

Therefore, as Example 12 depicts, LIFO produces (in a period of rising prices) (1) a lower ending inventory, (2) a higher cost of goods sold, and (3) a lower gross profit. FIFO will produce the opposite.

The IRS will permit companies to use LIFO for tax purposes only if they use LIFO for financial reporting purposes. Thus, if a business uses LIFO for tax purposes, it must also report inventory and income on the same valuation basis for its financial statements; however, it is allowed to report an alternative inventory amount in the notes to the financial statements. This is permitted because it affords true financial analysis by allowing comparison of one business with another on a similar basis. It should be noted that a business cannot change its inventory valuation method any time it chooses. Once a method has been adopted, the business should use the same procedure from one period to the next. If management feels a need to change, permission must be granted by the IRS. The business must then follow specific authoritative guides that will detail how the changes should be treated on financial statements.

(C) Costing Inventory: Average Cost Valuation

Known also as weighted average, this inventory measurement system is based on the average cost of inventory during the period and takes into consideration the quantity and the price of the inventory items by assigning the same amount of cost to identical items. In other words, it spreads the total dollar cost of the goods available for sale equally among all the units. The ending inventory is determined by the following procedure:

1. The cost of the total number of units available for sale (beginning inventory plus purchases) is divided by the total number of units available for sale.

2. The number of units in the ending inventory is multiplied by this weighted average figure.

EXAMPLE 13

Referring to the same data in Chart I, the cost of the 320 units on hand would be calculated as follows:

1. $6,100 ÷ 700$ units = $8.71 unit cost
2. $8.71 × 320$ units on hand = $2,787* ending inventory

---

*Rounded off to highest dollar.

EXAMPLE 14

The cost of goods sold is then calculated by subtracting the value of the ending inventory from the total value of the inventory available for sale ($6,100 − $2,787 = $3,313).

Because there were 700 units available for sale and 320 units on hand at the end of the period, the number of units sold was determined as 700 − 320 = 380 units. Therefore, another method of computation to determine the cost of goods sold would be $8.71 × 380 units (cost of goods sold) = $3,310.*

The average cost method is best used by firms that buy large amounts of goods that are similar in nature and stored in a common place. Grain-processing, gasoline, and coal are good examples of products that could logically be costed under weighted average.

There are some limitations that should be noted in this valuation procedure. Unit cost cannot be related to any physical purchase and does not represent any price changes. In those industries that are greatly affected by price and style change, this method will not yield specific cost determination.

The average cost method averages price fluctuation (up or down), in determining both gross profit and inventory cost, and the results will always be the same regardless of whether price trends are rising or falling.

EXAMPLE 15

Rising Price Market

Jan. 1	Beginning inventory	100 units @ $6 = $ 600
Mar. 20	1st purchase	100 units @ 7 = 700
Jul. 20	2nd purchase	100 units @ 8 = 800
Nov. 20	3rd purchase	100 units @ 9 = 900
	Available for sale	400 units $3,000

Falling Price Market

Jan. 1	Beginning inventory	100 units @ $9 = $ 900
Mar. 20	1st purchase	100 units @ 8 = 800
Jul. 20	2nd purchase	100 units @ 7 = 700
Nov. 20	3rd purchase	100 units @ 6 = 600
	Available for sale	400 units $3,000

Ending inventory consists of 150 units. Under the average cost method, the cost per unit is the same whether there is a rising or falling price market.

$$\$3,000 \div 400 = \$7.50 \text{ per unit}$$
$$150 \text{ units on hand} \times \$7.50 = \underline{\$1,125}$$

Thus, the ending inventory value of $1,125 will not change, regardless of the economic pricing trend. The cost of goods sold is then determined by

$$(400 − 150) = 250 \text{ units} \times \$7.50 = \underline{\$1,875}$$

Note that the cost of goods sold, whether in a rising or falling price market, will be valued at the same cost.

(D) Comparison of Inventory Methods

The three methods of inventory valuation discussed are based on an assumption as to the flow of costs. The FIFO method is based on the assumption that costs flow in the order in which they were incurred; the LIFO method assumes that costs flow in the reverse of the order in which they were

---

*Rounded off to highest dollar.

incurred; and weighted average assumes that costs should be assigned to the merchandise inventory based on an average cost per unit. Note that if the costs of all purchases remain the same, the three methods of inventory valuation will yield identical results. However, as prices never stay constant, in practice each of these three methods will result in a different cost for the ending inventory. Remember that the ending figure is subtracted from the cost of goods available for sale to arrive at the cost of goods sold (COGS). Therefore, the net income or loss will vary according to the inventory method chosen. Also, the ending inventory on the balance sheet will vary with each method.

In Example 16 below, we compare the results of the FIFO, LIFO, and weighted average methods, with regard to both ending inventory and cost of goods sold. Since the two amounts are related through the equation

$$\text{Goods available for sale} - \text{ending inventory} = \text{cost of goods sold}$$

it is seen that if the ending inventory is *overstated*, the cost of goods sold will be *understated* and net profit *overstated*. On the other hand, if inventory is *understated*, then cost of goods sold will be *overstated* and net profit *understated*. Clearly, the method chosen for inventory computation can have a marked effect on the profit of the firm. There is no *one* method that is the best for all firms, but careful consideration of the following factors will be helpful in making the decision: (1) the effect on the income statement and balance sheet, (2) the effect on taxable income, and (3) the effect on the selling price.

EXAMPLE 16

	First-In–First-Out	Last-In–First-Out	Weighted Average
Goods available for sale	$6,100	$6,100	$6,100
Ending inventory, Dec. 31	3,130	2,430	2,787
Cost of goods sold	$2,970	$3,670	$3,313

Summary From Chart I

Based upon Example 16, the following evaluation is considered:

FIFO

1. Yields the lowest amount of cost of goods sold
2. Yields the highest amount of gross profit
3. Yields the highest amount of ending inventory

Note: During a period of inflation or rising prices, the use of FIFO will have the results shown above, but in a declining price economy, the results will be reversed. The major criticism of this method is the tendency to maximize the effect of inflationary and deflationary trends on amounts reported as gross profit.

LIFO

1. Yields the highest amount of cost of goods sold
2. Yields the lowest amount of gross profit
3. Yields the lowest amount of ending inventory

Because the cost of the most recently acquired units approximates the cost of their replacement, this method can be defended on the basis that its use more nearly matches current costs with current revenues. The major justification for LIFO is that it minimizes the effect of price trends on gross profit.

Weighted Average

1. Yields results between FIFO and LIFO for cost of goods sold
2. Yields results between FIFO and LIFO for gross profit
3. Yields results between FIFO and LIFO for ending inventory

This compromise method of inventory costing reduces the effect of price trends (up or down) as all costs are averaged in the determination of both gross profit and inventory cost. For any given series of prices, the average cost will be the same, regardless of the direction of price trends.

Summary

1. When inventory is recorded based on a physical count at the end of an accounting period, we have the _____ method.

2. The inventory method used when units are generally of high value is the _____ method.

3. The _____ inventory method is most commonly used in retail establishments.

4. A method of inventory valuation based on the concept that the goods are sold in the order in which they are received is known as _____ .

5. The valuation of inventory based on the concept that the most recent costs incurred should be charged against income is known as _____ .

6. In a rising market, net income under _____ would be smaller, thus producing a smaller tax.

7. The inventory method based on the concept that the unit cost of merchandise sold is the average of all expenditures for inventory is known as _____ .

Answers: 1. periodic; 2. perpetual; 3. periodic; 4. first-in–first-out (FIFO); 5. last-in–first-out (LIFO); 6. LIFO; 7. weighted average.

Solved Problems

8.1.   (*a*)   Based upon the following records, determine the value of the inventory to be recorded.

Goods on hand (paid)	$ 59,000
Goods on hand (owed)	42,000
Goods on hand (consignment)	15,000
Goods ordered but not received (FOB sh. pt.)	24,000
Goods ordered but not received (FOB dest.)	12,000
	$152,000

(*b*)   How is this value treated?

SOLUTION

(*a*) The inventory is valued as follows:

Goods on hand (paid)	$ 59,000
Goods on hand (owed)	42,000
Goods ordered (FOB shipping point)	24,000
Total inventory on hand	$125,000

(*b*) Balance Sheet
    Current Assets
        Merchandise Inventory $125,000

8.2. In Prob. 8.1, if $25,000 of inventory had been sold but, at the time of the accounting valuation, had not been shipped, what would the value of the inventory then be?

SOLUTION

$$\$125,000 - \$25,000 = \underline{\$100,000}$$

Under the periodic system, no adjustment to the Inventory account is made until the end of the period, when a new count is made.

8.3. The inventory information for a product is given below:

Jan. 1	Inventory	12 units	$15
Feb. 16	Purchase	8 units	16
Mar. 4	Purchase	15 units	18
Oct. 15	Purchase	10 units	20

After taking a physical count, we find that we have 14 units on hand. Determine the ending inventory cost by the FIFO method.

SOLUTION

Most recent purchase	(Oct. 15)	10 units @ $20 = $200
Next most recent purchase	(Mar. 4)	4 units @ 18 = 72
Ending inventory		14 $272

Remember that values are assigned to the inventory based on the latest cost (the most recent purchases).

8.4. Assign a value to the ending inventory under FIFO using the following cost data:

Beginning inventory	200 units @ $10 = $2,000
First purchase	300 units @ 12 = 3,600
Second purchase	300 units @ 11 = 3,300
Available for sale	800 $8,900

An inventory count at the end of the period reveals that 450 units are still on hand.

SOLUTION

Second purchase	300 units @ $11 = $3,300
First purchase	150 units @ 12 = 1,800
Beginning inventory	450 $5,100

8.5.   Based upon the information in Prob. 8.4, determine the cost of goods sold for the period.

SOLUTION

There are two methods to determine the cost of those goods sold.

(a)   Total goods available $8,900
       Ending inventory   5,100
       Cost of goods sold $3,800

Alternative Method

(b)   Beginning inventory   200 units @ $10 = $2,000
       First purchase   150 units @ 12 = 1,800
       Cost of goods sold   350 units $3,800

Since there were a total of 800 units available and 450 were on hand at the end of the period, 350 units were sold (800 − 450 = 350).

8.6.   Product information for item 204 is as follows:

Jan. 1	Inventory	50 units @ $10 =	$ 500
Apr. 24	Purchase	30 units @ 8 =	240
July 10	Purchase	40 units @ 7 =	280
Nov. 15	Purchase	35 units @ 8 =	280
	Units available	155 Total cost	$1,300

By a physical count, it is estimated that 95 units are left in the ending inventory. (a) What is the value of the ending inventory under FIFO valuation? (b) Determine the cost of goods sold.

SOLUTION

(a)   Nov. 15   35   units @ $8 = $280
       July 10   40   units @ 7 = 280
       Apr. 24   20* units @ 8 = 160
       Ending inventory   95   units $720

_____

*A total of 95 units are on hand. Since you have 75 units (35 + 40) from the two most recent purchases, only 20 of 30 units of the April 24 purchase are needed.

(b) $1,300   Total amount of goods
        −720   Ending inventory
       $ 580   Cost of goods sold

Alternative Method

Jan. 1	50 units @ $10 = $500
Apr. 24	10 units @ 8 = 80
Cost of goods sold	60 units $580

Note that since there were 155 units available and 95 units were on hand, 60 units (155 − 95) were used to determine the cost of goods sold.

8.7. Based upon the following information, determine under LIFO valuation (*a*) ending inventory of 120 units and (*b*) its cost of goods sold.

Beginning inventory	100 units @ $15 =	$1,500
Apr. 30	100 units @ 17 =	1,700
Sept. 30	100 units @ 18 =	1,800
Dec. 30	100 units @ 21 =	2,100
Available for sale	400 units	$7,100

SOLUTION

(*a*)

Beginning inventory	100 units @ $15 =	$1,500
Apr. 30	20 units @ 17 =	340
Ending inventory	120 units	$1,840

(*b*)

Dec. 30	100 units @ $21 =	$2,100
Sept. 30	100 units @ 18 =	1,800
Apr. 30	80 units @ 17 =	1,360
Cost of goods sold	280 units	$5,260

Proof:

$7,100	Available units
−1,840	Ending inventory
$5,260	Cost of goods sold

8.8. Based upon the following information in a rising price market, determine (*a*) ending inventory of 260 units under LIFO and (*b*) the cost of goods sold.

Beginning inventory	100 units @ $ 5 =	$ 500
Mar. 30 purchase	100 units @ 6 =	600
Sept. 30 purchase	100 units @ 8 =	800
Nov. 30 purchase	100 units @ 9 =	900
Dec. 30 purchase	100 units @ 12 =	1,200
	500 units	$4,000

SOLUTION

(*a*)

Beginning inventory	100 units @ $5 =	$ 500
Mar. 30 purchase	100 units @ 6 =	600
Sept. 30 purchase	60 units @ 8 =	480
Ending inventory	260 units	$1,580

(*b*) The ending inventory is $1,580 and the cost of goods sold is ($4,000 − $1,580 = $2,420) or computed as

Dec. 30	100 units @ $12 =	$1,200
Nov. 30	100 units @ 9 =	900
Sept. 30	40 units @ 8 =	320
Cost of goods sold	240*	$2,420

*Since there were 500 units in the total inventory, and 260 remained, 240 units had been sold.

8.9.   If in Prob. 8.8 the management had decided to delay the Dec. 30 purchase until the following
year (in order to show a higher profit based on a lower cost) what would be the cost of goods
sold without the last December purchase?

SOLUTION

Four hundred units (the December purchase of 100 units is eliminated) were available to be sold and
260 units remained on hand. Thus the 140 units sold will be costed as follows:

Nov. 30*	100 units @ $9 =	$ 900
Sept. 30	40 units @ 8 =	320
Cost of goods sold	140	$1,220

*No December purchase is considered.

Therefore, management now has a cost of $1,220 rather than $2,420 (Prob. 8.8), thus meeting its
objective of higher profits. This lower cost will then yield a higher profit, yet it keeps the ending inventory
at the same figure.

8.10.   The beginning inventory and various purchases of product Y were as follows:

Jan. 1	Beginning inventory	8 units @ $10 =	$ 80
Apr. 4	First purchase	12 units @ 11 =	132
July 16	Second purchase	16 units @ 12 =	192
Aug. 25	Third purchase	15 units @ 13 =	195
Dec. 24	Fourth purchase	18 units @ 14 =	252
	Available for sale	69 units	$851

An inventory count disclosed that 30 units of product Y were on hand. (*a*) Determine
the ending inventory under the Weighted Average method. (*b*) Determine the cost of
goods sold.

SOLUTION

(*a*)   (1) $851 ÷ 69 = $12.33 per unit

(2) $12.33 × 30 = $370 Ending inventory*

*Rounded off to the nearest dollar.

(*b*)   Since 69 units were available for sale and 30 of those units were on hand, 69 − 30 = 39 units were
sold. To determine the total cost of goods sold, multiply the units sold by the average cost of each
unit. Therefore:

$$39 \text{ units} \times \$12.33 \text{ per unit} = \$481$$

Alternative Method

Total value of goods	$851
Ending inventory	−370
Cost of goods sold	$481

8.11. In an inflationary market, Essex Corp. bought the following items:

Jan. 1	Beginning inventory	150 units @ $2.00 =	$ 300
May 14	First purchase	300 units @ 4.00 =	1,200
Oct. 6	Second purchase	300 units @ 5.00 =	1,500
Nov. 14	Third purchase	250 units @ 6.00 =	1,500
Dec. 19	Fourth purchase	200 units @ 7.50 =	1,500
	Available for sale	1,200 units	$6,000

If 225 units are left on hand, determine (a) the ending inventory in this inflationary period under the average cost method and (b) the cost of goods sold.

SOLUTION

(a) $6,000 ÷ 1,200 units = $5 per unit
      225 units on hand × $5 per unit = $1,125 Ending inventory

(b)   1,200 units − 225 units on hand = 975 units sold
      975 × $5 per unit = $4,875 Cost of goods sold

To prove that both items (a) and (b) are correct:

$1,125	Ending inventory
+4,875	Cost of goods sold
$6,000	Goods available for sale

8.12. In a deflationary market, Robert Kincaid bought the following items:

Jan. 1	Beginning inventory	200 units @ $7.50 =	$1,500
May 14	First purchase	250 units @ 6.00 =	1,500
Oct. 6	Second purchase	300 units @ 5.00 =	1,500
Nov. 14	Third purchase	300 units @ 4.00 =	1,200
Dec. 19	Fourth purchase	150 units @ 2.00 =	300
	Available for sale	1,200 units	$6,000

If 225 units are left on hand, determine (a) the ending inventory in this deflationary period under the average cost method and (b) the cost of goods sold.

SOLUTION

(a) $6,000 ÷ 1,200 units = $5 per unit
      225 units on hand × $5 per unit = $1,125 Ending inventory

(b)   1,200 units − 225 units on hand = 975 units sold
      975 units × $5 per unit = $4,875 Cost of goods sold

Proof: $1,125 + $4,875 = $6,000 Goods available for sale

Note that in both this problem (8.12) and Prob. 8.11, the ending inventory value is the same regardless of inflation (rising prices) or deflation (falling prices). This occurs because you are averaging the entire accounting period. In the next problem, different values do occur, because the inventory will be valued under FIFO and LIFO as well as average cost.

8.13. The beginning inventory and various purchases of product B were as follows:

Jan.	1	Balance	8 units @ $10.00
Mar.	5	Purchase	12 units @ 11.00
June	9	Purchase	16 units @ 12.00
Aug.	20	Purchase	15 units @ 13.00
Nov.	1	Purchase	18 units @ 14.00

An inventory count under the periodic system disclosed that 30 units of product B were on hand. Determine the ending inventory cost by (*a*) first-in–first out; (*b*) last-in–first-out; (*c*) weighted average.

SOLUTION

(*a*) Most recent purchase (Nov. 1)   18 units @ $14 = $252
     Next most recent (Aug. 20)   12 units @ 13 = 156
                   Total units   30 Total cost $408

(*b*) Earliest cost (Jan. 1)   8 units @ $10 = $ 80
     Next earliest (Mar. 5)   12 units @ 11 = 132
     Next earliest (June 9)   10 units @ 12 = 120
                Total units   30 Total cost $332

(*c*)   8 units @ $10 = $ 80
                        12 units @ 11 = 132
                        16 units @ 12 = 192
                        15 units @ 13 = 195
                        18 units @ 14 = 252
                        69 Total cost $851
              Total units   30 Total cost $370*

The weighted average cost per unit is $851 ÷ 69 = $12.33. The cost of 30 units on hand is calculated as $12.33 × 30 = $370*.

---

*Rounded to the nearest dollar.

8.14. From the following information, determine the cost of inventory by the first-in–first-out (FIFO), the last-in–first out (LIFO), and the weighted average cost method.

Unit Number	Inventory January 1, 19X8	March Purchases	June Purchases	September Purchases	Number of Units in Inventory December 31, 19X8
101	3 @ $480	5 @ $490	6 @ $500	5 @ $510	6
103	6 @ 208	10 @ 210	11 @ 220	7 @ 222	7
105	4 @ 200	5 @ 200	4 @ 210	2 @ 215	3
107	3 @ 225	9 @ 240	7 @ 245	4 @ 250	5
109	1 @ 295	1 @ 300	3 @ 315	—	2

Unit Number	Quantity	Cost per Unit	Total Cost
FIRST-IN–FIRST-OUT			
Total inventory			

Unit Number	Quantity	Cost per Unit	Total Cost
LAST-IN–FIRST-OUT			
Total inventory			

Unit Number	Quantity	Cost per Unit	Total Cost
WEIGHTED AVERAGE COST			
Total inventory			

SOLUTION

Unit Number	Quantity	Cost per Unit	Total Cost
FIRST-IN–FIRST-OUT			
101	5	$510	$2,550
101	1	500	500
103	7	222	1,554
105	2	215	430
105	1	210	210
107	4	250	1,000
107	1	245	245
109	2	315	630
Total inventory			$7,119

Unit Number	Quantity	Cost per Unit	Total Cost
LAST-IN–FIRST-OUT			
101	3	$480	$1,440
101	3	490	1,470
103	6	208	1,248
103	1	210	210
105	3	200	600
107	3	225	675
107	2	240	480
109	1	295	295
109	1	300	300
Total inventory			$6,718

Unit Number	Quantity	Cost per Unit	Total Cost
WEIGHTED AVERAGE COST			
101	6	$496.84	$2,981.04
103	7	215.35	1,507.45
105	3	204.67	614.01
107	5	241.30	1,206.50
109	2	308.00	616.00
Total inventory			$6,925.00

8.15. Determine the gross profit under the (*a*) FIFO and (*b*) LIFO assumptions, given the following information:

Sales	$40,000
Goods available for sale	12,000
Ending inventory (under FIFO)	3,500
Ending inventory (under LIFO)	6,500

SOLUTION

		FIFO		LIFO
Sales		$40,000		$40,000
Cost of Goods Sold:				
Goods Available for Sale	$12,000		$12,000	
Less End. Inventory	3,500		6,500	
Cost of Goods Sold		8,500		5,500
Gross Profit		$31,500		$34,500

Since FIFO produced a lower ending inventory, the corresponding profit was lower. Also, as a proof, FIFO produced a higher cost of goods sold, therefore yielding a lower gross profit.

8.16. Based upon the following inventory information and other pertinent data, determine

(*a*) Ending inventory—36 units

(*b*) Cost of goods sold

(c)   Gross profit

Beginning inventory	20 units @ $9 = $180
First purchase	15 units @ 8 = 120
Second purchase	22 units @ 7 = 154
Third purchase	10 units @ 6 = 60
Available for sale	67 units $514

		FIFO		**LIFO**
Sales		$10,000		$10,000
Cost of Goods Sold:				
Goods Avail. for Sale	$514		$514	
Less Ending Inventory	(a)		(a)	
Cost of Goods Sold		(b)		(b)
Gross Profit		(c)		(c)

SOLUTION

In order to determine the gross profit, we must first determine the ending inventory and cost of goods sold under both the FIFO and LIFO methods.

Ending Inventory

FIFO

Third purchase	10 units @ $6 = $ 60	
Second purchase	22 units @ 7 = 154	
First purchase	4 units @ 8 = 32	
	36 units $246	(a)

LIFO

Beginning inventory	20 units @ $9 = $180	
First purchase	15 units @ 8 = 120	
Second purchase	1 unit @ 7 = 7	
	36 units $307	(a)

Cost of Goods Sold*

FIFO

Beginning inventory	20 units @ $9 = $180	
First purchase	11 units @ 8 = 88	
	31 units $268	(b)

LIFO

Third purchase	10 units @ $6 = $ 60	
Second purchase	21 units @ 7 = 147	
	31 units $207	(b)

---

*Since there are available 67 units and 36 remain as inventory, 31 units (67 − 36) have been sold.

		FIFO			**LIFO**	
Sales		$10,000			$10,000	
Cost of Goods Sold:						
Goods Avail. for Sale	$514			$514		
Less Ending Inventory	246	(*a*)		307	(*a*)	
Cost of Goods Sold		268	(*b*)		207	(*b*)
Gross Profit		$ 9,732	(*c*)		$ 9,793	(*c*)

CHAPTER 9

Alternative Inventory Valuation Methods

9.1 SPECIFIC IDENTIFICATION

Specific identification is a method of valuing inventory and determining the costs of goods sold by using the actual (specific) costs assigned to the units on hand and to those that were sold. In other words, the actual costs of the specific items sold constitute the cost of goods sold.

(A) Methodology

Under this method, it is necessary for the business to (1) keep records of the purchase price of each specific unit, (2) keep records of each specific unit sold, and (3) determine the ending inventory by totaling the original cost of all the specific units on hand. This cumbersome system should not be used for firms with large unit volumes and small unit prices (even computerized accounting systems and bar codes may not justify the use of this system), but it is ideal for small inventories of specifically identifiable items such as automobiles. This method gives the business the most accurate way of evaluating its inventory because actual costs and not valuations are used to determine the amount of the merchandise on hand at the end of the year.

EXAMPLE 1

A small auto business has the following three cars as of January 1, 19X8:

Item		Cost
Blue	642	$ 8,950
Green	795	12,420
Black	416	15,600

It purchased two additional cars during the month:

Item		Cost
Gray	814	$10,000
White	326	9,500

It sold one car during the month:

Item		Cost
Green	795	$12,420

In order to determine the cost of goods sold and the ending inventory as of January 31, 19X8, the following method is used:

Jan. 1	Inventory	642 (Blue)	$ 8,950	
		795 (Green)	12,420	
		416 (Black)	15,600	
				$36,970
Jan.	Purchases	814 (Gray)	$10,000	
		326 (White)	9,500	19,500
Jan.	Cost of sales	795 (Green)		(12,420)

Cost of goods sold (cost of sales) is determined by the amount of the specific items sold. In this case:

795 (Green)	$12,420

The ending inventory is identified as what remains on hand.

Jan. 1	642 (Blue)	$ 8,950
	416 (Black)	15,600
	814 (Gray)	10,000
	326 (White)	9,500
		$44,050

In other words, the beginning inventory plus purchases of $56,470 ($36,970 + $19,500) less the cost of goods sold of $12,420 would yield the value of the autos on hand as $44,050.

(B) Flow of Costs

When the cost of administering the specific identification method becomes too high in money and time, firms usually revert to the systems discussed previously, which use an arbitrary assumption as to the flow of costs of goods through the business. As stated in previous chapters, those assumptions would be

1. Cost flow is in the order of purchases—first-in–first-out.
2. Cost flow is in the reverse of the order of purchases—last-in–first-out.
3. Cost flow is the average of all purchases—weighted average.

However, even though many units are bought and sold, as long as they can be specifically identified, the method of specific identification can be justified.

EXAMPLE 2

			Units	Unit Cost	Total Cost
Jan.	1	Beginning inventory	10	$15	$150
Mar. 10		Purchase	20	18	360
June		Sales	(8)		
			22		$510

Assuming that six out of the eight units sold in June are identified as being from the beginning inventory and the balance (2) from the March 10 purchase, the cost of the goods sold would be determined as follows:

Jan. 1	6 units	@	$15 =	$ 90
Mar. 10	2 units	@	18 =	36
	8 units sold costing			$126

Thus, the cost of goods sold would be $126, the ending inventory would be $384 ($510 − $126), and the number of units on hand, by specific identification, would be 22 (30 − 8). In summary,

		Units	Unit Cost	Total Cost
Jan. 1	Beginning inventory	4	$15	$ 60
Mar. 10	Purchase	18	18	324
	Ending inventory	22		$384

Note that the costs remaining in the ending inventory are the actual costs of the specific items that were not sold.

9.2 NET REALIZABLE VALUE

The inventory methods mentioned in the preceding chapter all reported inventory at cost. When inventory items are damaged, become obsolete, or can be replaced at prices less than original cost, it may become necessary to report the inventory at an amount that is less than cost.

When it appears that inventory is obsolete or damaged, it should be reported at its net realizable value, which is the amount that the inventory can be sold for (minus selling costs).

EXAMPLE 3

Inventory with a cost of $8,000 is determined to be obsolete and can be sold for only $3,000. This inventory should be reported at its net realizable value determined by

Cost	$8,000
Less: Estimated selling price	3,000
Loss	$5,000

The above loss of $5,000 must be recognized as soon as it is known, even before the obsolete inventory is sold. The journal entry required to recognize this loss and to reduce the inventory amount would be

Loss on Write-down of Inventory*	5,000	
Inventory		5,000

*This is an expense account.

EXAMPLE 4

If it costs $200 to sell the inventory above, the loss would be $5,200 and the value of the inventory would be reduced by that amount. The entry would be

Loss on Write-down of Inventory	5,200	
Inventory		5,200

The net realizable value method allows a company to recognize a loss when it occurs; thus, the company will break even when the inventory is ultimately sold. The inventory is reported at its true value and is not carried at an amount which exceeds its future economic benefit.

9.3 LOWER OF COST OR MARKET (LCM)

(A) Introduction

When the value of the inventory has declined below its cost, a firm may choose the lower of cost or market (LCM) method. This method involves a comparison between the cost of inventory on hand and its current replacement cost. The lower of the two amounts is then used, which is a departure from the normal historical cost principle. Any loss in value should be recognized in the accounting period in which it occurred. This immediate recognition of loss is accomplished by an adjusting entry.

(B) The Theory of Conservatism

This method is used because accountants generally feel that assets should be valued conservatively, thereby not overstating their true value regardless of cost. Thus, when the price of an item is below its purchase cost, market price rather than cost may be used.

This method is acceptable in inventory valuation because a decline in the replacement cost can be accompanied by a reduction in the selling price of the merchandise, thus reducing the value of the inventory. It is used with the FIFO and weighted average methods of inventory valuation, but not with LIFO, for tax purposes. However, there is nothing to prevent its use for financial accounting purposes.

EXAMPLE 5

The total cost of the ending inventory was $1,605 by a physical inventory count under the FIFO method. However, because of a decline in the market price of goods, replacement of the inventory on an item-by-item basis could be obtained for $1,300. What is the effect of this market price revaluation?

There is a loss of $305 on the value of the inventory.

Inventory under FIFO	$1,605
Current replacement cost	1,300
Market value decline (loss)	($ 305)

If LCM is used, this loss will affect the cost of goods sold, producing a higher cost and reducing net income by $305.

However, if at year's end the inventory on the balance sheet is reported at $1,605 (cost), GAAP requires that under LCM inventory, an adjusting entry be made crediting the inventory and debiting the loss to be recognized in the current year.

(C) Application

The application of the item-by-item method is illustrated below:

EXAMPLE 6

		Unit Price			
Description	Quantity	Cost	Market	Valuation	LCM
Item A	200	$2.00	$2.25	Cost	$ 400
Item B	100	1.75	1.50	Market	150
Item C	150	1.80	1.00	Market	150
Item D	300	3.20	2.00	Market	600
					$1,300

Note that without LCM, the valuation of the merchandise would be:

Description	Quantity	Unit Price	Valuation
Item A	200	$2.00	$ 400
Item B	100	1.75	175
Item C	150	1.80	270
Item D	300	3.20	960
Total inventory cost			$1,805

(D) Total Replacement Cost (LCM)

Although item-by-item valuation is the most popular valuation method under LCM, the total replacement cost of the merchandise can also be used to value the inventory. Using the figures in Example 6, the total cost or market value would be computed as shown in Example 7.

EXAMPLE 7

Description	Quantity	Unit Price Cost	Unit Price Market	Total Cost	Total Market
Item A	200	$2.00	$2.25	$ 400	$ 450
Item B	100	1.75	1.50	175	150
Item C	150	1.80	1.00	270	150
Item D	300	3.20	2.00	960	600
				$1,805	$1,350

Inventory valuation, lower of total cost or total market $1,350

When the total replacement cost of the inventory is used (even though an item may cost more to replace than its original cost), the concept of conservation still applies.

9.4 ESTIMATING VS. PHYSICAL COUNT

Although a physical inventory is taken once a year, there are occasions when the value of the inventory must be known during the year. When interim financial statements are requested (monthly, quarterly, or semiannually), an inventory amount must be estimated. If no physical count is taken, the amount of inventory must be estimated. Also, in the event of fire or any other casualty, an amount must be reported as a loss. Two of the most popular methods of estimating inventory (when no physical count is used) are the gross profit method and the retail method.

(A) Gross Profit Method

This method rearranges the Cost of Goods Sold section of the income statement. As stated previously, the cost-of-goods-sold formula is

$$
\begin{array}{l}
\quad \text{Inventory (beginning)} \\
+ \ \underline{\text{Net purchases}} \\
\quad \text{Goods available for sale} \\
- \ \underline{\text{Inventory (ending)}} \\
\quad \text{Cost of goods sold}
\end{array}
$$

Note that when you subtract inventory (ending) from the goods available for sale, the cost of goods sold is determined. Conversely, if you subtract the estimated cost of goods sold from the goods available for sale, the value of the inventory (ending) will result. The estimated cost of goods sold figure is arrived at by using the past year's gross profit percentage and subtracting the resulting amount from sales.

EXAMPLE 8

During the past five years, a company's gross profit averaged 30% of sales. If the sales for this interim period are $70,000, the inventory at the beginning of the period is $30,000, and the net purchases are $50,000, you would estimate the inventory (ending) under the gross profit method as follows:

Inventory (beginning)		$30,000
Add: Net Purchases		50,000
Goods Available for Sale		$80,000
Sales	$70,000	
Estimated Gross Profit (30%)	21,000*	
Estimated Cost of Goods Sold		49,000
Estimated Inventory (Ending)		$31,000

*($70,000 × 30%)

This method of estimating ending inventory is also useful when a calamity such as a fire, flood, or theft destroys a company's inventory. It is obvious that a dollar amount must be assigned to the inventory lost before any insurance claim can be made. Although this may appear to be an impossible task, it is possible to build up to the inventory figure. For example, the dollar amounts of all the sales, purchases, and beginning inventory can be obtained from the previous year's financial statements. Also, information can be further provided by customers, suppliers, sellers, etc.

EXAMPLE 9

A fire occurred in a retail store and destroyed most records. If the average gross profit rate, based upon the last three years of operations, is 40%, and the net sales (according to various sales records) is $90,000, determine the ending inventory by the gross profit method of estimation. Assume that outside verification determined that the beginning inventory was $40,000 and all purchases (net) were $76,000.

	Inventory (beginning)	$ 40,000	
+	Net purchases	76,000	
	Goods available for sale	$116,000	
−	Estimated cost of goods sold	54,000*	
	Estimated ending inventory	$ 62,000	
*	Sales	$90,000	
−	Gross profit estimate	36,000	($90,000 × 40%)
	Cost of goods sold estimated	$54,000	

Bear in mind that the gross profit method is not intended to replace the physical inventory count but is used to estimate the inventory cost when a physical count is not deemed possible. This method is based on the assumption that the rate of gross profit has been fairly stable in the past periods under examination and will remain so in the future. Without this stability, calculations of inventory using the gross profit method will be inaccurate and not useful in any accounting procedure. Since this method is based solely on estimation, it is not acceptable for tax purposes unless no other physical inventory method is available.

(B) Retail Inventory Method

The retail inventory method of inventory costing is used by retail businesses, particularly department stores. Department stores usually determine gross profit monthly but take a physical inventory only on an annual basis. The retail inventory method permits a determination of inventory at any time of the year and also produces a comparison of the estimated ending inventory with the physical inventory ending inventory, both at retail prices. This will help to identify any inventory shortages resulting from theft and other causes.

This method, similar to the gross profit method previously mentioned, is used to estimate the dollar cost of inventory (ending) when a physical count cannot be done. The procedure for determination under the retail inventory method is as follows:

1. Beginning inventory and purchases must be recorded both at cost and at selling price.

2. Total goods available for sale are then computed on both bases, cost and selling price.

3. Sales for the period are deducted from the goods available for sale at selling price.

4. Ending inventory at selling price is the result of step (3). This amount is then converted to ending inventory at cost by multiplying by the appropriate markup ratio.

EXAMPLE 10

		Cost	Selling Price
Step 1.	Beginning Inventory	$280,000	$400,000
	+ Net Purchases for Period	110,000	180,000
Step 2.	Goods Available for Sales	$390,000	$580,000
Step 3.	− Net Sales for Period		340,000
	Ending Inventory at Selling Price		$240,000
Step 4.	Cost to Selling Price Ratio ($390,000 ÷ $580,000) = 67%		
	Ending Inventory at Cost ($240,000 × 67%) = $160,800		

In the above example, the cost percentage is 67%, which means that the inventory and purchases are marked up by an average of 33% (100% − 67%).

Certainly not all items in the goods available for sale are marked up exactly 33%. (Some will be marked higher and some lower than 33%.) In other words, the retail method will use a percentage that represents an average of markup cost. Suppose a retailer had different categories of inventory, each with a different cost ratio. How would the firm use the retail method to estimate the total cost of all the inventory on hand at any time of the year? The retailer would simply apply the retail inventory method to each category separately, using that category's specific cost ratio, then add the costs of the categories to determine the estimate of the overall cost of inventory.

(C) Summary of Both Methods

The major difference between the gross profit method and the retail inventory method is that the former uses the historical gross profit rates, and the latter uses the percentage markup (cost-to-selling-price ratio) from the current period. In other words, the gross profit method uses past experience as a basis, whereas the retail method uses current experience.

The gross profit method is usually less reliable because past situations may be different from current ones. Remember that both methods are useful because they allow the accountant to prepare financial statements more frequently without taking the time to make a physical count each time or maintaining perpetual inventory records. However, the annual physical count is necessary, as it will disclose any loss due to theft or other shrinkage conditions and will serve as the basis for an adjustment to all inventory records and the Inventory account.

Summary

1. The lower the value of the inventory, the _____ the profit.

2. Determining ending inventory by LCM is done at the _____ of the period.

3. A method of valuing inventory and determining the costs of goods sold by using the actual costs assigned to the units on hand and to those that are sold is known as _____ .

4. Under the specific identification method, _____ costs and not valuations are used to determine the ending inventory.

5. When it appears that inventory is obsolete or broken, it should be reported at its _____ .

6. The inventory valuation method that tax law prohibits using with LCM is _____ .

7. The most common method of inventory valuation under LCM is based on the _____ price.

8. The most accurate determination of inventory is by the _____ method.

Answers: 1. lower; 2. end; 3. specific identification; 4. actual; 5. net realizable value; 6. LIFO; 7. unit; 8. specific identification

Solved Problems

9.1.   Based upon the inventory transactions below, determine by means of specific identification (*a*) the cost of goods sold and (*b*) the ending inventory.

		Units	Unit Cost	Total Cost
Jan. 1	Beginning inventory	5	$6	$ 30
Feb. 5	Purchases	15	9	135
Apr. 9	Purchases	10	8	80
June	Sales	(12)		
				$245

Assume that the 12 units sold were

Jan 1	Inventory 4
Feb. 5	Purchases 4
Apr. 9	Purchases 4

SOLUTION

(a)   Cost of goods sold

Jan. 1	Inventory	4 units	@ $6 =	$24
Feb. 5	Purchases	4 units	@ 9 =	36
Apr. 9	Purchases	4 units	@ 8 =	32
Total cost of goods sold		12 units		$92

(b)   Ending inventory

Jan. 1		1 unit	@ $6 =	$ 6
Feb. 5		11 units	@ 9 =	99
Apr. 9		6 units	@ 8 =	48
		18		$153

Proof: Total inventory before sale		$245
Less: Cost of goods sold		92
Specific inventory on hand		$153

9.2. Based on the data below, determine the value of the inventory at the lower of cost or market by completing the table.

Item	Units	Unit Cost	Market Value
A	100	$1.00	$1.50
B	150	4.00	4.50
C	200	6.00	5.00
D	250	8.00	7.00

Item	Units	Basis	Lower of Cost or Market
A	100		
B	150		
C	200		
D	250		

Value of inventory ____

SOLUTION

Item	Units	Basis	Lower of Cost or Market
A	100	$1.00	$ 100
B	150	4.00	600
C	200	5.00	1,000
D	250	7.00	1,750

Value of inventory $3,450

9.3. Inventory costing $12,000 has been determined to be obsolete and can now be sold only for $8,000. (a) Record the journal entry needed to record this loss. (b) If there were costs of $600 to sell the merchandise in (a), what journal entry would be needed to record this information, and (c) what is the value of the inventory after the loss is considered?

SOLUTION

(a) Loss on Write-down of Inventory   4,000
     Inventory   4,000

(b) Loss on Write-down of Inventory   4,600
     Inventory   4,600

(c) The value of the inventory would be calculated as

Cost	$12,000
Loss	− 4,000
	$ 8,000
Selling costs	− 600
Ending inventory	$ 7,400

9.4. Using the following data, determine the value of the inventory under the item-by-item method of LCM valuation.

Items	Units	Valuation Cost	Valuation Market	LCM Cost	LCM Market
A	10	$22	$21		
B	15	8	10		
C	12	20	15		
D	10	29	19		

SOLUTION

Items	Units	Valuation Cost	Valuation Market	LCM Cost	LCM Market
A	10	$22	$21	$220	$210
B	15	8	10	120	150
C	12	20	15	240	180
D	10	29	19	290	190
				$870	$730

Item-by-Item — LCM

A	$210	(Market)
B	120	(Cost)
C	180	(Market)
D	190	(Market)
	$700	Ending inventory

9.5. Penny Corp. categorizes its items into specific groups. Determine the inventory by category by completing the table.

| | | Unit Price | | Total | Market | |
Descrip.	Quantity	Cost	Market	Cost	Cost	LCM
Categ. I 572	100	$ 5.00	$ 6.00			
684	150	3.00	2.00			
579	180	2.00	1.00			
Total cost Categ. I						
Categ. II 1065	50	$ 9.00	$10.00			
1259	100	12.00	14.00			
Total cost Categ. II						
Total Inventory Cost						

SOLUTION

| | | Unit Price | | Total | Market | |
Descrip.	Quantity	Cost	Market	Cost	Cost	LCM
Categ. I 572	100	$ 5.00	$ 6.00	$ 500	$ 600	
684	150	3.00	2.00	450	300	
579	180	2.00	1.00	360	180	
Total cost Categ. I				$1,310	$1,080	$1,080
Categ. II 1065	50	$ 9.00	$10.00	$ 450	$ 500	
1259	100	12.00	14.00	1,200	1,400	
Total cost Categ. II				$1,650	$1,900	1,650
Total Inventory Cost						$2,730

9.6. Using the following data furnished from various sources, determine the inventory of Adam Israel that was destroyed by fire, using the gross profit method.

Beginning inventory	$20,000
Net purchases	40,000
Net sales	65,000
Gross profit average	25%

SOLUTION

Inventory (beginning)		$20,000
Add: Net purchases		40,000
Goods available for sale		$60,000
Sales	$65,000	
Estimated gross profit	16,250	$(65,000 \times 25\%)$
Estimated cost of goods sold		48,750
Estimated ending inventory		$11,250

9.7. A flood destroyed most records and inventory of the Noah Company in March 19X8. After investigating outside records from various sources, the following information was obtained:

Inventory, 12/31/X7	$24,000
Purchases during 19X8	56,000
Purchase returns during 19X8	6,000
Net sales during 19X8	100,000
Gross profit rate:	
19X5 30%	
19X6 40%	
19X7 50%	

Determine the amount of the inventory loss to be claimed during 19X8 under the gross profit method.

SOLUTION

Inventory, 1/1/X8*		$24,000
Purchases	$56,000	
Less: Purchase returns	6,000	
Net purchases		50,000
Goods available for sale		$74,000
Sales	$100,000	
Estimated gross profit	40,000 (100,000 × 40%)**	
Estimated cost of goods sold		60,000
Estimated ending inventory, 12/31/X8		$14,000

---

*The ending inventory of 12/31/X7 becomes the beginning inventory of 1/1/X8.
**The average of 30% + 40% + 50% ÷ 3 = 40%.

9.8. Determine by the retail method the estimated cost of the December 31 inventory.

	Cost	Retail
December 1, inventory	$290,000	$400,000
Dec. 1–31, purchases	110,000	180,000
Goods available for sale	$400,000	$580,000
Sales for December		340,000

SOLUTION

	Cost	Retail
Dec. 1, inventory	$290,000	$400,000
Dec. 1–31, purchases	110,000	180,000
Goods available for sale	$400,000	$580,000
Sales for month		340,000
Dec. 31, inventory at retail		$240,000
Inventory at estimated cost		
($240,000 × 67%*)	$160,800	

---

*Cost ratio 67% ($400,000 ÷ $580,000)

9.9. Estimate the cost of inventory at May 31 by the retail method.

	Cost	Retail
May 1, inventory	$18,000	$24,000
May purchases	34,000	41,000
Sales for May		37,000

SOLUTION

	Cost	Retail
May 1, inventory	$18,000	$24,000
May purchases	34,000	41,000
Goods available for sale	$52,000	$65,000
($52,000 ÷ $65,000 = 80% ratio)		
Sales for May		37,000
May 31, inventory at retail		$28,000
May 31, inventory at estimated cost	$22,400*	

*($28,000 × 80%)

9.10. Determine by the retail method the estimated cost of the ending inventory on December 31.

	Cost	Retail
Inventory, Dec. 1	$200,000	$300,000
Purchases, Dec. 1–31	105,000	190,000
Goods available for sale	$305,000	$490,000
Sales, Dec. 1–31		$400,000

SOLUTION

	Cost	Retail
Inventory, Dec. 1	$200,000	$300,000
Purchases, Dec. 1–31	105,000	190,000
Goods available for sale	$305,000	$490,000
Net sales, Dec. 1–31		400,000
Inventory, Dec. 31		$ 90,000

Ratio of cost to retail $\dfrac{305,000}{490,000} = 62\%$

Ending inventory at cost ($90,000 × 62%) $55,800

9.11. A fire destroyed the inventory of the Chase Bike store. Based upon past records, it was determined that the gross profit rate averaged 45%, the net sales were $160,000, ending inventory of the previous year was $50,000, and net purchases during the year were $70,000. What is the amount the bike company can claim on its damaged inventory on hand?

SOLUTION

Inventory (beginning)		$ 50,000
Net purchases		70,000
Goods available for sale		$120,000
Sales	$160,000	
Estimated gross profit	72,000	($160,000 × 45%)
Estimated cost of goods sold		88,000
Estimated inventory (ending)		$ 32,000

9.12. Determine the total estimated inventory destroyed by fire under the retail inventory method for two different inventories of the Happy Department Store. (This problem is actually a combination of two former problems.)

	Cost	Retail
Inventory I	$280,000	$400,000
Net purchases	110,000	180,000
Net sales		340,000
Inventory II	$ 18,000	$ 24,000
Net purchases	34,000	41,000
Net sales		37,000

SOLUTION

Inventory I	Cost	Retail
Inventory (beginning)	$280,000	$400,000
Net purchases	110,000	180,000
Goods available for sale	$390,000	$580,000
Sales		340,000
Inventory at retail		$240,000
Inventory at estimated cost ($240,000 × 67%*)	$160,800	

*Cost ratio 67% ($390,000:$580,000)

Inventory II	Cost	Retail
Inventory (beginning)	$18,000	$24,000
Net purchases	34,000	41,000
Goods available for sale ($52,000 ÷ $65,000 = 80% ratio)	$52,000	$65,000
Sales		
Inventory at retail		37,000
Inventory at estimated cost	$22,400*	$28,000

*($28,000 × 80%)

Total estimated inventory at cost:	
Inventory I	$160,800
Inventory II	22,400
Total estimated inventory at cost	$183,200

9.13. Determine the ending inventory under the retail inventory method using the following merchandising data for two specific inventories.

		Cost	Retail
Inventory A	Inventory beginning	$25,000	$ 40,000
	Net purchases	53,000	90,000
	Net sales		110,000
Inventory B	Inventory beginning	$14,000	$ 22,000
	Net purchases	70,000	98,000
	Net sales		90,000

SOLUTION

Inventory A		Cost	Retail
	Inventory (beginning)	$25,000	$ 40,000
+	Net purchases	53,000	90,000
	Goods available for sale	$78,000	$130,000
−	Net sales		110,000
	Inventory (ending)		$ 20,000

Ratio of cost to retail price $\dfrac{\$78,000}{\$130,000} = 60\%$

Ending inventory at cost ($20,000 × 60%) $\hspace{3cm}$ $12,000

Inventory B		Cost	Retail
	Inventory (beginning)	$14,000	$ 22,000
+	Net purchases	70,000	98,000
	Goods available for sale	$84,000	$120,000
−	Net sales		90,000
	Ending inventory		$ 30,000

Ratio of cost to retail price $\dfrac{\$84,000}{\$120,000} = 70\%$

Ending inventory at cost ($30,000 × 70%) $\hspace{3cm}$ $21,000

Then add:

Ending inventory (A) at cost	$12,000
Ending inventory (B) at cost	21,000
Total ending inventory at cost	$33,000

Note that the total ending inventory at retail would be $50,000 ($20,000 + $30,000).

CHAPTER 10

Repetitive Transactions

10.1 INTRODUCTION

In earlier sections, the accounting principles discussed were illustrated in terms of small businesses with relatively few transactions. Each transaction was recorded by means of an entry in the general journal, then posted to the related account in the general ledger.

Such a simple system becomes altogether too slow and cumbersome when transactions in various categories occur by the hundreds or thousands each month. In that case, it is more practical to group the repetitive transactions according to type (sales, purchases, cash, etc.) and to provide a separate *special journal* for each type. Entries that are not of a repetitive nature, such as corrections, adjusting entries, and closing entries, will still be entered in the general journal.

The advantages of using special journals where there are numerous repetitive transactions may be summarized as follows:

1. *Reduces detailed recording.* In the special journal, each transaction is entered on a single line designed to provide all necessary information. For example, a sales transaction is recorded on a single line indicating a debit to the customer's account and giving the customer's name, the date, the amount, and any other desired data (such as the invoice number). Under the special-journal concept, individual posting is eliminated. Only one posting for the total amount is made to the appropriate ledger account at the end of the month. Thus, if a firm had 1,000 sales on account during the month, the Sales account would be credited once, not 1,000 times.

2. *Permits better division of labor.* Each special journal can be handled by a different person, who will become more familiar with the special work and therefore more efficient. Just as important, journalizing can be done by a number of people working simultaneously, rather than consecutively.

3. *Permits better internal control.* In large firms, having separate journals allows the work to be arranged in such a way that no one person has conflicting responsibilities, for example, the receipt and the recording of cash. Thus, no employee can steal received cash and then make a journal entry to conceal the theft.

10.2 SPECIAL LEDGERS (SUBSIDIARY LEDGERS)

Further simplification of the general ledger is brought about by the use of subsidiary ledgers. In particular, for those businesses that sell goods on credit and find it necessary to maintain a separate account for each customer and each creditor, a special *accounts receivable ledger* and an *accounts payable ledger* eliminate multiple entries in the general ledger.

The advantages of special or subsidiary ledgers are similar to those of special journals. These are

1. **Reduces ledger detail.** Most of the information will be in the subsidiary ledger, and the general ledger will be reserved chiefly for summary or total figures. Therefore, it will be easier to prepare the financial statements.

2. **Permits better division of labor.** Here again, each special or subsidiary ledger may be handled by a different person. Therefore, one person may work on the general ledger accounts, while another person may work simultaneously on the subsidiary ledger.

3. **Permits a different sequence of accounts.** In the general ledger, it is desirable to have the accounts in the same sequence as in the balance sheet and income statement. As a further aid, it is desirable to use numbers to locate and reference the accounts, as explained in Sec. 3.5. However, for accounts receivable and accounts payable, which involve names of customers or companies, it is preferable to have the accounts in *alphabetical* sequence.

4. **Permits better internal control.** Better control is maintained if a person other than the person responsible for the general ledger is responsible for the subsidiary ledger. For example, the accounts receivable or customers' ledger trial balance must agree with the balance of the Accounts Receivable account in the general ledger. The general ledger account acts as a *controlling account*, and the subsidiary ledger must agree with the control. No unauthorized entry could be made in the subsidiary ledger, as it would immediately put that record out of balance with the control account.

The idea of control accounts introduced above is an important one in accounting. Any group of similar accounts may be removed from the general ledger and a controlling account substituted for it. Not only is another level of error protection thereby provided, but the time needed to prepare the general ledger trial balance and the financial statements is further reduced.

10.3 USE OF SPECIAL JOURNALS

The principal special journals are the sales journal, purchases journal, cash receipts journal, and cash disbursements journal.

We shall describe each and illustrate the relationship between the special journal and the general ledger, on the one hand, and the relationship between the special journal and the subsidiary ledger, on the other hand. Also, it is desirable to point out in each case the relationship of the controlling account to the subsidiary ledger.

(A) Sales Journal

The entry for the individual sale on account is a debit to Accounts Receivable (and to the customer's account) and a credit to Sales. Only sales on account are recorded in the sales journal. Cash sales ordinarily do not require the customer's name and are recorded in the cash receipts journal, usually in a daily total.

Referring to Example 1 below, we have the following procedure for recording and posting the sales journal:

1. Record the sale on account in the sales journal.

2. Post from the sales journal to the individual accounts in the subsidiary ledger.

3. Record the posting of the individual accounts in the post reference (P.R.) column. A check indicates that the posting has been made.

4. At the end of the month, total the amount of sales made on account. This total is posted in the general ledger to the Accounts Receivable account (12) as a debit and to the Sales account (41) as a credit. In the general ledger the source of the entry (S-1) is entered in each account.

EXAMPLE 1

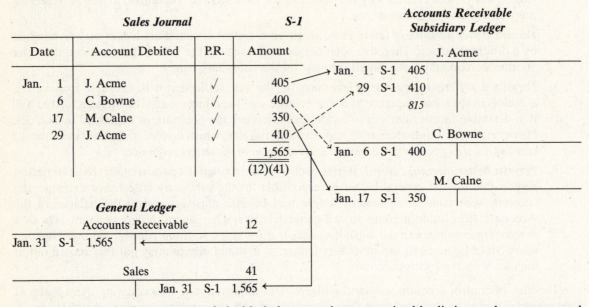

The balances in the accounts receivable ledger may be summarized by listing each customer and the amount he or she owes. The accounts receivable trial balance, known as a *schedule of accounts receivable*, should agree with the controlling account.

EXAMPLE 2

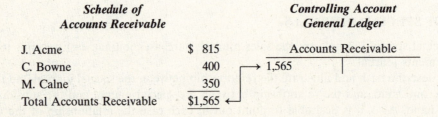

(B) Purchases Journal

In most businesses, purchases are made regularly and are evidenced by purchase invoices issued to creditors. In previous chapters the entry to record the purchase of goods on account had the following form:

> Purchases   (Debts)
>
>   Accounts Payable   (Credit)

Where there are many transactions involving purchases of merchandise for resale, of supplies to be used in the business, of equipment, etc., the labor-saving features of a special purchases journal may be utilized. The basic principles that apply to the sales journal also apply to the purchases journal. However, because of the variety of items that are purchased, more columns are needed in the purchases journal.

For the sales journal (see Example 2), the schedule of accounts receivable total equaled the controlling account in the general ledger. In the purchases journal, the individual transactions with the creditors (accounts payable) are posted to the creditor's account in the subsidiary ledger, while the total is posted to the controlling account, Accounts Payable.

EXAMPLE 3

Jan. 2 Purchased merchandise on account from Altman Company, $2,000
      8 Purchased supplies on account from Bay Company, $600
     15 Purchased equipment on account from Calloway Company, $5,000
     15 Purchased land from J. Smith on account, $1,000
     21 Purchased additional supplies on account from Bay Company, $200
     28 Purchased additional merchandise on account from Altman Company, $1,000

Purchases Journal   P-1 (1)

Date	Account Credited	P.R.	Acct. Pay. Cr.	Purch. Dr.	Supp. Dr.	Sundry Accounts Dr.	P.R.	Amt.
Jan. 2	Altman Company	✓	2,000	2,000				
8	Bay Company	✓	600		600			
15	Calloway Company	✓	5,000			Equipment	18	5,000
15	J. Smith	✓	1,000			Land	17	1,000
21	Bay Company	✓	200		200			
28	Altman Company	✓	1,000	1,000				
			9,800	3,000	800			6,000
			(21)	(51)	(14)			(✓)
		(2)	(3)	(3)	(3)			(4)

Notes:

(1) P-1 denotes the page number (1) of the purchases journal.

(2) The individual amounts will be posted as credits to their respective accounts in the accounts payable subsidiary ledger. The check marks in the purchases journal indicate such postings.

(3) Accounts Payable, Purchases, and Supplies are posted to the respective accounts in the general ledger as totals only.

(4) The sundry amount of $6,000 is not posted as a total; instead, the individual amounts are posted, as many different accounts may be affected each month.

General Ledger

Supplies	14		Accounts Payable	21
Jan. 31 P-1 800			Jan. 31 P-1 9,800	

Land	17
Jan. 15 P-1 1,000	

Equipment	18		Purchases	51
Jan. 15 P-1 5,000			Jan. 31 P-1 3,000	

Accounts Payable Subsidiary Ledger

Altman Company				Bay Company			
	Jan. 2	P-1	2,000		Jan. 8	P-1	600
	28	P-1	1,000		21	P-1	200
			3,000				*800*

Calloway Company				J. Smith			
	Jan. 15	P-1	5,000		Jan. 15	P-1	1,000

To prove that the accounts payable ledger is in balance, the total owed to the four companies must agree with the balance in the Accounts Payable control account.

Schedule of Accounts Payable

Altman Company	$3,000
Bay Company	800
Calloway Company	5,000
J. Smith	1,000
Total	$9,800

Accounts Payable		
	P-1	$9,800

(C)   Cash Receipts Journal

Transactions involving cash are recorded in either the cash receipts or the cash disbursements journal. Items that increase the firm's cash position are recorded in the cash receipts journal. Increases in cash may come from such sources as collections from customers, receipts from cash sales, investments, and collection of interest and principal on notes held by the firm (notes receivable).

The procedure for recording and posting the cash receipts journal is described below and illustrated in Example 4.

1.   The total of the cash column is posted as a debit to the Cash account.

2.   Each amount is posted to the individual customer's account. The total is posted as a credit to the Accounts Receivable account in the general ledger.

3.   The total of the sales credit column is posted as a credit to the Sales account.

4.   Each item in the sundry column is posted individually to the general ledger. The total of the sundry column is not posted.

5.   The accuracy of the journal (that is, the equality of debits and credits) is verified by adding the three credit columns and comparing the total with the debit column.

EXAMPLE 4

The month of February saw the following cash-increasing transactions:

Feb. 2   Received $600 from J. Acme in partial settlement of his bill
      5   Returned defective merchandise bought for cash and received $80 in settlement [see Sec. 10.4 (B)]
      14 Cash sales for the first half of the month, $3,800
      24 Received a check from C. Bowne in full settlement of her account, $400
      28 Cash sales for the second half of the month, $3,720

As shown in Example 2, there are balances in Mr. Acme's, Ms. Bowne's, and Mr. Calne's accounts of $815, $400, and $350 respectively.

Cash Receipts Journal   CR-1

Date	Account Credited	P.R.	Cash Dr.	Acct. Rec. Cr.	Sales Income Cr.	Sundry Cr.
Feb. 2	J. Acme	✓	600	600		
5	Purchase Returns	52	80			80
14	Cash Sales	✓	3,800		3,800	
24	C. Bowne	✓	400	400		
28	Sales	✓	3,720		3,720	
			8,600	1,000	7,520	80
			(11)	(12)	(41)	(✓)

General Ledger

Cash		11
Feb. 28 CR-1 8,600		

Sales Income		41
	Feb. 28 CR-1	7,520

Accounts Receivable		12
Bal. 1,565	Feb. 28 CR-1	1,000
565		

Purchase Returns		52
	Feb. 5 CR-1	80

Accounts Payable Subsidiary Ledger

J. Acme		
Bal. 815	Feb. 2 CR-1	600

C. Bowne		
Bal. 400	Feb. 24 CR-1	400

M. Calne	
Bal. 350	

(D) Cash Disbursements Journal

The cash disbursements journal, also known as the cash payments journal, is used to record all transactions that *reduce* cash. These transactions may arise from payments to creditors, cash purchases (of supplies, equipment, or merchandise), the payment of expenses (salary, rent, insurance, etc.), or personal withdrawals.

The procedure for recording and posting the cash disbursements journal parallels that for the cash receipts journal:

1. A check is written each time a payment is made; the check numbers provide a convenient reference, and they help in controlling cash and in reconciling the bank account.

2. The cash credit column is posted in total to the general ledger at the end of the month.

3. Debits to Accounts Payable represent cash paid to creditors. These individual amounts will be posted to the creditors' accounts in the accounts payable subsidiary ledger. At the end of the month, the total of the accounts payable column is posted to the general ledger.

4. The sundry column is used to record debits for any account that cannot be entered in the other special columns. These would include cash purchases of equipment and inventory, payment of expenses, and cash withdrawals. Each item is posted separately to the general ledger. The total of the sundry column is not posted.

EXAMPLE 5

Cash Disbursements Journal   CD-1

Date	Check No.	Account Debited	P.R.	Cash Cr.	Acct. Pay Dr.	Sundry Dr.
Feb. 2	1	Bay Company	✓	600	600	
8	2	Rent Expense	52	220		220
15	3	Salaries Expense	53	1,900		1,900
21	4	Purchases	51	1,600		1,600
24	5	Salaries Expense	53	1,900		1,900
				6,220	600	5,620
				(11)	(21)	(✓)

General Ledger

Cash   11
Bal. 8,600* | Feb. 28 CD-1 6,220

Accounts Payable   21
Feb. 18 CD-1 600 | Bal. 9,800**
                            9,200

Purchases   51
Feb. 21 CD-1 1,600 |

Rent Expense   52
Feb. 8 CD-1 220 |

Salaries Expense   53
Feb. 15 CD-1 1,900 |
24 CD-1 1,900 |
3,800

Accounts Payable Subsidiary Ledger

Bay Company
Feb. 2 CD-1 600 | Bal. 800**
                   200

Altman Company
| Bal. 3,000**

Calloway Company
| Bal. 5,000**

J. Smith
| Bal. 1,000**

*From the cash receipts journal, Example 4.

**From the purchases journal, Example 3.

10.4 SPECIAL SITUATIONS

(A) Discounts

To induce a buyer to make payment before the amount is due, the seller may allow the buyer to deduct a certain percentage of the bill. If payment is due within a stated number of days after the date of invoice, the number of days will usually be preceded by the letter "n," signifying net. For example, bills due in 30 days would be indicated by n/30.

A 2 percent discount offered if payment is made within 10 days would be indicated by 2/10. If the buyer has a choice of either paying the amount less 2 percent within the 10-day period or paying the entire bill within 30 days, the terms would be written as 2/10, n/30.

EXAMPLE 6

A sales invoice totaling $800 and dated January 2 has discount terms of 2/10, n/30. If the purchaser pays on or before January 12 (10 days after the date of purchase), he may deduct $16 ($800 × 2%) from the bill and pay only $784. If he chooses not to pay within the discount period, he is obligated to pay the entire amount of $800 by February 1.

Some companies offer a varied cash discount depending on when payment is made, for example, 2/10, 1/20, net 30. This means that the company offers a 2 percent discount if the buyer pays within 10 days; if he or she pays after 10 days but within 20 days of purchase, he or she gets a 1 percent discount; the net amount is due within 30 days.

EXAMPLE 7

A $600 invoice dated April 6 has terms of 3/10, 2/15, n/30. If the bill is paid by April 16, the discount will be $18. If it is paid after April 16 but by April 21, the discount will be $12. The entire bill of $600 must be paid by May 6.

Although in most cases the cash discount period is computed from the invoice or purchase date, it may also be computed from either the date of the receipt of the goods (**ROG**) or the end of the month (**EOM**).

ROG is used primarily when there is a significant gap between the date of the sale and the delivery date. This eliminates the necessity for the buyer to pay for goods before receiving them in order to get a discount.

EOM is used primarily as a convenience, with traditional end-of-month billing practices followed by most companies.

EXAMPLE 8

The last date on which a discount can be taken is shown below.

	Invoice Date	Goods Received	Terms	Last Day on Which Discount Can Be Taken
Invoice $500	October 3	October 8	2/10, n/30 ROG	October 18
Invoice $700	October 3	October 8	2/10, n/30 EOM	November 10*

*10 days after the end of the month (EOM).

From the point of view of the seller, the discount is a sales discount; the purchaser would consider it a purchase discount. If a business experiences a large number of sales and purchase discounts, then special columns would be added in the cash receipts and cash disbursements journals, respectively.

Sales Discount appears as a reduction of Sales in the income statement. Purchase Discount appears as a reduction of Purchases in the Cost of Goods section of the income statement.

(B) Return of Merchandise

Many factors in business will cause a return of merchandise: damaged goods, incorrect size or style, or a price not agreed upon. Returns associated with purchases are recorded as purchase returns, and those associated with sales are recorded as sales returns.

Purchase Returns. If a firm has many purchase returns, a purchase returns journal should be used. However, for illustrative purposes, entries for the return of purchases (bought on account) are made here in the general journal:

	P.R.	Debit	Credit
Accounts Payable, Smith and Company	✓ 21	420	
Purchase Returns	52		420

The debit portion of the entry is posted to the Accounts Payable account in the general ledger (21), and also to the accounts payable subsidiary ledger (✓) under Smith and Company. Because the controlling account and the customer's account are both debited, a diagonal line is needed in the Post Reference column to show both postings. For items involving a return for cash, the cash receipts journal is used.

Accounts Payable Ledger   **General Ledger**

Smith and Company		Accounts Payable 21		Purchase Returns 52
J-1 420	Bal. 800	J-1 420 Bal. 800		J-1 420

Purchase Returns appears in the income statement as a reduction of Purchases.

Sales Returns.   If many transactions occur during the year in which customers return goods bought on account, a special journal known as the sales returns journal is used. However, where sales returns are infrequent, the general journal is sufficient.

The entry to record returns of sales on account in the general journal would be

	P.R.	Debit	Credit
Sales Returns	42	600	
Accounts Receivable, Murphey Company	✓ 12		600

The Accounts Receivable account, which is credited, is posted both in the Accounts Receivable controlling account (12) and in the accounts receivable ledger (✓), under Murphey Company.

Accounts Receivable Ledger   **General Ledger**

Murphey Company		Accounts Receivable 12		Sales Returns 42
Bal. 900	J-1 600	Bal. 900 J-1 600		J-1 600
_300_		_300_		

If the sales returns involve the payment of cash, it will appear in the cash disbursements journal. Sales Returns appears in the income statement as a reduction of Sales Income.

(C)   Types of Ledger Account Forms

The T account has been used for most illustrations of accounts thus far. The disadvantage of the T account is that it requires totaling the debit and the credit columns in order to find the balance. If it is necessary to have the balance of a customer's or creditor's account available at any given moment, an alternative form of the ledger, the three-column account, may be used. The advantage of the form is that an extra column, "Balance," is provided, so that the amount the customer owes, or the creditor is owed, is always shown. As each transaction is recorded, the balance is updated. Below is an illustration of an Accounts Receivable ledger account using this form.

A. Lapinsky

Date	P.R.	Debit	Credit	Balance
Jan. 2	S-1	650		650
4	S-1	409		1,059
8	CD-1		500	559

Summary

1. The journal used to record sales of merchandise on account is known as the _____ journal.

2. The sale of merchandise for cash would appear in the _____ journal.

3. It is common practice to divide the ledger in a large business into three separate ledgers, known as the _____, _____, and _____ ledgers.

4. The total of the sales journal is posted at the end of the month as a debit to Accounts Receivable and a credit to _____.

5. The only column in the purchases journal that will not be posted in total at the end of the month is the _____ column.

6. Sales Discount and Purchase Discount appear in the _____ statement as reductions of Sales and of Purchases, respectively.

7. Terms of 2/10, n/30 on a $750 purchase of January 4, paid within the discount period, would provide a discount of $_____.

8. Accounts Receivable and Accounts Payable in the general ledger may be classified as _____.

9. Merchandise purchased on account would be entered in the _____ journal.

10. Merchandise sold on account would be entered in the _____ journal.

11. Merchandise sold for cash would be entered in the _____ journal.

12. Merchandise purchased for cash would be entered in the _____ journal.

13. Equipment purchased on account would be entered in the _____ journal.

Answers: 1. sales; 2. cash receipts; 3. general, accounts receivable, accounts payable; 4. Sales; 5. sundry;, 6. income; 7. 15; 8. controlling accounts; 9. purchases; 10. sales; 11. cash receipts; 12. cash disbursements; 13. purchases.

Solved Problems

10.1. For each of the following transactions, indicate with a check mark the journal in which it should be recorded.

(a) Purchase of merchandise on account

(b) Purchase of merchandise for cash

(c) Receipt of cash from a customer in settlement of an account

(d) Cash sales for the month

(e) Payment of salaries

(f) Sales of merchandise for cash

(g) Sales of merchandise on account

(h) Cash refunded to customer

(i) Sale of a fixed asset for cash

(j) Notes payable sent to creditor in settlement of an account

	Cash Receipts Journal	Cash Disburs. Journal	Sales Journal	Purchases Journal	General Journal
(a)					
(b)					
(c)					
(d)					
(e)					
(f)					
(g)					
(h)					
(i)					
(j)					

SOLUTION

	Cash Receipts Journal	Cash Disburs. Journal	Sales Journal	Purchases Journal	General Journal
(a)				✓	
(b)		✓			
(c)	✓				
(d)	✓				
(e)		✓			
(f)	✓				
(g)			✓		
(h)		✓			
(i)	✓				
(j)					✓

10.2. Listed below are some selected transactions. Enter these transactions in a general journal form.

Mar. 1 Sold merchandise on account, $2,150 with terms of 2/15, n/30
    4 Purchased merchandise on account, $4,150 with terms of 3/10, n/30
    5 Issued credit memorandum for defective merchandise, $190
    7 Paid for merchandise purchased on Mar. 4
    9 Received credit memorandum for merchandise returned, $285
  11 Sold merchandise on account, $1,640 with terms of 2/10, n/30
  14 Received payment for Mar. 1 transaction
  17 Purchased merchandise on account, $2,178 with terms of 2/10, n/30
  24 Received full payment from Mar. 11 transaction
  29 Paid for merchandise from Mar. 17 transaction

SOLUTION

Mar. 1	Accounts Receivable	2,150	
	Sales		2,150
4	Purchases	4,150	
	Accounts Payable		4,150
5	Sales Returns and Allowances	190	
	Accounts Receivable		190
7	Accounts Payable	4,150	
	Purchases Discount		83
	Cash		4,067
9	Accounts Payable	285	
	Purchase Returns		285
11	Accounts Receivable	1,640	
	Sales		1,640
14	Cash	2,107	
	Sales Discount	43	
	Accounts Receivable		2,150
17	Purchases	2,178	
	Accounts Payable		2,178
24	Cash	1,640	
	Accounts Receivable		1,640
29	Accounts Payable	2,178	
	Cash		2,178

10.3. Record the following transactions in the sales journal.

Jan. 1 Sold merchandise on account to Fleischer Company, $550
    4 Sold merchandise on account to Gerard Company, $650
  18 Sold merchandise on account to Harke Company, $300
  29 Sold additional merchandise on account to Harke Company, $100

Sales Journal   *S-1*

Date	Account Debited	P.R.	Amount

SOLUTION

Sales Journal   *S-1*

Date	Account Debited	P.R.	Amount
Jan. 1	Fleischer Company	✓	550
4	Gerard Company	✓	650
18	Harke Company	✓	300
29	Harke Company	✓	100
			1,600

10.4. Post the customers' accounts in Prob. 10.3 to the accounts receivable subsidiary ledger and prepare a schedule of accounts receivable.

Fleischer Company

Gerard Company

Harke Company

Schedule of Accounts Receivable

Fleischer Company	
Gerard Company	
Harke Company	

SOLUTION

Fleischer Company

Jan. 1	S-1	550

Gerard Company

Jan. 4	S-1	650

Harke Company

Jan. 18	S1	300
29	S-1	100
		400

Schedule of Accounts Receivable

Fleischer Company	550
Gerard Company	650
Harke Company	400
	1,600

10.5. For Prob. 10.3, make the entries needed to record the sales for the month.

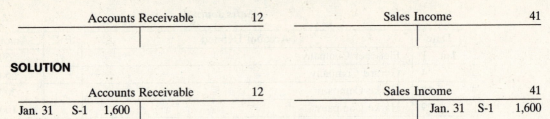

Accounts Receivable	12

Sales Income	41

SOLUTION

Accounts Receivable	12
Jan. 31 S-1 1,600	

Sales Income	41
	Jan. 31 S-1 1,600

10.6. Based on the following sales journal, post each transaction to its respective Accounts Receivable account.

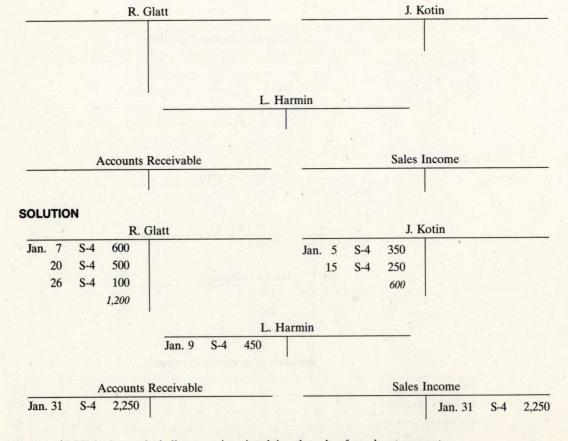

Date	*Sales Journal* Account Debited	P.R.	*S-4* Amount
Jan. 5	J. Kotin	✓	350
7	R. Glatt	✓	600
9	L. Harmin	✓	450
15	J. Kotin	✓	250
20	R. Glatt	✓	500
26	R. Glatt	✓	100
31			2,250

R. Glatt

J. Kotin

L. Harmin

Accounts Receivable

Sales Income

SOLUTION

R. Glatt	
Jan. 7 S-4 600	
20 S-4 500	
26 S-4 100	
1,200	

J. Kotin	
Jan. 5 S-4 350	
15 S-4 250	
600	

L. Harmin	
Jan. 9 S-4 450	

Accounts Receivable	
Jan. 31 S-4 2,250	

Sales Income	
	Jan. 31 S-4 2,250

Note: $2,250 is the total of all transactions involving the sale of goods on account.

10.7. Vitman Company was established in December of the current year. Its sales of merchandise on account and related returns and allowances during the remainder of the month are described below.

Dec. 15   Sold merchandise on account to Acme Co., $850
19   Sold merchandise on account to Balt Corp, $800
20   Sold merchandise on account to Conway, Inc., $1,200
22   Issued credit memorandum for $40 to Balt Corp. for merchandise returned
24   Sold merchandise on account to Davy Company, $1,650
25   Sold additional merchandise on account to Balt Corp., $900
26   Issued credit memorandum for $25 to Acme Co. for merchandise returned
27   Sold additional merchandise on account to Conway, Inc., $1,600

Record the transactions for December in the sales journal and general journal below.

Sales Journal   S-6

Date	Account Debited	P.R.	Amount

General Journal   J-8

Date	Description	P.R.	Dr.	Cr.

SOLUTION

Sales Journal   S-6

Date	Account Debited	P.R.	Amount
Dec. 15	Acme Co.		850
19	Balt Corp.		800
20	Conway, Inc.		1,200
24	Davy Company		1,650
25	Balt Corp.		900
27	Conway, Inc.		1,600
			7,000

General Journal   J-8

Date	Description	P.R.	Dr.	Cr.
Dec. 22	Sales Returns		40	
	Accounts Receivable, Balt Corp.			40
26	Sales Returns		25	
	Accounts Receivable, Acme Corp.			25

10.8. Based on the information in Prob. 10.7, post to the customers' accounts.

```
            Acme Co.                              Conway, Inc.
    _____|_____     _____|_____


            Balt. Corp.                           Davy Company
    _____|_____     _____|_____
```

SOLUTION

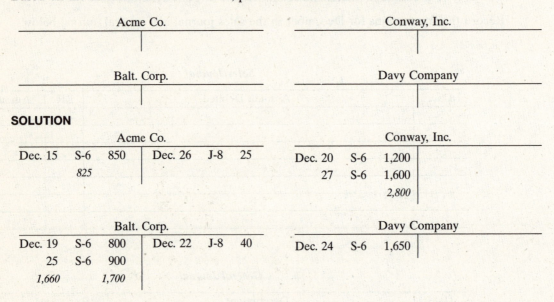

```
              Acme Co.                                Conway, Inc.
Dec. 15  S-6  850  | Dec. 26  J-8  25      Dec. 20  S-6  1,200 |
         825       |                            27  S-6  1,600 |
                                                       2,800   |

              Balt. Corp.                             Davy Company
Dec. 19  S-6  800  | Dec. 22  J-8  40      Dec. 24  S-6  1,650 |
     25  S-6  900  |
  1,660      1,700 |
```

10.9. Post the general journal and the sales journal to the three accounts below using the data supplied in Prob. 10.7. What is the sum of the balances of the accounts in the subsidiary ledger (Prob. 10.8)? What is the balance of the controlling account?

```
        Accounts Receivable                       Sales Income
    _____|_____     _____|_____


               Sales Returns
            _____|_____
```

SOLUTION

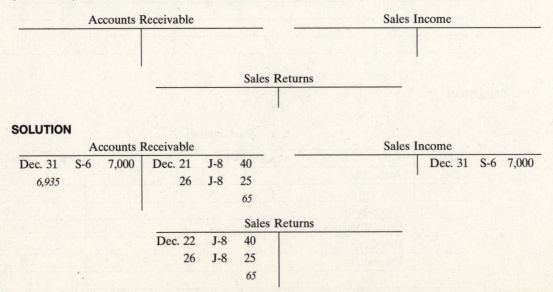

```
          Accounts Receivable                        Sales Income
Dec. 31  S-6  7,000 | Dec. 21  J-8  40                | Dec. 31  S-6  7,000
        6,935       |      26  J-8  25
                    |             65

               Sales Returns
            Dec. 22  J-8  40   |
                26  J-8  25   |
                       65
```

The balance in the subsidiary ledger is $6,935 and the balance in the Accounts Receivable account (control) is the same.

10.10. What are the net proceeds of goods sold on March 10 for $750, terms 2/10, n/30, if payment is made (*a*) on March 18? (*b*) on March 22?

SOLUTION

(*a*) $750 × 2% = $15
       $750 − $15 = $735

(*b*) $750 (the discount period ended March 20)

10.11. What entries are needed for parts (*a*) and (*b*) of Prob. 10.10?

(*a*)

(*b*)

SOLUTION

(*a*)	Cash	735	
	Sales Discount	15	
	Accounts Receivable		750
(*b*)	Cash	750	
	Accounts Receivable		750

10.12. Assuming that Prob. 10.10 involved cash payments rather than cash receipts, what entries would be needed to record parts (*a*) and (*b*)?

(*a*)

(*b*)

SOLUTION

(*a*)	Accounts Payable	750	
	Purchase Discount		15
	Cash		735
(*b*)	Accounts Payable	750	
	Cash		750

10.13. Vane Co. receives an invoice that totals $189.75, including a shipping charge of $50. Terms are 3/10, n/60. If the invoice is paid within 9 days of receipt, what is the amount of the payment?

SOLUTION

$$\text{Total amount} - \text{shipping charge} = \text{amount for discounting}$$
$$\$189.75 - \$50 = \$139.75$$

$$\text{Net cost} = \text{list price} - (\text{list price} \times \text{discount rate})$$
$$= \$139.75 - (\$139.75 \times 0.03) = \$139.75 - \$4.19 = \$135.56$$

$$\text{Total cost} = \text{net cost} + \text{additional costs}$$
$$= \$135.56 + \$50 \text{ shipping cost} = \$185.56$$

10.14. An invoice for $859.78 dated August 10 offers terms of 2/10 ROG. The shipment of goods arrived on September 29, and the bill was paid on October 8. Find the amount due.

SOLUTION

We must first determine whether the bill was paid within the discount period. Since the terms are ROG (receipt of goods), we use the delivery date as the first day of the discount period.

Sept. 29	Delivery date
+10	Discount period
39	
−30	Days in Sept.
Oct. 9	Last date for discount

Since the bill was paid within the discount period, the discount applies.

$$\text{Net cost} = \text{list price} \times \text{complement of discount}$$
$$= \$859.78 \times (100\% - 2\%) = \$859.78 \times 0.98 = \$842.58$$

10.15. Kim's Fabric Shop received an invoice dated April 8 for $675, with terms of 5/20 EOM. (*a*) What is the last date for the discount and (*b*) what amount is due on that date?

SOLUTION

(*a*) The last date for the discount is May 20.

(*b*) Net cost = list price × complement of discount
$$= \$675 \times (100\% - 5\%) = \$675 \times 0.95 = \$641.25$$

10.16. For each of the following, find the final discount date and the final net invoice date. (Assume that February has 28 days.)

	Invoice Date	Terms	Delivery Date
(*a*)	Jan. 11	3/10, n/30 EOM	Feb. 2
(*b*)	July. 14	2/20, n/30 ROG	Sept. 4
(*c*)	Oct. 4	2/10, n/60	Nov. 1

SOLUTION

(a) Final discount date: Feb. 10
Final invoice date:

30	Payment period (begins Feb. 1)
−28	Days in Feb.
Mar. 2	

(b) Final discount date:

Sept. 4	Delivery date
+20	Discount period
Sept. 24	

Final invoice date:

Sept. 4	Delivery date
+30	Payment period
34	
−30	Days in Sept.
Oct. 4	

(c) Final discount date:

Oct. 4	Invoice date
+10	Discount period
Oct. 14	

Final invoice date:

Oct. 4	Invoice date
+60	Payment period
64	
−31	Days in Oct.
33	
−30	Days in Nov.
Dec. 3	

10.17. Record the following transactions in general journal form.

May 1 Sold goods on account to Kay Munoz, $600, terms 2/10, n/30
     6 Kay Munoz returned $100 of the merchandise because of damages
     10 Received a check from Kay Munoz for the amount owed

	Dr.	Cr.

SOLUTION

		Dr.	Cr.
May 1	Accounts Receivable, Kay Munoz	600	
	Sales		600
6	Sales Return	100	
	Accounts Receivable, Kay Munoz		100
10	Cash	490	
	Sales Discount	10*	
	Accounts Receivable, Kay Munoz		500

*($600 − $100 × 2%)

10.18. Record the following transactions in the purchases journal.

Apr. 2   Purchased merchandise on account from Kane Company, $450
    5   Purchased supplies on account from Lane Supply, $180
  20   Purchased merchandise on account from Hanson Company, $400
  24   Purchased additional supplies on account from Lane Supply, $50
  29   Purchased equipment on account from Olin Equipment, $1,600

Purchases Journal   *P-1*

Date	Account Credited	P.R.	Acct. Pay. Cr.	Purch. Dr.	Supp. Dr.	Sundry Acct. Dr.	P.R.	Amt.

SOLUTION

Purchases Journal   *P-1*

Date	Account Credited	P.R.	Acct. Pay. Cr.	Purch. Dr.	Supp. Dr.	Sundry Acct. Dr.	P.R.	Amt.
Apr. 2	Kane Company		450	450				
5	Lane Supply		180		180			
20	Hanson Company		400	400				
24	Lane Supply		50		50			
29	Olin Equipment		1,600			Equipment		1,600
			2,680	850	230			1,600

10.19. Post the information from Prob. 10.18 into the accounts payable subsidiary ledger and prepare a schedule of accounts payable.

Kane Company
_____|_____

Lane Supply
_____|_____

Hanson Company
_____|_____

Olin Equipment
_____|_____

Schedule of Accounts Payable

Kane Company		
Lane Supply		
Hanson Company		
Olin Equipment		

SOLUTION

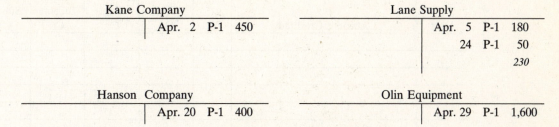

				Kane Company			
				Apr. 2	P-1	450	

				Lane Supply		
			Apr. 5	P-1	180
			24	P-1	50
					230

		Hanson Company		
		Apr. 20	P-1	400

	Olin Equipment		
	Apr. 29	P-1	1,600

Schedule of Accounts Payable

Kane Company		450
Lane Supply		230
Hanson Company		400
Olin Equipment		1,600
		2,680

10.20. Post the purchases journal totals from Prob. 10.18 to the accounts in the general ledger.

General Ledger

Supplies	14

Accounts Payable	21

Equipment	17

Purchases	51

SOLUTION

General Ledger

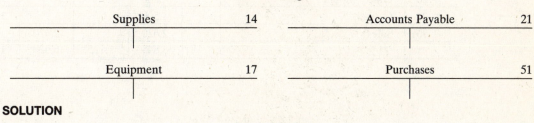

Supplies		14
Apr. 30　P-1　230		

Accounts Payable		21
	Apr. 30　P-1　2,680	

Equipment		17
Apr. 29　P-1　1,600		

Purchases		51
Apr. 30　P-1　850		

10.21. Record the following transactions in the cash receipts journal.

Jan.　2　Received $510 from L. Harmon in full settlement of his account
　　　10　Received $615 from B. Elder in settlement of her account
　　　14　Cash sales for the past 2 weeks, $3,400

20 Sold $200 of office supplies (not a merchandise item) to Smith Company as a service
24 The owner made an additional investment of $1,500
30 Cash sales for the last 2 weeks, $2,620

Cash Receipts Journal CR-1

Date	Account Credited	P.R.	Cash Dr.	Acct. Rec. Cr.	Sales Income Cr.	Sundry Cr.

SOLUTION

Cash Receipts Journal CR-1

Date	Account Credited	P.R.	Cash Dr.	Acct. Rec. Cr.	Sales Income Cr.	Sundry Cr.
Jan. 2	L. Harmon		510	510		
10	B. Elder		615	615		
14	Sales		3,400		3,400	
20	Office Supplies		200			200
24	Capital		1,500			1,500
30	Sales		2,620		2,620	
			8,845	1,125	6,020	1,700

10.22. Post the information from Prob. 10.21 into the accounts receivable subsidiary ledger.

Accounts Receivable Ledger

	L. Harmon			B. Elder	
Bal.	510		Bal.	615	

SOLUTION

Accounts Receivable Ledger

	L. Harmon				B. Elder		
Bal.	510	Jan. 2 CR-1 510		Bal.	615	Jan. 10 CR-1 615	

10.23. Post the cash receipts journal totals from Prob. 10.21 to the accounts in the general ledger.

General Ledger

Cash	11		Capital	31
			Bal.	6,500

Accounts Receivable	12
Bal.	3,000

Office Supplies	15
Bal.	3,500

Sales Income	41

SOLUTION

General Ledger

Cash		11		Capital		31
Jan. 31 CR-1 8,845				Bal.		6,500
				Jan. 24 CR-1		1,500
						8,000

Accounts Receivable		12
Bal. 3,000	Jan. 31 CR-1	1,125
1,875		

Sales Income		41
	Jan. 31 CR-1	6,020

Office Supplies		15
Bal. 3,500	Jan. 20 CR-1	200
3,300		

10.24. Record the following transactions in the cash disbursements journal.

Mar. 1 Paid rent for the month, $320 (Check 16)
   7 Paid J. Becker $615 for his Feb. invoice (Check 17)
  10 Bought store supplies for cash, $110 (Check 18)
  15 Paid salaries for the first half of the month, $685 (Check 19)
  23 Paid B. Cone for Feb. invoice, $600 (Check 20)
  30 Paid salaries for the second half of the month, $714 (Check 21)

Cash Disbursements Journal   CD-1

Date	Check No.	Account Dr.	P.R.	Cash Cr.	Acct. Pay. Dr.	Sundry Dr.

SOLUTION

Cash Disbursements Journal   CD-1

Date	Check No.	Account Dr.	P.R.	Cash Cr.	Acct. Pay. Dr.	Sundry Dr.
Mar. 1	16	Rent Expense		320		320
7	17	J. Becker		615	615	
10	18	Store Supplies		110		110
15	19	Salaries Expense		685		685
23	20	B. Cone		600	600	
30	21	Salaries Expense		714		714
				3,044	1,215	1,829

10.25. Post the information from Prob. 10.24 into the accounts payable subsidiary ledger.

Accounts Payable Ledger

J. Becker				B. Cone		
		Bal.	615			Bal.	600

SOLUTION

Accounts Payable Ledger

J. Becker					B. Cone			
Mar. 7	CD-1	615	Bal.	615	Mar. 23	CD-1	600	Bal.	600

10.26. Post the cash disbursements journal from Prob. 10.24 to the accounts in the general ledger.

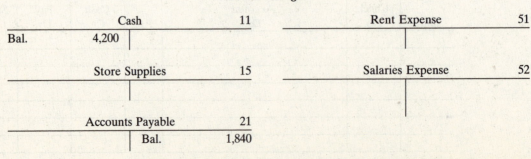

General Ledger

Cash		11		Rent Expense		51
Bal.	4,200					

Store Supplies		15		Salaries Expense		52

Accounts Payable		21
	Bal.	1,840

SOLUTION

General Ledger

Cash			11		Rent Expense			51
Bal.	4,200	Mar. 31 CD-1	3,044		Mar. 1 CD-1	320		

Store Supplies			15		Salaries Expense			52
Mar. 10 CD-1	110				Mar. 15 CD-1	685		
					30 CD-1	714		

Accounts Payable			21
Mar. 31 CD-1	1,215	Bal.	1,840

10.27. The cash receipts journal below utilizes a special column for sales discount. Record the following cash transactions in the journal.

May 2   Received a check for $588 from A. Banks in settlement of his $600 Apr. 25 bill
  12   Received $686 in settlement of the May 3 invoice of $700 from J. Johnson
  26   Received a check for $495 in settlement of B. Simpson's May 17 bill of $500

Cash Receipts Journal   CR-1

Date	Account Cr.	P.R.	Cash Dr.	Sales Disc. Dr.	Acct. Rec. Cr.	Sundry Cr.

SOLUTION

Cash Receipts Journal   CR-1

Date	Account Cr.	P.R.	Cash Dr.	Sales Disc. Dr.	Acct. Rec. Cr.	Sundry Cr.
May 2	A. Banks		588	12	600	
12	J. Johnson		686	14	700	
26	B. Simpson		495	5	500	
			1,769	31	1,800	

10.28. The cash disbursements journal below utilizes the special column Purchases Discount. Record the following cash transactions in the cash disbursements journal.

June 2   Paid J. Thompson $490 in settlement of their May 25 invoice for $500, Check 24
  10   Sent check to B. Rang, $297, in settlement of their June 1 invoice of $300, Check 25
  21   Paid A. Johnson $588 in settlement of the $600 invoice of last month, Check 26

Cash Disbursements Journal **CD-1**

Date	Check No.	Account Dr.	P.R.	Cash Cr.	Pur. Disc. Cr.	Acct. Pay. Dr.	Sundry Dr.

SOLUTION

Cash Disbursements Journal **CD-1**

Date	Check No.	Account Dr.	P.R.	Cash Cr.	Pur. Disc. Cr.	Acct. Pay. Dr.	Sundry Dr.
June 2	24	J. Thompson		490	10	500	
10	25	B. Rang		297	3	300	
21	26	A. Johnson		588	12	600	
				1,375	25	1,400	

10.29. All transactions affecting the Cash account of M & M Company for the month of January 19X8, are presented below.

Jan. 1 Received cash from Alden Company for the balance due on the account, $1,600, less 2% discount

    5 Received payment from Walk Company on account, $1,550

    8 Paid rent for the month, $650, Check 165

   10 Purchased supplies for cash, $614, Check 166

   14 Cash sales for the first half of the month, $5,280

   15 Paid salaries for the first half of the month, $1,600, Check 167

   19 Received $406 in settlement of a $400 note receivable plus interest

   19 Received payment from J. Cork of $500, less 1% discount

   20 Paid B. Simmons $686 in settlement of $700 invoice, Check 168

   24 Paid $450 on account to L. Hann, Check 169

   27 Paid H. Hiram $800, less 2%, on account, Check 170

   30 Paid salaries for the second half of the month, $1,680, Check 171

Record the above transactions in both the cash receipts and cash disbursements journals.

Cash Receipts Journal   CR-1

Date	Account Cr.	P.R.	Cash Dr.	Sales Disc. Dr.	Sales Income Cr.	Acct. Rec. Cr.	Sundry Cr.

Cash Disbursements Journal   CD-1

Date	Check No.	Account Dr.	P.R.	Cash Cr.	Pur. Disc. Cr.	Acct. Pay. Dr.	Sundry Dr.

SOLUTION

Cash Receipts Journal   CR-1

Date	Account Cr.	P.R.	Cash Dr.	Sales Disc. Dr.	Sales Income Cr.	Acct. Rec. Cr.	Sundry Cr.
Jan. 1	Alden Co.	√	1,568	32		1,600	
5	Walk Co.	√	1,550			1,550	
14	Sales	√	5,280		5,280		
19	Notes Rec.		406				400
19	Interest Inc.						6
19	J. Cork	√	495	5		500	
			9,299	37	5,280	3,650	406

Cash Disbursements Journal   **CD-1**

Date	Check No.	Account Dr.	P.R.	Cash Cr.	Pur. Disc. Cr.	Acct. Pay. Dr.	Sundry Dr.
Jan. 8	165	Rent Expense		650			650
10	166	Supplies		614			614
15	167	Salaries Expense		1,600			1,600
20	168	B. Simmons	√	686	14	700	
24	169	L. Hann	√	450		450	
27	170	H. Hiram	√	784	16	800	
30	171	Salaries Expense		1,680			1,680
				6,464	30	1,950	4,544

10.30. The Johnston Company transactions involving purchases and sales for the month of January are presented below. All purchases and sales are made on account.

Jan. 3   Sold merchandise to Acme Supply Company, $440

    5 Purchased merchandise from Balfour Corporation, $7,200

  10   Sold merchandise to Mennon Company, $345

  10   Sold merchandise to Blant Company, $2,400

  14   Purchased from Wyde Equipment $750 worth of equipment

  17   Purchased office supplies from Gold Supply, $850

  21   Purchased merchandise from Caldon Company, $6,240

  28   Returned damaged merchandise purchased from Balfour Corporation, receiving credit of $300

  30   Issued credit of $60 to Acme Supply Company for defective goods returned to us

Record the transactions in the sales, purchases, and general journals.

Sales Journal   **S-1**

Date	Account Debited	P.R.	Amount

Purchases Journal   **P-1**

Date	Account Cr.	P.R.	Acct. Pay. Cr.	Pur. Dr.	Supp. Dr.	Sundry Accounts Dr.	P.R.	Amt.

General Journal   *J-1*

Date	Description	P.R.	Debit	Credit

SOLUTION

Sales Journal   *S-1*

Date	Account Debited	P.R.	Amount
Jan. 3	Acme Supply Company	√	440
10	Mennon Company	√	345
10	Blant Company	√	2,400
			3,185

Purchases Journal   *P-1*

Date	Account Cr.	P.R.	Acct. Pay. Cr.	Pur. Dr.	Supp. Dr.	Sundry Account Dr.	P.R.	Amt.
Jan. 5	Balfour Corp.	√	7,200	7,200				
14	Wyde Equipment	√	750			Equipment		750
17	Gold Supply	√	850		850			
21	Caldon Company	√	6,240	6,240				
			15,040	13,440	850			750

General Journal   *J-1*

Date	Description	P.R.	Debit	Credit
Jan. 28	Accounts Payable, Balfour Corp.		300	
	Purchase Returns			300
30	Sales Returns		60	
	Accounts Receivable, Acme Supply			60

10.31. William Drew began business on March 1. The transactions completed by the Drew Company for the month of March are listed below. Record these transactions, using the various journals provided.

Mar. 1 Deposited $14,000 in a bank account for the operation of Drew Company
2 Paid rent for the month, $600, Check 1
4 Purchased equipment on account from Andon Equipment, $10,000
7 Purchased merchandise on account from Baily Company, $1,200
7 Cash sales for the week, $1,650
10 Issued Check 2 for $150, for store supplies
11 Sold merchandise on account to Manny Company, $600
12 Sold merchandise on account to Nant Company, $350
14 Paid biweekly salaries of $740, Check 3

14   Cash sales for the week, $1,800
16   Purchased merchandise on account from Cotin Company, $1,100
17   Issued Check 4 to Baily Company for March 7 purchase, less 2%
18   Bought $250 worth of store supplies from Salio Supply House on account
19   Returned defective merchandise of $200 to Cotin Company and received credit
19   Sold merchandise on account to Olin Company, $645
21   Issued Check 5 to Andon Equipment for $500, in part payment of equipment purchase
21   Cash sales for the week, $1,845
22   Received check from Nant Company in settlement of their March 12 purchase, less 2% discount
22   Purchased merchandise from Canny Corporation for cash, $750, Check 6
24   Purchased merchandise on account from Daily Corporation, $850
25   Sold merchandise on account to Pallit Corporation, $740
26   Purchased additional supplies, $325, from Salio Supply House on account
27   Received check from Manny Company in settlement of their account, less 1% discount
28   Paid biweekly salaries, $810, Check 7
28   Cash sales for the week, $1,920
30   Received $300 on account from Olin Company

General Journal   J-1

Date	Description	P.R.	Debit	Credit

Cash Receipts Journal   CR-1

Date	Account Cr.	P.R.	Cash Dr.	Sales Disc. Dr.	Acct. Rec Cr.	Sales Income Cr.	Sundry Cr.

Cash Disbursements Journal   CD-1

Date	Check No.	Account Dr.	P.R.	Cash Cr.	Pur. Disc. Cr.	Acct. Pay. Dr.	Sundry Dr.

Purchases Journal   P-1

Date	Account Cr.	P.R.	Acct. Pay. Cr.	Pur. Dr.	Store Supp. Dr.	Sundry Acct. Dr.		
						Acct.	P.R.	Amount

Sales Journal   S-1

Date	Account Debited	P.R.	Amount

SOLUTION

General Journal   J-1

Date	Description	P.R.	Dr.	Cr.
Mar. 19	Accounts Payable, Cotin Co.	√ 21	200	
	Purchase Returns	52		200
	Defective goods			

Cash Receipts Journal CR-1

Date	Account Cr.	P.R.	Cash Dr.	Sales Disc. Dr.	Acct. Rec. Cr.	Sales Income Cr.	Sundry Cr.
Mar. 1	Drew Company, Capital	31	14,000				14,000
7	Cash Sales	√	1,650			1,650	
14	Cash Sales	√	1,800			1,800	
22	Nant Company	√	343	7	350		
23	Cash Sales	√	1,845			1,845	
27	Manny Company	√	594	6	600		
30	Cash Sales	√	1,920			1,920	
30	Olin Company	√	300		300		
			22,452	13	1,250	7,215	14,000
			(11)	(42)	(12)	(41)	(√)

Cash Disbursements Journal CD-1

Date	Check No.	Account Dr.	P.R.	Cash Cr.	Pur. Disc. Cr.	Acct. Pay. Dr.	Sundry Dr.
Mar. 2	1	Rent Expense	54	600			600
10	2	Store Supplies	14	150			150
14	3	Salaries Expense	55	740			740
17	4	Baily Company	√	1,176	24	1,200	
21	5	Andon Equipment	√	500		500	
22	6	Purchases	51	750			750
31	7	Salaries Expense	55	810			810
				4,726	24	1,700	3,050
				(11)	(53)	(21)	(√)

Purchases Journal P-1

Date	Account Cr.	P.R.	Acct. Pay. Cr.	Pur. Dr.	Store Supp. Dr.	Sundry Acct. Dr.		
						Acct.	P.R.	Amount
Mar. 4	Andon Equipment	√	10,000			Equipment	19	10,000
7	Baily Company	√	1,200	1,200				
16	Cotin Company	√	1,100	1,100				
18	Salio Supply House	√	250		250			
24	Daily Corporation	√	850	850				
26	Salio Supply House	√	325		325			
			13,725	3,150	575			10,000
			(21)	(51)	(14)			(√)

Sales Journal   *S-1*

Date	Account Debited	P.R.	Amount
Mar. 11	Manny Company	√	600
12	Nant Company	√	350
19	Olin Company	√	645
25	Pallit Corporation	√	740
			2,335
			(12)(41)

10.32. Based on the work in Prob. 10.31, post all transactions to the appropriate accounts in the general ledger, the accounts receivable ledger, and the accounts payable ledger.

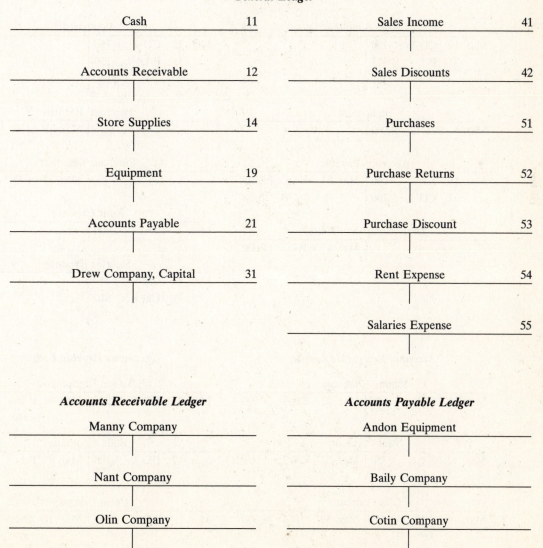

General Ledger

| Cash | 11 | Sales Income | 41 |

| Accounts Receivable | 12 | Sales Discounts | 42 |

| Store Supplies | 14 | Purchases | 51 |

| Equipment | 19 | Purchase Returns | 52 |

| Accounts Payable | 21 | Purchase Discount | 53 |

| Drew Company, Capital | 31 | Rent Expense | 54 |

| | | Salaries Expense | 55 |

Accounts Receivable Ledger   *Accounts Payable Ledger*

Manny Company   Andon Equipment

Nant Company   Baily Company

Olin Company   Cotin Company

	Pallit Corporation			Daily Corporation	

				Salio Supply House	

SOLUTION

General Ledger

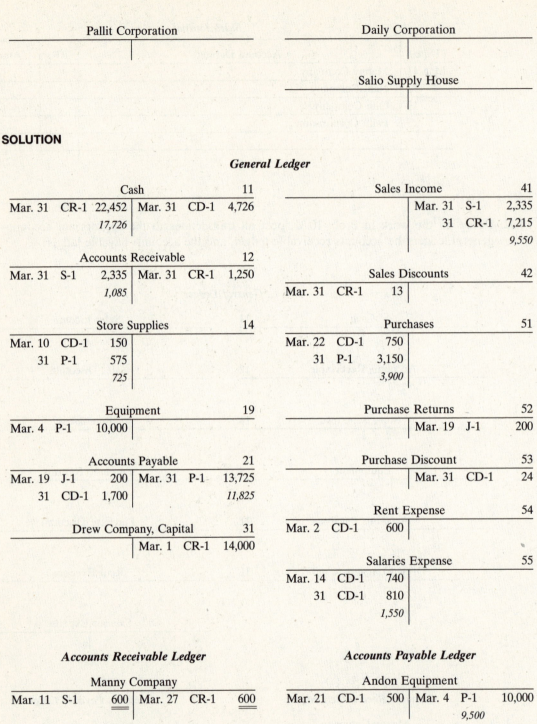

Cash 11

Mar. 31	CR-1	22,452	Mar. 31	CD-1	4,726
		17,726			

Accounts Receivable 12

Mar. 31	S-1	2,335	Mar. 31	CR-1	1,250
		1,085			

Store Supplies 14

Mar. 10	CD-1	150			
31	P-1	575			
		725			

Equipment 19

Mar. 4	P-1	10,000			

Accounts Payable 21

Mar. 19	J-1	200	Mar. 31	P-1	13,725
31	CD-1	1,700			11,825

Drew Company, Capital 31

			Mar. 1	CR-1	14,000

Sales Income 41

			Mar. 31	S-1	2,335
			31	CR-1	7,215
					9,550

Sales Discounts 42

Mar. 31	CR-1	13			

Purchases 51

Mar. 22	CD-1	750			
31	P-1	3,150			
		3,900			

Purchase Returns 52

			Mar. 19	J-1	200

Purchase Discount 53

			Mar. 31	CD-1	24

Rent Expense 54

Mar. 2	CD-1	600			

Salaries Expense 55

Mar. 14	CD-1	740			
31	CD-1	810			
		1,550			

Accounts Receivable Ledger

Manny Company

Mar. 11	S-1	600	Mar. 27	CR-1	600

Nant Company

Mar. 12	S-1	350	Mar. 22	CR-1	350

Olin Company

Mar. 19	S-1	645	Mar. 30	CR-1	300
		345			

Accounts Payable Ledger

Andon Equipment

Mar. 21	CD-1	500	Mar. 4	P-1	10,000
					9,500

Baily Company

Mar. 17	CD-1	1,200	Mar. 7	P-1	1,200

Cotin Company

Mar. 19	J-1	200	Mar. 16	P-1	1,100
					900

Pallit Corporation				Daily Corporation			
Mar. 25	S-1	740			Mar. 24	P-1	850

				Salio Supply House			
				Mar. 18	P-1	250	
				26	P-1	325	
							575

10.33. Based on the information in Probs. 10.31 and 10.32, prepare (*a*) a schedule of accounts receivable, (*b*) a schedule of accounts payable, (*c*) a trial balance.

(*a*)

Drew Company	
Schedule of Accounts Receivable	
March 31, 19X8	
Olin Company	
Pallit Corporation	

(*b*)

Drew Company	
Schedule of Accounts Payable	
March 31, 19X8	
Andon Equipment	
Cotin Company	
Daily Corporation	
Salio Supply House	

(*c*)

Drew Company		
Trial Balance		
March 31, 19X8		
Cash		
Accounts Receivable		
Store Supplies		
Equipment		
Accounts Payable		
Drew Company, Capital		
Sales		
Sales Discount		
Purchases		
Purchase Returns		
Purchase Discount		
Rent Expense		
Salaries Expense		

SOLUTION

(a)

Drew Company	
Schedule of Accounts Receivable	
March 31, 19X8	
Olin Company	$ 345
Pallit Corporation	740
	$ 1,085

(b)

Drew Company	
Schedule of Accounts Payable	
March 31, 19X8	
Andon Equipment	$ 9,500
Cotin Company	900
Daily Corporation	850
Salio Supply House	575
	$11,825

(c)

Drew Company		
Trial Balance		
March 31, 19X8		
Cash	$17,726	
Accounts Receivable	1,085	
Store Supplies	725	
Equipment	10,000	
Accounts Payable		$11,825
Drew Company, Capital		14,000
Sales		9,550
Sales Discount	13	
Purchases	3,900	
Purchase Returns		200
Purchase Discount		24
Rent Expense	600	
Salaries Expense	1,550	4
	$35,599	$35,599

CHAPTER 11

Capital and Equity

11.1 INTRODUCTION

Throughout this book, the emphasis has been placed on the capital section of the single (sole) proprietorship's books, with just a mention given to the equity section of the corporation's books and none at all to partnership capital. The first chapter of *Schaum's Outline of Accounting II* will treat this area at length, but it is important for your understanding of the fundamentals of accounting to introduce this topic at this time.

11.2 SOLE PROPRIETORSHIP

A sole proprietorship is a business owned by one individual. It is a separate business entity, but it is not a separate *legal entity*. The proprietor owns the assets and owes the creditors personally, not as a business, as in the case of a corporation.

The equity of the sole proprietor consists of three accounts: a capital account, a drawing account, and an income summary account. These accounts are described and illustrated below.

Capital account. The proprietor's capital account reflects the changes in his or her equity during the year. Examples 1 through 3 follow the sequence of events in the business of Aaron Baker.

EXAMPLE 1

On January 1, Aaron Baker invested $10,000 in his business. The entry is as follows:

Jan. 1	Cash	10,000	
	Aaron Baker, Capital		10,000

Drawing account. Before earnings are made, the proprietor usually has to draw compensation for his living expenses. He is not an employee, and therefore he does not earn a salary; his earnings result from profits of the company. Such drawings reduce his equity and reduce cash.

EXAMPLE 2

Aaron Baker decided that he would withdraw $500 a month for personal expenses. He expects this equity reduction to be more than offset by earnings, which will be determined at the end of the year. The entry to be made each month is

Aaron Baker, Drawing	500	
Cash		500

The account Aaron Baker, Drawing is used to accumulate the details of the drawings so that only one figure, the total, is transferred to the capital account at the end of the year.

When the drawings of $6,000 for the year are transferred, the entry is as follows:

Dec. 31   Aaron Baker, Capital   6,000
                 Aron Baker, Drawing   6,000

Income Summary account. When the accounts are summarized and closed, the various expenses are debited in total to Income Summary and the individual expense accounts are credited. The income is credited in total to Income Summary and the individual income accounts are debited. The net difference, a profit or a loss, is transferred to the capital account. The process is treated in Chap. 5 (see, in particular, Sec. 5.3).

EXAMPLE 3

The business of Aaron Baker had income from fees of $20,000 and expenses of $9,000. The income of $20,000, less total expenses of $9,000, results in net income of $11,000. The account is closed out and the balance transferred to the capital account with the following entry:

Dec. 31   Income Summary   11,000
             Aron Baker, Drawing   11,000

The account Aaron Baker, Capital (see Examples 1 and 2) will now reflect the proprietor's investment, drawings, and income:

Aaron Baker, Capital

Dec. 31, 19X8 Drawings	6,000	Jan. 1, 19X8 Investment	10,000
31, 19X8 Balance	15,000	Net Income	11,000
	21,000		21,000
		Jan. 1, 19X9 Balance	15,000

Instead of showing a single capital item on the closing balance sheet, it is preferable to present the opening balance, the increase and decrease for the period, and the closing balance, as shown below.

OWNER'S EQUITY

Aaron Baker, Capital		
Balance, January 1, 19X8		$10,000
Net Income for Year	$11,000	
Drawings for Year	6,000	5,000
Balance, December 31, 19X8		$15,000

11.3 PARTNERSHIP

A partnership, according to the Uniform Partnership Act, is "an association of two or more persons to carry on as co-owners of a business for profit." Such an association should preferably be expressed in a partnership agreement. Profits may be shared equally, according to invested capital, or on any other basis. A partner's share is called his or her *interest* in the business.

The partnership capital accounts consist of a capital account for each partner, a drawing account for each partner, and an income summary account. These accounts are described and illustrated on the following page.

Capital accounts. Like the sole proprietor's account (Example 3), each partner's account reflects the changes in his or her equity during the year.

EXAMPLE 4

On January 1, Joseph Kelso invested $15,000 and James Murray invested $10,000 to begin a retail hardware business. The entry is as follows:

Jan. 1	Cash	25,000	
	Joseph Kelso, Capital		15,000
	James Murray, Capital		10,000

Drawing accounts. The individual drawing accounts will also be similar to the sole proprietor's drawing account.

EXAMPLE 5

It was agreed that Joseph Kelso would draw $400 a month and James Murray $300 a month. The entry each month will be as follows:

Joseph Kelso, Drawing	400	
James Murray, Drawing	300	
Cash		700

The monthly amounts will be accumulated in each partner's drawing accounts as in Example 2. At the end of the year, the totals for the year will be transferred to the partners' accounts as follows:

Dec. 31	Joseph Kelso, Capital	4,800	
	James Murray, Capital	3,600	
	Joseph Kelso, Drawing		4,800
	James Murray, Drawing		3,600

Income Summary account. The expense and income accounts are closed into Income Summary as described for a single proprietor (Example 3). However, the profit or loss will be transferred to two or more accounts rather than a single account. The Income Summary, like the drawing accounts, will be closed out for the period.

Partnership profits and losses may be divided in any manner the partners agree upon. In general, a partner may be expected to share in proportion to the amount of capital and/or services he or she contributes. In the absence of a clear agreement, the law provides that all partners share equally, regardless of the differences in time devoted or capital contributed.

Below are outlined the principal methods for profit and loss distribution. For simplicity, the examples are limited to only two partners.

Fixed or capital basis. Profits and losses are generally divided equally, in a fixed ratio, or in a ratio based on the amounts of capital contributed by the partners.

EXAMPLE 6

Perez and Roth have capital balances of $30,000 and $20,000, respectively. The net income for the first year of operations was $15,000. If the partners have decided to share on an equal basis, the journal entry for the allocation of the net income will be

Income Summary	15,000	
Perez, Capital		7,500
Roth, Capital		7,500

If, however, capital investment is to be the determining factor, the entry will run as follows:

Income Summary	15,000	
Perez, Capital		9,000*
Roth, Capital		6,000**

$$* \frac{30,000}{30,000 + 20,000}(15,000)$$

$$** \frac{20,000}{30,000 + 20,000}(15,000)$$

Interest basis. Under this method, each partner is paid interest on his or her capital investment, and the remaining net income is divided in a fixed ratio or on some other basis. Thus, a partner's share depends *partially* on his or her capital investment.

EXAMPLE 7

Instead of the equal split as in Example 6, each partner is to receive 6 percent interest on his or her capital balance, with the remaining net income to be shared equally. The entry would be:

Income Summary	15,000	
Perez, Capital		7,800
Roth, Capital		7,200

the computation being

	Perez	Roth	Total
Interest on investment	$1,800	$1,200	$ 3,000
Balance	6,000	6,000	12,000
Totals	$7,800	$7,200	$15,000

Salary basis. The partners may agree to give recognition to contributions in the form of services, while the remaining net income may be divided equally or in a fixed ratio.

EXAMPLE 8

Assume that the partnership of Perez and Roth (Example 6) agrees that a yearly salary allowance of $4,000 be given to Perez and $3,000 to Roth, the balance to be divided equally. The entry would be

Income Summary	15,000	
Perez, Capital		8,000
Roth, Capital		7,000

the computation being

	Perez	Roth	Total
Salary	$4,000	$3,000	$ 7,000
Balance	4,000	4,000	8,000
Totals	$8,000	$7,000	$15,000

Salary-plus-interest basis. Here, services rendered to the business and capital contribution jointly determine the income division. Each partner gets a salary and, at the same time, interest on capital. If any balance remains, it is divided in an agreed-upon ratio.

EXAMPLE 9

Perez and Roth (Example 6) decide to allow a credit of 6 percent interest on capital balances, respective salaries of $4,000 and $3,000, and equal division of any remainder. The entry would be

Income Summary	15,000	
Perez, Capital		8,300
Roth, Capital		6,700

11.4 CORPORATION

Equity Accounting for the Corporation

Accounting for the corporation is distinguished from accounting for the sole proprietorship or the partnership by the treatment of owners' (stockholders') equity, which, in the corporation, is separated into *paid-in capital* and *retained earnings*. The reason for this separation is that most states prohibit corporations from paying dividends from other than retained earnings. Paid-in capital is further divided, and so we have two major capital accounts:

Capital stock. Corporate capital stock is evidenced by stock certificates. There are a specified number of shares of stock authorized by the state, generally at a specified par value. No-par stock also can be issued in most states. When stock is issued at a price above par, the amount above par is termed a *premium*. If stock is issued below par, the difference is termed a *discount*. If only one type of stock is issued, it may be termed *capital stock* or, specifically, *common stock*. Capital stock that has been issued, fully paid, and reacquired by the company, but not canceled, is called *treasury stock*.

Retained earnings. Retained earnings represent stockholders' equity that has accumulated from profitable operation of the business. Generally they represent total net income less dividends declared. Retained earnings result only from operation of the business; no entries for transactions involving company stock are made to the account. The account is debited for dividends declared and credited for net income for the period. At the end of the year, Income Summary is debited and Retained Earnings credited for net income.

EXAMPLE 10   Operation at a Profit

Assume that on January 1 two separate businesses are formed, a sole proprietorship operated by Ira Sochet and a corporation having four stockholders. Assume further that the single owner invested $20,000, whereas the four stockholders each bought 500 shares of common stock at $10 per share. The entries to record the investments are

Sole Proprietorship			**Corporation**		
Cash	20,000		Cash	20,000	
Ira Sochet, Capital		20,000	Common Stock		20,000

After a year's operations, the net income of each enterprise was $5,000. In the sole proprietorship, the Income Summary balance is transferred to the capital account; in the corporation, the balance is transferred to Retained Earnings. Thus:

Sole Proprietorship			Corporation		
Income Summary	5,000		Income Summary	5,000	
Ira Sochet, Capital		5,000	Retained Earnings		5,000

The balance sheets of the two firms are identical except for the owner's equity sections, which appear as follows:

Sole Proprietorship		Corporation	
Ira Sochet, Capital, January 1, 19X8	$20,000	Common Stock, $10 par (2,000 shares authorized and issued)	$20,000
Add: Net Income	5,000	Retained Earnings	5,000
Ira Sochet, Capital, December 31, 19X8	$25,000	Stockholders' Equity	$25,000

EXAMPLE 11   Operation at a Loss

During the second year of operations, both firms in Example 10 lost $7,000, an amount that exceeds the first year's profits. Observe the difference in the two balance sheets:

Sole Proprietorship		Corporation	
Ira Sochet, Capital, January 1, 19X9	$25,000	Common Stock, $10 par (2,000 shares authorized and issued)	$20,000
Deduct: Net Loss	(7,000)	Deduct: Deficit	(2,000)*
Ira Sochet, Capital, December 31, 19X9	$18,000	Stockholders' Equity	$18,000

*Retained Earnings		
(19X9) 7,000	5,000	(19X8)

Summary

1. If there is a credit balance in the Income Summary after closing the accounts, then a(n) _____ has been made for the period.

2. When the proprietor invests $10,000 cash in the business, the debit is to Cash and the credit is to _____.

3. A business operated for profit by two or more co-owners is called a(n) _____.

4. The price at which the stock of a corporation is selling on the stock exchange is the _____ of the stock.

5. The two principal sections of the stockholders' equity section are _____ and _____ .

Answers: 1. profit; 2. Capital; 3. partnership; 4. market value; 5. paid-in capital, retained earnings.

Solved Problems

11.1   The capital accounts of Allie and Hallie have balances of $35,000 and $25,000, respectively. The articles of copartnership refer to the distribution of net income in the following manner:

1.   Allie and Hallie are to receive salaries of $9,000 and $6,000, respectively.

2.   Each is to receive 6 percent on her capital account.

3.   The balance is to be divided equally.

If the net income for the firm is $32,000, (*a*) determine the division of net income and (*b*) present the entry to close the expense and income summary account.

(*a*)

	Allie	Hallie	Total
Salary			
Interest			
Balance			
Share of net income			

(*b*)

SOLUTION

(*a*)

	Allie	Hallie	Total
Salary	$ 9,000	$ 6,000	$15,000
Interest	2,100	1,500	3,600
	$11,100	$ 7,500	$18,600
Balance	6,700	6,700	13,400
Share of net income	$17,800	$14,200	$32,000

(*b*)

Income Summary	32,000	
Allie, Capital		17,800
Hallie, Capital		14,200

11.2. Redo Prob. 11.1 for a net income of $12,000.

(a)

	Allie	Hallie	Total
Salary			
Interest			
Balance			
Share of net income			

(b)

SOLUTION

(a)

	Allie	Hallie	Total
Salary	$ 9,000	$ 6,000	$15,000
Interest	2,100	1,500	3,600
	$11,100	$ 7,500	$18,600
Balance	−3,300	−3,300	−6,600
Share of net income	$ 7,800	$ 4,200	$12,000

(b)

Income Summary		12,000	
Allie Capital			7,800
Hallie Capital			4,200

11.3. Baggetta and Cohen have capital accounts of $20,000 and $40,000, respectively. The partners divide net income in the following manner:

1.   Salaries of $10,000 to Baggetta and $12,000 to Cohen.
2.   Each partner receives 5 percent on his capital investment.
3.   The balance is divided in the ratio of 1:2.

Determine the division of net income if net income is (a) $34,000; (b) $22,000.

(a)

	Baggetta	Cohen	Total
Salary			
Interest			
Balance			
Total share			

(b)

	Baggetta	Cohen	Total
Salary			
Interest			
Balance			
Total share			

SOLUTION

(a)

	Baggetta	Cohen	Total
Salary	$10,000	$12,000	$22,000
Interest	1,000	2,000	3,000
	$11,000	$14,000	$25,000
Balance	3,000	6,000	9,000
Total share	$14,000	$20,000	$34,000

(b)

	Baggetta	Cohen	Total
Salary	$10,000	$12,000	$22,000
Interest	1,000	2,000	3,000
	$11,000	$14,000	$25,000
Balance	−1,000	−2,000	−3,000
Total share	$10,000	$12,000	$22,000

11.4. What entry is needed to record the issuance of 10,000 shares of capital stock at $40 par value? In what section of the balance sheet would this information be placed?

SOLUTION

Cash	400,000	
Capital Stock		400,000

Cash is a current asset, whereas Capital Stock would appear in the stockholders' equity section.

11.5. On December 10, 19X8, the directors of the Costa Corporation declared an annual dividend of $2 per share on the 6,000 shares of capital stock outstanding. What entry is needed to record the above information? How is Dividends Payable treated on the balance sheet?

SOLUTION

Dec. 10	Retained Earnings	12,000	
	Dividends Payable		12,000

The dividend becomes a current liability when declared and appears as such on the balance sheet.

11.6. (*a*) If the net income of the Black Corporation was determined to be $26,000, what entry would be made? (*b*) Assume a loss of $5,000.

(*a*)

(*b*)

SOLUTION

(*a*)	Income Summary	26,000	
	Retained Earnings		26,000
(*b*)	Retained Earnings	5,000	
	Income Summary		5,000

11.7. What entries are needed to close the accounts below?

All Income		All Expenses		Income Summary
	84,000	62,000		

Retained Earnings	Capital Stock
	100,000

SOLUTION

	All Income		All Expenses			Income Summary		
(*a*)	84,000	84,000	62,000	62,000	(*b*)	(*b*)	62,000	84,000	(*a*)
						(*c*)	22,000	

Retained Earnings		Capital Stock
	22,000 (*c*)	100,000

11.8. Based on the information from the above accounts, if dividends of $12,000 were declared, (*a*) prepare the needed entry, and (*b*) prepare the stockholders' equity section of the balance sheet.

Retained Earnings	Dividends Payable
	22,000	

SOLUTION

	Retained Earnings		Dividends Payable	
(*a*)	12,000	22,000	12,000	(*a*)

Stockholders' Equity

Capital Stock	$100,000
Retained Earnings	10,000*
Total Stockholders' Equity	$110,000

_____

*Net income	$22,000
Less: Dividends	12,000
Balance, end of period	$10,000

Examination III

Chapters 6–11

1. Prepare an eight-column work sheet for the Honest Taxi Company for the month of September. Adjustment data for September 30 are as follows:

(a)	Supplies on hand		$1,800
(b)	Expired insurance		200
(c)	Depreciation on equipment		350
(d)	Salaries payable		190

Honest Taxi Company
Work Sheet
Month Ended September 30, 19X8

Account Title	Trial Balance Dr.	Trial Balance Cr.	Adjustments Dr.	Adjustments Cr.	Income Statement Dr.	Income Statement Cr.	Balance Sheet Dr.	Balance Sheet Cr.
Cash	2,230							
Supplies	5,100							
Prepaid Ins.	600							
Equipment	15,000							
Accum. Deprec.		3,000						
Capital		19,600						
Drawing	700							
Fares Income		3,950						
Salaries Exp.	1,400							
Maint. Exp.	620							
Misc. Exp.	900							
	26,550	26,550						

2. On the basis of Question 1, journalize the closing entries needed.

3. The trial balance of the Harmin Company, before adjustments of December 31, 19X8, includes the following selected accounts:

Merchandise Inventory	$160,000
Sales	840,000
Sales Returns	40,000
Purchases	620,000
Transportation-In	2,000

Merchandise inventory on December 31 totals $135,000.

(*a*) Present the income statement, through Gross Profit on Sales, for the Harmin Company.

(*b*) Present journal entries necessary to adjust the merchandise inventory at December 31.

4. The accounts and the balances appearing in the ledger of the Capo Company, as of December 31, 19X8, are listed below.

Cash	$73,200
Accounts Receivable	11,000
Merchandise Inventory	33,000
Supplies	3,600
Prepaid Insurance	1,400
Equipment	10,000
Accumulated Depreciation	2,000
Accounts Payable	8,200
Notes Payable	6,000
J. Capo, Capital	22,500
J. Capo, Drawing	3,000
Sales	244,000
Sales Returns	1,200
Purchases	115,000
Transportation-In	2,000
Salaries Expense	18,000
Rent Expense	4,000
Advertising Expense	2,600
Maintenance Expense	3,000
Miscellaneous Expense	1,700

The data for the year-end adjustments are as follows:

(*a*)	Merchandise inventory on December 31	$28,600
(*b*)	Supplies inventory on December 31	1,100
(*c*)	Insurance expired during the year	950
(*d*)	Depreciation for the current year	750
(*e*)	Salaries accrued at December 31	350

Complete the eight-column work sheet below.

Capo Company
Work Sheet
Month Ended December 31, 19X8

Account Title	Trial Balance Dr.	Trial Balance Cr.	Adjustments Dr.	Adjustments Cr.	Income Statement Dr.	Income Statement Cr.	Balance Sheet Dr.	Balance Sheet Cr.
Cash	73,200							
Acct. Rec.	11,000							
Merch. Inv.	33,000							
Supplies	3,600							
Prepaid Ins.	1,400							
Equipment	10,000							
Accum. Deprec.		2,000						
Acct. Pay.		8,200						
Notes Pay.		6,000						
Capo, Capital		22,500						
Capo, Drawing	3,000							
Sales		244,000						
Sales Returns	1,200							
Purchases	115,000							
Transportation-In	2,000							
Salaries Exp.	18,000							
Rent Exp.	4,000							
Adv. Exp.	2,600							
Maint. Exp.	3,000							
Misc. Exp.	1,700							
	282,700	282,700						

5. The beginning inventory and purchases of product X for the year are given below:

Beginning inventory	7 units @ $41 each
Purchase, March 10	8 units @ $43 each
Purchase, July 22	5 units @ $45 each
Purchase, October 9	5 units @ $46 each

At the end of the year there were 8 units on hand. Determine the inventory cost by (a) first-in–first-out; (b) last-in–first-out; (c) weighted average.

6. Based on the above problem, determine the cost of goods sold under the first-in–first-out, last-in–first-out, and weighted average methods.

7. Based on the data below, determine the inventory cost at March 31 by the retail method.

	Cost	Retail
Inventory, March 1	$39,700	$63,000
Purchases in March (net)	24,000	31,600
Sales for March		56,000

Answers to Examination III

1.

Honest Taxi Company
Work Sheet
Month Ended September 30, 19X8

Account Title	Trial Balance Dr.	Trial Balance Cr.	Adjustments Dr.	Adjustments Cr.	Income Statement Dr.	Income Statement Cr.	Balance Sheet Dr.	Balance Sheet Cr.
Cash	2,230						2,230	
Supplies	5,100			(a) 3,300			1,800	
Prepaid Ins.	600			(b) 200			400	
Equipment	15,000						15,000	
Accum. Deprec.		3,000		(c) 350				3,350
Capital		19,600						19,600
Drawing	700						700	
Fares Income		3,950				3,950		
Salaries Exp.	1,400		(d) 190		1,590			
Maint. Exp.	620				620			
Misc. Exp.	900				900			
	26,550	26,550						
Supp. Exp.			(a) 3,300		3,300			
Ins. Exp.			(b) 200		200			
Deprec. Exp.			(c) 350		350			
Salaries Pay.				(d) 190				190
			4,040	4,040	6,960	3,950	20,130	23,140
Net Loss						3,010	3,010	
					6,960	6,960	23,140	23,140

2.

Fares Income	3,950	
Income Summary		3,950
Income Summary	6,960	
Salaries Expense		1,590
Maintenance Expense		620
Miscellaneous Expense		900
Supplies Expense		3,300
Insurance Expense		200
Depreciation Expense		350
Capital	3,010	
Income Summary		3,010
Capital	700	
Drawing		700

3. (*a*)

Harmin Company
Income Statement
Period Ended December 31, 19X8

Sales		$840,000	
Less: Sales Returns		40,000	$800,000
Cost of Goods Sold			
Merchandise Inv. (beg.)		$160,000	
Purchases	$620,000		
Transportation-In	2,000	622,000	
Goods Available for Sale		$782,000	
Less: Merchandise Inv. (end)		135,000	
Total Cost of Goods Sold			647,000
Gross Profit on Sales			$153,000

(*b*)

Income Summary	160,000	
Merchandise Inventory		160,000
Merchandise Inventory	135,000	
Income Summary		135,000

Capo Company
Work Sheet
Month Ended December 31, 19X8

Account Title	Trial Balance Dr.	Trial Balance Cr.	Adjustments Dr.	Adjustments Cr.	Income Statement Dr.	Income Statement Cr.	Balance Sheet Dr.	Balance Sheet Cr.
Cash	73,200						73,200	
Acct. Rec.	11,000						11,000	
Merch. Inv.	33,000		(a) 28,600	(a) 33,000			28,600	
Supplies	3,600			(b) 2,500			1,100	
Prepaid Ins.	1,400			(c) 950			450	
Equipment	10,000						10,000	
Accum. Deprec.		2,000		(d) 750				2,750
Acct. Pay.		8,200						8,200
Notes Pay.		6,000						6,000
Capo, Capital		22,500						22,500
Capo, Drawing	3,000						3,000	
Sales		244,000				244,000		
Sales Returns	1,200				1,200			
Purchases	115,000				115,000			
Transportation-In	2,000				2,000			
Salaries Exp.	18,000		(e) 350		18,350			
Rent Exp.	4,000				4,000			
Adv. Exp.	2,600				2,600			
Maint. Exp.	3,000				3,000			
Misc. Exp.	1,700				1,700			
	282,700	282,700						
Inc. Sum.			(a) 33,000	(a) 28,600	33,000	28,600		
Supplies Exp.			(b) 2,500		2,500			
Ins. Exp.			(c) 950		950			
Deprec. Exp.			(d) 750		750			
Salaries Pay.				(e) 350				350
			66,150	66,150	185,050	272,600	127,350	39,800
Net Income					87,550			87,550
					272,600	272,600	127,350	127,350

5. (a)

Most recent cost		5 units @ $46 =	$230
Next most recent cost		3 units @ 45 =	135
Inventory, Dec. 31	Total units	8 Total cost	$ 365

(b)

Earliest cost		7 units @ $41 =	$287
Next earliest cost		1 unit @ 43 =	43
Inventory, Dec. 31	Total units	8 Total cost	$ 330

(c)

Beginning		7 units @ $41 =	$287
First purchase		8 units @ 43 =	344
Second purchase		5 units @ 45 =	225
Third purchase		5 units @ 46 =	230
	Total units	25 Total cost	$1,086*
Inventory, Dec. 31	Total units	8 Total cost	$ 347.52

*Average cost per unit $43.44 ($1,086 ÷ 25)

6.

	First-In–First-Out	Last-In–First-Out	Weighted Average
Merchandise Available for Sale	$1,086	$1,086	$1,086
Merchandise Inventory, Dec. 31	365	330	348
Cost of Goods Sold	$ 721	$ 756	$ 738

7.

	Cost	Retail
Inventory	$39,700	$63,000
Purchases in March	24,000	31,600
Merchandise available for sale	$63,700	$94,600
Cost ratio ($63,700 ÷ $94,600)	67%	
Less: Sales		56,000
Inventory, March 31, at retail		$38,600
Inventory, March 31, at cost	$25,862*	

*($38,600 × 67%)

CHAPTER 12

Receivables and Payables

12.1 INTRODUCTION

A large portion of all business transactions are credit transactions. One way of extending credit is by the acceptance of a *promissory note*, a contract in which one person (the maker) promises to pay another person (the payee) a specific sum of money at a specific time, with or without interest. A promissory note is used for the following reasons:

1. The holder of a note can usually obtain money by taking the note to the bank and selling it (*discounting* the note).
2. The note is a written acknowledgement of a debt and is better evidence than an open account. It takes precedence over open accounts in the event that the debtor becomes bankrupt.
3. It facilitates the sale of merchandise on long-term or installment plans.

For a note to be negotiable, it must meet the requirements of the Uniform Commercial Code (UCC). The requirements are that the note must

1. Be in writing and signed by the maker.
2. Contain an order to pay a definite sum of money.
3. Be payable to order on demand or at a fixed future time.

12.2 METHODS OF COMPUTING INTEREST

For the sake of simplicity, interest is commonly computed on the basis of a 360-day year divided into 12 months of 30 days each. Two widely used manual methods are (1) the cancellation method and (2) the 6 percent, 60-days method. However, the use of a calculator is certainly the most preferred way.

EXAMPLE 1   The Cancellation Method

The basic formula is

$$\text{Interest} = \text{Principal} \times \text{Rate} \times \text{Time}$$

Consider a note for $400 at 6 percent for 90 days. The *principal* is the face amount of the note ($400). The *rate of interest* is written as a fraction: 6%/100% = 6/100. The *time*, if less than a year, is expressed as a fraction by placing the number of days the note runs over the number of days in a year: 90/360. Thus,

$$\text{Interest} = \$400 \times \frac{6}{100} \times \frac{90}{360} = \$6$$

EXAMPLE 2   The 6 Percent, 60-Days Method

This is a variation of the cancellation method, based on the fact that 60 days, or 1/6 year, at 6 percent is equivalent to 1 percent, so that the interest is obtained simply by shifting the decimal point of the principal two places to the left. The method also applies to other time periods or other interest rates. For instance:

	$400 Note	**30 Days**	**6 Percent**
(a)	Determine the interest for 60 days		$4.00
(b)	Divide the result by 2 (30 days is one-half of 60 days)	*Ans.*	$2.00

	$400 Note	**45 Days**	**6 Percent**
(a)	Determine the interest for 30 days		$2.00
(b)	Determine the interest for 15 days		1.00
(c)	Add the interest for 30 days and 15 days	*Ans.*	$3.00

	$400 Note	**60 Days**	**5 Percent**
(a)	Determine the interest at 6 percent		$4.00
(b)	Determine the interest at 1 percent by taking one-sixth of the above amount		0.67
(c)	Multiply the interest at 1 percent by the rate desired, 0.67×5	*Ans.*	$3.35

Determining Maturity Date

The maturity date is the number of specified days after the note has been issued and may be determined by

1. Subtracting the date of the note from the number of days in the month in which it was written.

2. Adding the number of days in each of the succeeding full months, stopping with the last full month before the number of days in the note are exceeded.

3. Subtracting the total days of the result of steps 1 and 2 above from the time of the note. The resulting number is the due date in the upcoming month.

EXAMPLE 3

The maturity date of a 90-day note dated April 4 would be computed as follows:

Period of note			90
April	30		
Date of note	4	26	
May		31	
June		30	
Total		87	
Maturity date		July	3

If the due date of a note is expressed in months, the maturity date can be determined by counting that number of expressed months from the date of writing.

EXAMPLE 4

A 5-month note dated March 17 would be due for payment on August 17. A 1-month note dated March 31 would mature on April 30.

12.3 ACCOUNTING FOR NOTES

(A) Notes Payable

A promissory note is a note payable from the standpoint of the maker, whereas it is a note receivable from the standpoint of the payee.

A note payable is a written promise to pay a creditor an amount of money in the future. Notes are used by a business to

1. Make purchases
2. Settle an open account
3. Borrow money from a bank

Make Purchases

EXAMPLE 5

Assume that you, as the owner, bought office equipment costing $2,000 by giving a note.

Office Equipment	2,000	
Notes Payable		2,000

Settle an Open Account

EXAMPLE 6

There are times when a note is issued in settlement of an account payable. Assume that the Johnson Agency bought merchandise from Shambley Corporation for $500, terms 2/10, n/30. The entry would be recorded in the purchases journal and would appear in the general ledger as

Purchases		Accounts Payable	
500			500

However, 30 days later, the agency is unable to pay and gives to Shambley Corporation a 60-day, 6 percent note for $500 to replace its open account. When the Johnson Agency issues the note payable, an entry is made in the general journal that will decrease the accounts payable and increase the notes payable.

Accounts Payable	500	
Notes Payable		500

Accounts Payable		Notes Payable	
500	500		500

Note that the Johnson Agency still owes the debt to Shambley Corporation. However, it now becomes a different form of obligation, as it is a written, signed promise in the form of a note payable.

EXAMPLE 7

When the maker pays the note in 60 days at 6 percent, the amount of the payment will be the total of the principal and interest and will be recorded in the cash disbursements journal.

Notes Payable	500	
Interest Expense	5	
Cash		505

Borrow Money from a Bank. On occasion, businesses find that it is necessary to borrow money by giving a note payable to a bank. Frequently, banks require the interest to be paid in advance. This is accomplished by deducting the amount of the interest from the principal when the loan is made and is known as *discounting a note payable*. The proceeds will be the amount of money the maker of the note receives after the discount has been taken from the principal.

EXAMPLE 8

Assume that the Rhulen Agency seeks to borrow $3,000 for 60 days at 12 percent from the Commercial National Bank. The bank will deduct the interest ($60.00) from the $3,000 principal and will give the difference of $2,940 (proceeds) to the Rhulen Agency.

The entry recorded in the cash receipts journal is

Cash	2,940	
Interest Expense	60	
Notes Payable		3,000

Sixty days after the issuance of the instrument, the note becomes due, and the Rhulen Agency sends a check for the face value of the note ($3,000). Because the interest was deducted immediately when the loan was made, no further interest will be paid at that time. The entry to record the payment of the note will be made in the cash payments journal.

Notes Payable	3,000	
Cash		3,000

Note: When a business issues many notes payable, a special subsidiary book, known as the notes payable register, may be used. This register will give the complete data for all notes issued and paid by the business. It must be noted, however, that this is merely a source of information and not a journal, as no postings to the ledger are made from it.

(B) Notes Receivable

A note received from a customer is an asset because it becomes a claim against the buyer for the amount due.

EXAMPLE 9

Assume that Howard Cogan owes David Rasnich $400 and gives him a 90-day, 12 percent note in settlement. Mr. Cogan still owes the debt, but his obligation is now of a different type. On Mr. Rasnich's books the entry is

Notes Receivable	400	
Accounts Receivable		400

Only the principal ($400) is recorded when the note is received, since it represents the amount of the unpaid account. The interest is not due until the date of collection, 90 days later. At that time, the interest earned (income) will be part of the entry recognizing the receipt of the proceeds from the note:

Cash	412	
Notes Receivable		400
Interest Income		12

(C) Drafts

Sometimes drafts rather than promissory notes are used in settlement of a business obligation. A draft is an order by the seller (drawer) to the buyer (drawee) stating that the buyer must pay a certain amount of money to a third party (payee).

EXAMPLE 10

If the seller is not acquainted with the buyer, he or she may draw a draft on the buyer and attach to it a bill of lading for the purchase. (A bill of lading is prepared by the transportation company.) The draft and bill of lading are sent to the bank, at which time the bank presents the documents to the buyer. When the buyer pays the amount of the draft to the bank, he or she receives the bill of lading and obtains the purchase from the transportation company. The bank forwards the amount collected to the seller, deducting from it a service charge.

12.4 DISCOUNTING

The negotiability of a note receivable enables the holder to receive cash from the bank before the due date. This is known as *discounting*.

Once the interest to be paid has been determined, the procedure for discounting a note is quite simple. The *maturity value* of a note is

(1)   Face of note + interest income = maturity value

where the *face* is the principal and the interest income is computed as in Sec. 12.2. The holder of a note may discount it at the bank *prior to its due date*. He will receive the maturity value less the *discount*, or interest charge imposed by the bank for holding the note for the unexpired portion of its term. In other words,

(2)   Maturity value $\times$ discount rate $\times$ unexpired time = discount

and

(3)   Maturity value $-$ discount = net proceeds

EXAMPLE 11

Mr. Rasnich holds a $400, 90-day, 12 percent note written by Howard Cogan on April 10 (see Example 9). It is discounted at 12 percent on May 10. The interest on the note amounts to $12. Hence,

(1)   Maturity value = $400 + $12 = $412

Since, at the time of discounting, Mr. Rasnich has held the note for only 30 days, the bank will have to wait $90 - 30 = 60$ days until it can receive the maturity value. The discount charge is then

(2)   Discount = $\$412 \times \dfrac{12}{100} \times \dfrac{60}{360} = \$8.24$

and Mr. Rasnich receives

(3) $$\text{Net proceeds} = \$412 - \$8.24 = \$403.76$$

In this example the bank's discount rate happened to be equal to the interest rate of the note; this need not always be the case (see Prob. 12.12).

12.5   DISHONORED NOTES RECEIVABLE

If the issuer of a note does not make payment on the due date, the note is said to be *dishonored*. It is no longer negotiable, and the amount is charged back to Accounts Receivable. The reasons for transferring the dishonored notes receivable to the Accounts Receivable accounts are: (1) the Notes Receivable account is then limited to current notes that have not yet matured; and (2) the Accounts Receivable account will then show the dishonoring of the note, giving a better picture of the transaction.

EXAMPLE 12

A $500, 60-day, 12 percent note written by F. Saltzman was dishonored on the date of maturity. The entry is

Accounts Receivable, F. Saltzman	510	
Notes Receivable		500
Interest Income		10

Observe that the interest income is recorded and is charged to the customer's account.

When a payee discounts a note receivable, he or she creates a *contingent* (potential) *liability*. This occurs because there is a possibility that the maker may dishonor the note. Bear in mind that the payee has already received payment from the bank in advance of the maturity date. He or she is, therefore, contingently liable to the bank to make good on the amount (maturity value) in the event of default by the maker. Any *protest fee* arising from the default of the note is charged to the maker of the note and is added to the amount to be charged against his or her account.

EXAMPLE 13

In Example 11, assume that Howard Cogan dishonored the note when due. The entry for Mr. Rasnich would be

Accounts Receivable	412*	
Cash		412

*$400   (face)
  12   (interest)
$412   (maturity value)

Had the bank issued a protest fee of $15, the amount charged to the customer would be $427.

12.6 UNCOLLECTIBLE ACCOUNTS

(A) Recording

Businesses must expect to sustain some losses from uncollectible accounts and should therefore show on the balance sheet the *net amount of accounts receivable*, the amount expected to be collected, rather than the gross amount. The difference between the gross and net amounts represents the estimated uncollectible accounts, or bad debts. These expenses are attributed to the year in which the sale is made, though they may be realized at a later date.

There are two methods of recording uncollectible accounts, the direct write-off method and the allowance method.

Direct Write-Off Method. In small businesses, losses that arise from uncollectible accounts are recognized in the accounts *in the period in which they become uncollectible*. Under this method, when an account is deemed uncollectible, it is written off the books by a debit to the expense account, Uncollectible Accounts Expense, and a credit to the individual customer's account and to the controlling account.

EXAMPLE 14

If William Anderson's $300 account receivable, dated May 15, 19X7, was deemed uncollectible in January of 19X8, the entry in 19X8 would be

Uncollectible Accounts Expense	300	
Accounts Receivable, William Anderson		300

Allowance Method. As has been stated before, one of the fundamentals of accounting is that revenue be matched with expenses in the same year. Under the direct write-off method, in Example 14, the loss was not recorded until a year after the revenue had been recognized. The allowance method does not permit this. The income statement for each period must include all losses and expenses related to the income earned *in that period*. Therefore, losses from uncollectible accounts should be deducted in the year in which the sale was made. Since it is impossible to predict which particular accounts will not be collected, an adjusting entry is made, usually at the end of the year.

EXAMPLE 15

Assume that in the first year of operation, a firm has estimated that $2,000 of accounts receivable will be uncollectible. The adjusting entry would be

Uncollectible Accounts Expense	2,000	
Allowance for Uncollectible Accounts		2,000

The credit balance of Allowance for Uncollectible Accounts (contra asset) appears on the balance sheet as a deduction from the total amount of Accounts Receivable:

Accounts Receivable	$29,920	
Less: Allowance for Uncollectible Accounts	2,000	$27,920

The $27,920 will become the estimated realizable value of the accounts receivable at that date. The uncollectible accounts expense will appear as an operating expense in the income statement.

(B)   Computation

There are two generally accepted methods of calculating the amount of uncollectible accounts. One method is to use a flat percentage of the net sales for the year. The other method takes into consideration the ages of the individual accounts at the end of the fiscal year.

Percentage of Sales Method.   Under the percentage of sales method, a fixed percentage of the total sales on account is taken. For example, if charge sales were $200,000 and experience has shown that approximately 1 percent of such sales will become uncollectible at a future date, the adjusting entry for the uncollectible accounts would be

Uncollectible Accounts Expense	2,000	
Allowance for Uncollectible Accounts		2,000

The same amount is used whether or not there is a balance in Allowance for Uncollectible Accounts. However, if any substantial balance should accumulate in the allowance account, a change in the percentage figure would become appropriate.

Balance Sheet Method.   Under the balance sheet method, every account is "aged"; that is, each item in the balance is related to its sale date. The further past due the account, the more probable it is that the customer is unwilling or unable to pay. A typical analysis is shown in Example 16.

EXAMPLE 16

Age of Account	Accounts Receivable Balance	Estimated Percent Uncollectible	Amount
1–30 days	$ 8,000	1%	$ 80
31–60 days	12,000	3%	360
61–90 days	6,000	5%	300
91–180 days	3,000	20%	600
Over 180 days	920	50%	460
	$29,920		$1,800

The calculated allowance for uncollectible accounts ($1,800 in Example 16) is reconciled at the end of the year with the actual balance in the allowance account, and an adjusting entry is made. The amount of the adjusting entry must take into consideration the balance of the Allowance for Uncollectible Accounts. The percentage of sales method does not follow this procedure.

EXAMPLE 17

The analysis showed that $1,800 would be required in the Allowance for Uncollectible Accounts at the end of the period. The Allowance for Uncollectible Accounts has a credit balance of $200. The adjusting entry at the end of the year would be

Uncollectible Accounts Expense	1,600*	
Allowance for Uncollectible Accounts		1,600

---

*($1,800 − $200)

If, however, there had been a debit balance of $200, a credit to Allowance for Uncollectible Accounts of $2,000 would be necessary to bring the closing balance to $1,800.

When it becomes evident that a customer's account is uncollectible, it is written off the books. This is done by crediting Accounts Receivable (the individual customer's account in the subsidiary ledger) for the amount deemed uncollectible and debiting Allowance for Uncollectible Accounts. Note that there is no expense at this time, as it was already estimated in the previous year.

EXAMPLE 18

John Andrew's account (a) was deemed uncollectible.

Allowance for Uncollectible Accounts	600	
Accounts Receivable, J. Andrew		600

General Ledger	*Accounts Receivable Ledger*

Allowance for Uncollectible Accounts		John Andrew	
(a) 600	Bal. 1,800	Bal. 600	(a) 600

Accounts Receivable	
Bal. 29,200	(a) 600

12.7   RECOVERY OF BAD DEBTS

If a written-off account is later collected in full or in part (a *recovery of bad debts*), the write-off will be reversed for the amount received.

EXAMPLE 19

At a later date, Mr. Andrew (see Example 18) pays his account in full. The reversing entry (b) to restore his account will be

Accounts Receivable, John Andrew	600	
Allowance for Uncollectible Accounts		600

A separate entry, (c), will then be made in the cash receipts journal to record the collection, debiting Cash $600 and crediting Accounts Receivable, John Andrew. If a partial collection was made, the reversing entry should be made for the amount recovered.

General Ledger	*Accounts Receivable Ledger*

Cash		John Andrew	
(c) 600		Bal. 600	(a) 600
		(b) 600	(c) 600

Accounts Receivable	
29,200	(a) 600
(b) 600	(c) 600

Allowance for Uncollectible Accounts	
(a) 600	Bal. 1,800
	(b) 600

Summary

1. The practice of transferring a customer's note to the bank is called _____ .

2. The face of a note plus the interest due is known as _____ .

3. Under the _____ method, uncollectible accounts are charged to expense when they become uncollectible.

4. Uncollectible Accounts Expense appears in the _____ statement, whereas Allowance for Uncollectible Accounts appears in the _____ .

5. The method based on the age of the accounts receivable is known as the _____ approach.

6. Ascertaining the amount and time outstanding for each account is known as _____ .

7. If Myer Levy issues to Sam Borod a $400 note, Myer Levy is called the _____ and Sam Borod the _____ .

8. The interest on a $800, 90-day, 6 percent note would be _____ .

9. Normally, banks will base their discount on the _____ of the note.

10. What effect does the acceptance of a note receivable have on the total assets of a firm? _____ .

Answers: 1. discounting; 2. maturity value; 3. direct write-off, 4. income, balance sheet; 5. balance sheet; 6. aging; 7. maker, payee; 8. $12; 9. maturity value; 10. No effect

Solved Problems

12.1. The Hudson Corp. borrowed $5,000 for 90 days at 12 percent from the Sullivan National Bank. What entries are needed to (*a*) record the loan, and (*b*) record the payment? Assume that the interest payment must be made in advance.

(*a*)

(*b*)

SOLUTION

(a)	Cash	4,850	
	Interest Expense	150*	
	Notes Payable		5,000

*Interest for 90 days at 12 percent deducted in advance.

(b)	Notes Payable	5,000	
	Cash		5,000

12.2. Based on the information in Prob. 12.1, what entry would be necessary if after 90 days, Hudson Corporation was unable to repay the loan and was granted another 90-day renewal?

SOLUTION

Interest Expense	150*	
Cash		150

*Only the interest has to be paid, since the note is renewed.

12.3. Assume in Prob. 12.1 that Mr. Hudson's note required the interest payment upon the maturity of the note. What entries are needed to (a) record the loan and (b) record the payment?

(a)			
(b)			

SOLUTION

(a)	Cash	5,000	
	Notes Payable		5,000
(b)	Notes Payable	5,000	
	Interest Expense	150	
	Cash		5,150

12.4. Below is an example of a note receivable.

July 1, 19X8

I, Charles Babcock, promise to pay Acme Stores $800, 60 days from date, at 15% interest.

Charles Babcock

(*a*) Who is the maker of the note? (*b*) Who is the payee of the note? (*c*) What is the maturity date of the note? (*d*) What is the maturity value of the note?

SOLUTION

    (*a*)   Charles Babcock

    (*b*)   Acme Stores

    (*c*)   August 30

    (*d*) $820

12.5. A note written on August 1 and due on November 15 was discounted on October 15. (*a*) For how many days was the note written? (*b*) For how many days did the bank charge in discounting the note?

SOLUTION

(*a*)

	August 1–31	30 days
	September	30 days
	October	31 days
	November	15 days
		106 days

(*b*)

	October 15–31	16 days
	November 1–15	15 days
		31 days

12.6. Determine the interest on the following notes: (*a*) $750 principal, 6 percent interest, 96 days; (*b*) $800 principal, 9 percent interest, 90 days. Use the 60-day, 6% method.

SOLUTION

(*a*)

$750	6%	60 days	$ 7.50
	6%	30 days	3.75
	6%	6 days	.75
	6%	96 days	$12.00

(*b*)

$800	6%	60 days	$ 8.00
	6%	30 days	4.00
		90 days	$12.00

The interest at 9% is then

$$\frac{9\%}{6\%} \times \$12.00 = \underline{\$18.00}$$

12.7. On July 10, Jay Company issued a 60-day, 12.5 percent note for $6,000. Determine (*a*) the due date, (*b*) the interest, (*c*) the maturity value.

SOLUTION

(*a*)

Term of note		60
July	31	
Issuing date July	10	21
Days left to maturity		39
Days in August		31
Due date September		8

(*b*)

$$\$6,000 \times 12.5\% \times \frac{60}{360} = \$125$$

(*c*)

$6,000	Principal
+125	Interest
$6,125	Maturity value

12.8. Below is a list of notes payable from the books of March Company. Determine (*a*) the due date, (*b*) the interest, (*c*) the maturity value for each note (not a leap year). As you can see, a calculator is your best accounting tool for mathematics.

	Date Issued	Principal	Rate	Time, Days	Due Date	Interest	Maturity Value
(1)	Jan. 10	$ 4,200	12.5%	60			
(2)	Feb. 12	7,900	14%	30			
(3)	Mar. 15	6,000	12.75%	90			
(4)	Apr. 10	3,800	14.50%	120			
(5)	June 17	2,800	13.25%	30			
(6)	July 15	7,000	12.75%	60			
(7)	Aug. 21	7,000	12.50%	60			
(8)	Sept. 11	10,000	14%	90			
(9)	Oct. 30	2,000	13.5%	60			
(10)	Nov. 2	2,500	12%	30			

SOLUTION

	Due Date	Interest	Maturity Value
(1)	Mar. 11	$ 87.50	$ 4,287.50
(2)	Mar. 14	92.17	7,992.17
(3)	June 13	191.25	6,191.25
(4)	Aug. 8	183.67	3,983.67
(5)	July 17	30.92	2,830.92
(6)	Sept. 13	148.75	7,148.75
(7)	Oct. 20	145.83	7,145.83
(8)	Dec. 10	350.00	10,350.00
(9)	Dec. 29	45.00	2,045.00
(10)	Dec. 2	25.00	2,525.00

12.9. From the following information, prepare the necessary journal entries.

1. On June 10, received a 30-day, 12 percent, $5,000 note dated June 9 from Price Rite in settlement of his account.

2. July 9, received payment from Price Rite on note.

SOLUTION

June 10	Notes Receivable	5,000	
	Accounts Receivable, Price Rite		5,000
July 9	Cash	5,050	
	Notes Receivable		5,000
	Interest Income		50

12.10. A 90-day, 12 percent, $4,000 note receivable in settlement of an account, dated June 1, is discounted at 12 percent on July 1. Compute the proceeds of the note.

SOLUTION

$4,000.00	Principal
120.00	Interest income (90 days, 12%)
$4,120.00	Maturity value
82.40	Discount (60 days, 12% of maturity value)
$4,037.60	Proceeds, July 1–August 30 (due date)

12.11. What are the entries needed to record the information in Prob. 12.10 (*a*) on June 1? (*b*) on July 1?

(*a*)

(*b*)

SOLUTION

(*a*)	Notes Receivable	4,000.00	
	Accounts Receivable		4,000.00
(*b*)	Cash	4,037.60	
	Interest Income		37.60
	Notes Receivable		4,000.00

12.12. Record the following transactions in the books of Mary Sudolle Company.

(*a*)   May 1   Received a $6,000, 90-day, 12 percent note in settlement of the Happy Valley account

(*b*)   May 31   Discounted the note at 10 percent at the bank

(*c*)   July 30   Happy Valley paid the note in full

(*a*)

(*b*)

(*c*)

SOLUTION

(a)	Notes Receivable	6,000	
	Accounts Receivable, Happy Valley		6,000

(b)	Cash	6,077	
	Interest Income		77*
	Notes Receivable		6,000

*$6,000.00	Principal
180.00	Interest Income
$6,180.00	Maturity value
103.00	Discount $\left(\$6,180 \times \dfrac{10}{100} \times \dfrac{60}{360}\right)$
$6,077.00	Proceeds

(c) No entry

12.13. If in Prob. 12.12 Happy Valley dishonored its obligation on July 30 and a $5 protest fee was imposed by the bank, what entry would be required to record this information?

SOLUTION

Accounts Receivable, Happy Valley	6,185*	
Cash		6,185

*$6,180 (maturity value) + $5 (protest fee)

12.14. Record the following transactions in the books of Carl Klein:

(a) Sept. 5   Received an $8,000, 90-day, 6 percent note in settlement of the M. Ribble account and immediately discounted it at 6 percent at the bank

(b) Dec. 4   M. Ribble dishonored the note, and a protest fee of $2 was imposed

(c) Dec. 31   M. Ribble paid her obligation, including the protest fee

(a)			

(b)			

(c)			

SOLUTION

(a)	Notes Receivable	8,000	
	Accounts Receivable, M. Ribble		8,000
	Cash	7,998.20*	
	Interest Expense	1.80	
	Notes Receivable		8,000

*$8,000.00	Principal
120.00	Interest Income
$8,120.00	Maturity value
121.80	Discount
$7,998.20	Proceeds

(b)	Accounts Receivable, M. Ribble	8,122*	
	Cash		8,122

*(Maturity value + protest fee)

(c)	Cash	8,122	
	Accounts Receivable, M. Ribble		8,122

12.15. Shown are balances for Caren Jill Associates.

Accounts Receivable		Sales		Allowance for Uncollectible Accounts	
120,000			350,000		400

What is the adjusting entry needed to record the provision for uncollectible accounts if the uncollectible expense is estimated (a) as 1 percent of net sales? (b) by aging the accounts receivable, the allowance balance being estimated as $3,600?

(a)			

(b)			

SOLUTION

(a)	Uncollectible Accounts Expense	3,500*	
	Allowance for Uncollectible Accounts		3,500

(b)	Uncollectible Accounts Expense	3,200**	
	Allowance for Uncollectible Accounts		3,200

*1% of $350,000
**$3,600 − $400. The credit balance of $400 in allowance must be taken into consideration.

12.16. Using the aging schedule below, prepare the adjusting entry providing for the uncollectible accounts expense.

Amount	Age	Estimated Percent Uncollectible
$24,000	1–30 days	1%
18,000	31–60 days	3%
10,000	61–180 days	25%
6,000	181 days and over	60%

SOLUTION

Uncollectible Accounts Expense	6,880*	
Allowance for Uncollectible Accounts		6,880

*$ 240 1–30 days ($24,000 × 1%)
$ 540 31–60 days ($18,000 × 3%)
$2,500 61–180 days ($10,000 × 25%)
$3,600 181 days and over ($6,000 × 60%)

12.17. Below are some accounts of the Jay Balding Company, as of January 19X8.

General Ledger   *Accounts Receivable Ledger*

Accounts Receivable   D. Grego
210,000 | 1,400 |

Allowance for Uncollectible Accounts   J. Philips
| 2,600   1,200 |

Prepare the entries needed to record the following information:

(a) Mar. 5 D. Grego account was determined to be uncollectible
(b) Apr. 14 Wrote off J. Philips account as uncollectible

(a)			
(b)			

SOLUTION

(a)	Allowance for Uncollectible Accounts	1,400	
	Accounts Receivable, D. Grego		1,400
(b)	Allowance for Uncollectible Accounts	1,200	
	Accounts Receivable, J. Philips		1,200

12.18. If, in Prob. 12.17, J. Philips later paid his account in full, what entries would be necessary?

SOLUTION

Accounts Receivable, J. Philips	1,200	
Allowance for Uncollectible Accounts		1,200
Cash	1,200	
Accounts Receivable, J. Philips		1,200

CHAPTER 13

Cash and Its Control

13.1 INTRODUCTION

In most firms transactions involving the receipt and disbursement of cash far outnumber any other kinds of transactions. Cash is, moreover, the most liquid asset and the most subject to theft and fraud. It thus becomes essential to have a system of accounting procedures and records that will maintain adequate control over cash.

13.2 CLASSIFICATION OF CASH

Roughly speaking, cash is anything that a bank will accept for deposit and will credit to the depositor's account. More precisely:

1. *Cash is a medium of exchange.* Thus, such items as currency, coin, demand deposits, savings deposits, petty cash funds, bank drafts, cashier's checks, personal checks, and money orders qualify as cash. There are other items that are usually under the control of the company cashier that are not cash, such as postage stamps, postdated checks, and IOUs. Postage is a prepaid expense; postdated checks are receivables; and IOUs are receivables or prepaid expenses, depending on whether they are to be collected or applied against employee expenses.

2. *Cash is immediately available for payment of current debts.* Certificates of deposit (CDs) are temporary investments rather than cash, since they cannot be immediately withdrawn. (Technically, savings accounts may not be withdrawn without notice to the bank, but generally this requirement is not enforced; hence, savings deposits were listed above as cash.) Likewise, a sinking fund specifically established to pay bond requirements or a deposit with a manufacturer for purchase of equipment is not available to pay other current obligations and, therefore, is not cash. Such items are generally shown on the balance sheet as noncurrent assets, whereas cash is listed as a current asset.

13.3 CONTROLLING CASH

(A) Cash Receipts

In a very small business the owner-manager can maintain control through personal contact and supervision. This kind of direct intervention must, in a firm of any size, be replaced by a system of internal control, namely, the separation of duties. No person assigned to handle cash should, at the same time, be in a position to make entries in the records affecting his or her own activities.

The specific controls applied to cash receipts may be summarized as

1. All receipts should be banked promptly.
2. Receipts from cash sales should be supported by sales tickets, cash register tapes, etc.
3. Accountability should be established each time cash is transferred.
4. Persons receiving cash should not make disbursements of cash, record cash transactions, or reconcile bank accounts.

(B) Cash Disbursements

The main ideas here are that payments should be made only by properly authorized persons, that equivalent value be received, and that documents adequately support the payment. Following are specific internal controls relating to cash disbursements.

1. All disbursements, except petty cash payments, should be made by prenumbered check.
2. Vouchers and supporting documents should be submitted for review when checks are signed.
3. Persons who sign checks should not have access to cash receipts, should not have a custody of funds or record cash entries, and should not reconcile bank accounts.

It is seen that special procedures will be needed for petty cash; these will be treated in Sec. 13.6.

(C) Cash Balances

The basic principle of separation of duties is evident in the specific controls for cash balances:

1. Bank reconciliations should be prepared by persons who do not receive cash or sign checks.
2. Bank statements and paid checks should be received unopened by the person reconciling the account.
3. All cash funds on hand should be closely watched and surprise counts made at intervals.

If the requirement that all cash receipts be banked is followed, then it is clear that the monthly bank statement can be made a powerful control over cash balances. Hence the importance of reconciling bank balances.

13.4 BANK STATEMENTS

Checks

A business opens a checking account to gain the privilege of placing its deposits in a safe place and also to be able to write checks. When an account is opened, each person who is authorized to write checks on that account must sign a signature card. The bank keeps the signature card on file and compares it when checks are submitted. A check is a written notice by the depositor directing the bank to deduct a specific sum of money from the checking account and to pay that amount to the person or company written on the check. A check involves three parties:

1. **Drawer:** the one who writes the check
2. **Drawee:** the bank on which the check is drawn
3. **Payee:** the person or company to whom the check is to be paid

Checks offer several advantages. The checkbook stubs provide a record of the cash paid out, while the canceled checks provide proof that money has been paid to the person legally entitled to it. Also, the use of checks is the most convenient way of paying bills, because checks can safely be sent through the mail. If a check is lost or stolen, the depositors can request the bank not to pay (a stop order).

Endorsements

When a check is given to the bank for deposit, the depositor signs the check on the back to show that he or she accepts responsibility for the amount of that check. The depositor's signature is known as an *endorsement*. This endorsement transfers the ownership of the check and guarantees to the individual that the depositor will guarantee its payment. Different kinds of endorsements serve different needs.

1.   **Blank endorsement.** This is an endorsement that consists only of the name of the endorser. Its disadvantage lies in the fact that a lost or stolen check with a blank endorsement may be cashed by the finder or thief. Therefore, this type of endorsement should not be used unless the depositor is at the bank already to make a deposit (Fig. 13-1).

2.   **Endorsement in full.** This type of endorsement states that the check can be cashed or transferred only on the order of the person named in the endorsement (Fig. 13-2).

3.   **Restrictive endorsement.** This type of endorsement limits the receiver of the check as to the use he or she can make of the funds collected. Usually this type of endorsement is done when checks are prepared for deposit (Fig. 13-3).

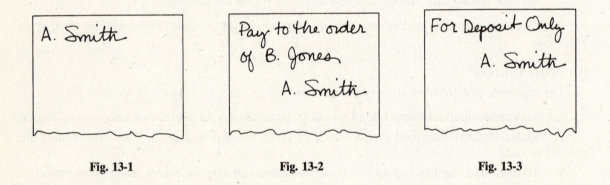

| Fig. 13-1 | Fig. 13-2 | Fig. 13-3 |

13.5   RECONCILING THE BANK BALANCE

Each month, generally, the bank forwards to the depositor a statement of his or her account showing:

1.   Beginning balance
2.   Deposits made and other credits
3.   Checks paid and other charges (debits)
4.   Ending balance

Included in the envelope with the statement are the paid, or "canceled," checks and any other deductions (debit memorandum) or additions (credit memorandum) to the account. A deduction may be a debit memorandum for bank service charges; an addition may be a credit memorandum for the proceeds of a note collected by the bank for the depositor.

Usually the balance of the bank statement and the balance of the depositor's account will not agree. To prove the accuracy of both records, the reconciling differences have to be found and any necessary entries made. The reconciling items will fall into two broad groups: (1) those on the depositor's books but not recorded by the bank, and (2) those on the bank statement but not on the depositor's books. The statement used to reconcile this difference is known as the bank reconciliation statement.

Items on Books but Not on Bank Statement

Deposits in transit. These are cash receipts recorded by a company but too late to be deposited. The total of such deposits is to be *added* to the bank balance.

Outstanding check. These are checks issued by the depositor but not yet presented to the bank for payment. The total of these checks is to be *deducted* from the bank balance.

Errors. Errors may be made in recording amounts of checks, for example, a transposition of figures. The item should be added to the bank balance if it was overstated and deducted if understated.

Items on Bank Statement but Not on Books

Service charges. The bank generally deducts amounts for bank services. The exact amount is usually not known by the depositor until he or she receives the statement. The amount should be deducted from the book balance.

NSF (not sufficient funds) checks. These are checks that have been deposited but cannot be collected because of insufficient funds in the account of the drawer of the check. The bank then issues a debit memorandum charging the depositor's account. The amount should be deducted from the book balance.

Collections. The bank collects notes and other items for a small fee. The bank then adds the proceeds to the account and issues a credit memorandum to the depositor. Often there are unrecorded amounts at the end of the month. These amounts should be added to the book balance.

Errors. Journal entries should be made for any adjustments to the book accounts. Bank errors should not be entered on the books. They should be brought to the attention of the bank and corrected by the bank.

EXAMPLE 1

The following information was available when the John Hennessey Company began to reconcile its bank balance on May 31, 19X8: balance per depositor's books, $1,638; balance per bank statement, $2,420; deposit in transit, $150; checks outstanding— #650, $300 and #654, $240; collection of $400 note plus interest of $8; collection fee for note, $10; bank service charge, $6.

John Hennessey Company
Bank Reconciliation
May 31, 19X8

Balance per bank		$2,420	Balance per checkbook		$1,638
Add: Deposit in transit		150	Add: Notes receivable	$400	
		$2,570	Interest income	8	408
					$2,046
Less:			Less:		
Outstanding checks			Collection fee	$10	
#650	$300		Service charge	6	16
#654	240	540			
Adjusted balance		$2,030	Adjusted balance		$2,030

Only reconciling items in the depositor's section (right side) are to be recorded on the books. The reconciling items in the bank section (left side) have already been recorded on the books and merely have not yet reached the bank. They will normally be included in the next bank statement.

To complete the reconcilement, the following two journal entries will be needed.

Entry 1	Cash	408	
	Notes Receivable		400
	Interest Income		8

| Entry 2 | Bank Service Expense | 16 | |
| | Cash | | 16 |

13.6 PETTY CASH

Funds spent through the cash disbursements journal take the form of checks issued in payment of various liabilities. In addition, a business will have many expenditures of small amounts for which it is not practical to issue checks. Examples are postage, delivery expense, supplies, and miscellaneous small items, which are paid for in cash through a petty cash fund.

Under the so-called *imprest system*, a fund is established for a fixed petty cash amount, which is periodically reimbursed by a single check for amounts expended. The steps in setting up and maintaining the petty cash fund are as follows:

1. An estimate is made of the total of the small amounts likely to be disbursed over a short period, usually a month. A check is drawn for the estimated total and put into the fund. The only time an entry is made in the Petty Cash account is for the initial establishment of the fund, unless at some later time it is determined that this fund must be increased or decreased.

EXAMPLE 2

A petty cash fund of $40 has been established.

| Petty Cash | 40 | |
| Cash | | 40 |

2. The individual in charge of petty cash usually keeps the money in a locked box along with petty cash vouchers, such as illustrated below. The petty cash voucher, when signed by the recipient, acts as a receipt and provides information concerning the transaction. As each payment is made, the voucher is entered in the petty cash record and placed with the balance of the money in the petty cash box.

Petty Cash Voucher

No. _____   Date _____
Paid To _____   Amount _____
Reason _____
Received By _____

EXAMPLE 3

Petty Cash Record

Date	Explanation	Voucher	Receipts	Payments	Postage	Del.	Sundry
Jan. 1	Established		$40.00				
2	Postage on Sales	1		$ 4.50	$ 4.50		
4	Telegram	2		4.00	4.00		
8	Taxi Fare	3		5.00		$5.00	
10	Coffee for Overtime	4		2.00			$ 2.00
15	Stamps	5		8.00	8.00		
26	Cleaning Windows	6		8.00			8.00
			$40.00	$31.50	$16.50	$5.00	$10.00
	Bal.			8.50			
			$40.00	$40.00			
Feb. 1	Bal.		$ 8.50				
	Replenished Fund		31.50				

EXAMPLE 4

The petty cash fund established in Example 2 might yield the following entries for the first month:

Postage Expense	16.50	
Delivery Expense	5.00	
Miscellaneous General Expense	10.00	
Cash		31.50

3. Proof of petty cash is obtained by counting the currency and adding the amounts of all the vouchers in the cash box. The total should agree with the amount in the ledger for the petty cash fund. If it does not, the entry in the cash disbursements journal recording the reimbursement of the petty cash fund will have to include an account known as Cash Short and Over. A cash shortage is debited and a cash overage is credited to this account. Cash Short and Over is closed out at the end of the year into the Income Summary account and is treated as a general expense (if a debit balance) or miscellaneous income (if a credit balance).

EXAMPLE 5

If in Example 4 the amount of cash remaining was not $8.50 but $6.50, the $2.00 difference would be considered to be short. The entry would then become

Postage Expense	16.50	
Delivery Expense	5.00	
Miscellaneous General Expense	10.00	
Cash Short and Over	2.00	
Cash		33.50

Summary

1. The most liquid asset and also the one most subject to theft and fraud is _____ .

2. All disbursements, except petty cash payments, should be made by _____ .

3. A written notice by a depositor instructing his or her bank to deduct a specific sum from his or her account and to pay it to the person assigned is known as a(n) _____ .

4. A check involves three parties: the _____ , who writes the check; the _____ , the bank on which it is drawn; and the _____ , the person to whom it is to be paid.

5. The signature on the back of a check showing that the individual accepts responsibility for that amount is known as a(n) _____ .

6. The _____ endorsement poses the greatest potential loss in the event of a lost or stolen check.

7. A bank service charge is evidenced by a(n) _____ .

8. A check that has been deposited but cannot be collected because of insufficient funds is labeled _____ by the bank and is deducted from the _____ balance.

9. Under the _____ , a fund is established for a fixed petty cash amount, which is reimbursed by a single check for amounts expended.

10. For small differences in the petty cash account, a(n) _____ account is generally used.

Answers: 1. cash; 2. prenumbered check; 3. check; 4. drawer, drawee, payee; 5. endorsement; 6. blank; 7. debit memorandum; 8. NSF, book; 9. imprest system; 10. Cash Short and Over.

Solved Problems

13.1. Name five sources of cash receipts.

SOLUTION

The following list contains the principal sources (any five sources could be named):

1. Sales of goods and services for cash
2. Collections of accounts and notes from customers
3. Renting of property
4. Loans from individuals
5. Loans from banks
6. Customers' notes discounted
7. New bonds issued

8. New capital stock issued
9. Sale of scrap, waste, and by-products
10. Disposal of equipment
11. Sale of other assets

13.2. Name five types of cash disbursements.

SOLUTION

　　Any five of the following types could be named:

1. Purchase of goods
2. Purchase of supplies
3. Payment of wages and salaries
4. Purchase of equipment
5. Payment of other operating expenses
6. Purchase of securities
7. Retirement of bank loans
8. Retirement of stocks and bonds
9. Miscellaneous payments (dividend payments, etc.)

13.3. Answer the following questions about the check shown below. (*a*) Who is the drawer? (*b*) Who is the drawee? (*c*) Who is the payee?

SOLUTION

(*a*) B. Smith
(*b*) Whiteside County Bank
(*c*) Jason Sloane

13.4. (*a*) Assume that J. Lerner, banking at 1st City Bank, wishes a full endorsement for A. Levy. Prepare a full endorsement.

(*b*) Prepare a blank endorsement.

(*c*) Prepare a restrictive endorsement for a deposit.

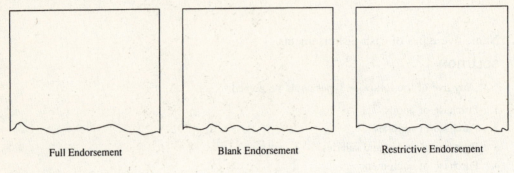

Full Endorsement   Blank Endorsement   Restrictive Endorsement

SOLUTION

Full Endorsement   Blank Endorsement   Restrictive Endorsement

13.5. For items 1 to 8 below, in order to produce equal adjusted balances for Blake Company, indicate whether they should be

(*a*) Added to the bank statement balance

(*b*) Deducted from the bank statement balance

(*c*) Added to the depositor's balance

(*d*) Deducted from the depositor's balance

(*e*) Exempted from the bank reconciliation statement

1. Statement includes a credit memorandum, $402, representing the collection of the proceeds of a note left at the bank.

2. Statement includes a credit memorandum representing the proceeds of a loan, $4,200, made to Blake Company by the bank.

3. Deposits in transit totaled $3,000.

4. Seven outstanding checks totaling $9,000 were not recorded on the statement.

5. A $150 customer's check that Blake Company had deposited was returned with "not sufficient funds" stamped across the face.

6. The bank erroneously charged someone else's check for $200 against Blake's account.

7. Blake Company was incorrectly credited with the deposit of $240 made by another depositor.

8. A $96 check was erroneously recorded in Blake's check stubs as $69.

SOLUTION

1. (c)   5. (d)
2. (c)   6. (a)
3. (a)   7. (b)
4. (b)   8. (d)

13.6. Of the following transactions involving the bank reconciliation statement, which ones necessitate an adjusting entry on the depositor's books? Prepare the necessary entries.

(a) Outstanding checks of $3,000 did not appear on the bank statement.

(b) The last 2 days' deposited receipts, $2,850, did not appear on the bank statement.

(c) The depositor's check for $120 for supplies was written in the records as $210.

(d) Bank service charge, $4.

(e)   A note left at the bank for collection, $822, was paid and credited to the depositor's account.

SOLUTION

(a) and (b) do not require any adjusting entries.

(c)	Cash	90	
	Supplies		90
(d)	Bank Service Expense	4	
	Cash		4
(e)	Cash	822	
	Notes Receivable		822

13.7. Using the following data, reconcile the bank account of the Kemper Motor Company.

1. Bank balance, $7,780

2. Depositor's balance, $6,500

3. Note collected by bank, $1,000, plus interest of $30; a collection charge of $10 was made by the bank.

4. Outstanding checks, $410.

5. Deposit in transit, $150.

SOLUTION

Balance per bank statement	$7,780	Balance per Kemper's books		$6,500
Add: Deposit in transit	150	Add: Note collected by bank		
	$7,930	Note	$1,000	
Less:		Interest	30	1,030
Outstanding checks	410			$7,530
		Less: Collection charge		10
Adjusted balance	$7,520	Adjusted balance		$7,520

13.8. Prepare the adjusting entries needed for Prob. 13.7.

	Dr.	Cr.

SOLUTION

	Dr.	Cr.
Cash	1,030	
Notes Receivable		1,000
Interest Income		30
Bank Service Expense	10	
Cash		10

13.9. Based on the following information, (a) prepare a bank reconciliation and (b) journalize the adjusting entries.

1. Bank balance per statement, $7,349.46.
2. Cash account balance, $5,432.76.
3. Check outstanding, $2,131.85.
4. Deposit in transit not recorded by bank, $1,243.15.
5. Note collected by bank, $1,015, including $15 interest.
6. A check for $46 for supplies was erroneously entered as $64.
7. Service charges not entered, $5.

SOLUTION

(a)   *Bank Reconciliation*

Balance per bank statement	$7,349.46	Balance per checkbook	$5,432.76
Add: Deposit in transit	1,243.15	Add: Note collected by bank	
	$8,592.61	Note $1,000	
Less: Outstanding check	2,131.85	Interest 15	1,015.00
		Error in recording check	18.00
			$6,465.76
		Less: Service charge	5.00
Adjusted balance	$6,460.76	Adjusted balance	$6,460.76

(b)   *Adjusting Entries*

Cash	1,033	
Notes Receivable		1,000
Interest Income		15
Supplies		18
Bank Service Expense	5	
Cash		5

13.10. Based on the following information, (a) prepare a bank reconciliation and (b) journalize the adjusting entries.

1. Bank balance per statement, $3,712.44.
2. Checkbook balance, $5,212.19.
3. Checks outstanding:

Check Numbers	Amount
934	$ 67.92
937	121.31
938	432.01
943	611.00

4. Deposit in transit not recorded by bank, $3,141.
5. Note collected by bank for $525, including $25 interest.
6. A check paid in advance for $251 for insurance was inadvertently entered as $151.
7. Bank service charge was $15.99.

SOLUTION

(*a*)   *Bank Reconciliation*

Balance per bank statement	$3,712.44	Checkbook balance	$5,212.19
Add: Deposit in transit	3,141.00	Add: Note $500	
	$6,853.44	Interest 25	525.00
			$5,737.19
		Less: Error in recording check	100.00
			$5,637.19
			15.99
Less: Outstanding checks	1,232.24	Less: Service charge	
Adjusted bank balance	$5,621.20	Adjusted bank balance	$5,621.20

(*b*)   *Adjusting Entries*

Cash	425.00	
Prepaid Insurance	100.00	
Notes Receivable		500.00
Interest Income		25.00
Miscellaneous Expense	15.99	
Cash		15.99

13.11. Correct the following incorrect bank reconciliation.

Kaney Company
Bank Reconciliation
December 31, 19X8

Balance per depositor's books	$7,250	
Add:		
Note collected by bank including interest	515	
Deposit in transit	1,200	
Bank error charging Kane's check to Kaney account	860	
Total		$9,825
Deduct:		
Check from customer of Kaney's deposited and returned by bank as NSF	$ 150	
Service charge	5	
Check for $250 written in Kaney's ledger and checkbook stubs as $150	100	
Outstanding checks	1,100	1,355
		$8,470
Less: Unexplained difference		1,920
Balance per bank statement		$6,550

SOLUTION

Kaney Company
Bank Reconciliation
December 31, 19X8

Balance per bank statement	$6,550	Balance per depositor's books	$7,250
Add: Deposit in transit	1,200	Add: Note collected by bank	515
Error	860		$7,765
	$8,610	Less:	
		NSF check	$150
		Bank service charge	5
Less: Outstanding checks	1,100	Error	100		255
Adjusted balance	$7,510	Adjusted balance	$7,510

13.12. Prepare the adjusting entries needed for Prob. 13.11.

SOLUTION

Cash	515	
Notes Receivable		515
Bank Service Expense	5	
Accounts Receivable	150	
Supplies	100	
Cash		255

13.13. Based on the following information, prepare a reconciliation of the Armando Company's bank account at December 31.

1. Balance per bank statement, December 31, $88,489.12.
2. Balance per books, December 31, $58,983.46.
3. Outstanding checks, December 31, $32,108.42.
4. Receipts of December 31, 19X8 deposited January 2, $5,317.20.
5. Service charge for November per bank memorandum of December 15, $3.85.
6. Proceeds of bank loan, December 15, omitted from company books, $9,875.00.
7. Deposit of December 23, omitted from bank statement, $2,892.41.
8. Check of Rome Products Company charged back by bank on December 22 for absence of countersignature. No entry was made on the books for the chargeback, $417.50.

9. Error on bank statement in entering deposit of December 16:

Current amount	$3,182.40
Entered in statement	3,181.40
	$ 1.00

10. Check 3917 of Arandon Manufacturing Company charged by bank in error to company's account, $2,690.00.

11. Proceeds of note of J. Somers & Company, collected by bank on December 10, not entered in cash book:

Principal	$2,000.00
Interest	20.00
	$2,020.00
Less: Collection charge	5.00
	$2,015.00

12. Erroneous debit memorandum of December 23 to charge company's account with settlement of bank loan, which was paid by check 8714 on same date, $5,000.00.

13. Error on bank statement in entering deposit of December 4:

Entered as	$4,817.10
Correct amount	4,807.10
	$ 10.00

14. Deposit of Arandon Manufacturing Company of December 6 credited in error to this company, $1,819.20.

Bank statement balance		
Add:		
Deduct:		
Adjusted bank balance		

Checkbook balance		
Add:		
Deduct:		
Adjusted checkbook balance		

SOLUTION

Bank statement balance		$ 88,489.12
Add:		
Deposit in transit	$ 5,317.20	
Error in deposit	2,892.41	
Dec. 16 deposit error	1.00	
Arandon Manufacturing Co. error	2,690.00	
Debit memorandum of Dec. 23	5,000.00	15,900.61
		$104,389.73
Deduct:		
Outstanding checks	$32,108.42	
Dec. 4 error in deposit	10.00	
Arandon Manufacturing Co. deposit in error	1,819.20	33,937.62
Adjusted bank balance		$ 70,452.11
Checkbook balance		$ 58,983.46
Add:		
Bank loan proceeds	$ 9,875.00	
Loan collection: Principal $2,000		
Interest 20	2,020.00	11,895.00
		$70,878.46
Deduct:		
Service charge	$ 3.85	
Collection charge	5.00	
Rome Co. (chargeback)	417.50	426.35
Adjusted checkbook balance		$ 70,452.11

13.14. What adjusting entries are needed to record the above data?

SOLUTION

Cash	11,895.00	
Notes Payable		9,875.00
Notes Receivable, J. Somers & Co.		2,000.00
Interest Income		20.00
Bank Service Expense	8.85	
Accounts Receivable, Rome Products Co.	417.50	
Cash		426.35

13.15. Transactions for the Eagan Company for the month of January, pertaining to the establishment of a petty cash fund, were as follows:

Jan. 1   Established an imprest petty cash fund of $50
      31   Box contained $6 cash and paid vouchers for transportation, $14; freight, $16; charity, $4; office supplies, $6; miscellaneous expense, $4

What are the journal entries necessary to record the petty cash information?

SOLUTION

Petty Cash	50	
Cash		50
Transportation Expense	14	
Freight Expense	16	
Charity Expense	4	
Office Supplies Expense	6	
Miscellaneous Expense	4	
Cash		44

13.16. If in Prob. 13.15 the cash on hand was $9, record the January 31 reimbursement.

SOLUTION

Transportation Expense	14	
Freight Expense	16	
Charity Expense	4	
Office Supplies Expense	6	
Miscellaneous Expense	4	
Cash		41
Cash Short and Over		3

13.17. If in Prob. 13.15 the cash on hand was only $2, record the January 31 reimbursement. What will happen to the Cash Short and Over account?

SOLUTION

Transportation Expense	14	
Freight Expense	16	
Charity Expense	4	
Office Supplies Expense	6	
Miscellaneous Expense	4	
Cash Short and Over	4	
Cash		48

At the end of the period the balance of the Cash Short and Over account is closed out to the Income Summary account.

13.18. At the close of the day, the total cash sales as determined by the sales registers were $1,480. However, the total cash receipts were only $1,472. The error cannot be located at the present time. What entry should be made to record the cash sales for the day?

SOLUTION

Cash	1,472	
Cash Short and Over	8	
Sales		1,480

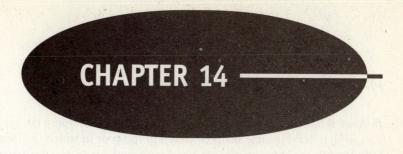

CHAPTER 14

Payroll

14.1 GROSS PAY

The pay rate at which employees are paid is generally arrived at through negotiations between the employer and the employees. The employer, however, must conform with all applicable federal and state laws (minimum wage, and so on). One law requires that certain workers be compensated at $1\frac{1}{2}$ times their regular pay for hours worked over 40.

Gross pay for wage earners is generally computed by using an individual time card.

EXAMPLE 1

Based on the time card, the computation of Ms. Stephenson's gross pay appears below. Note that 1 hour is allowed for lunch each day.

Time Card

Name	Carol Stephenson		Pay Rate/Hour	$9.00
Week Ended	12/25/X8			

	Time In	Time Out	Working Hours
Monday	8:00 A.M.	5:00 P.M.	8
Tuesday	8:00 A.M.	7:00 P.M.	10
Wednesday	8:00 A.M.	8:00 P.M.	11
Thursday	8:00 A.M.	5:00 P.M.	8
Friday	8:00 A.M.	6:00 P.M.	9

Approved	J. L.	Total Hours for Week	46

Regular pay: 40 hours × $9.00	$360.00
Overtime pay: 6 hours × $1\frac{1}{2}$ × $9.00	81.00
Gross pay	$441.00

14.2 DEDUCTIONS FROM GROSS PAY

Federal Withholding Taxes.   Under the federal withholding tax system (commonly known as "pay as you go"), federal income tax is collected in the year in which the income is received, rather than in the following year. Thus, employers must withhold funds for the payment of their employees' federal income taxes. The amount to be withheld depends on the number of exemptions the employee is allowed (Form W-4, see Fig. 14-1), the amount of the employee's earnings, and the employee's marital status. An employee is entitled to one personal exemption and one for his or her spouse and each dependent.

Fig. 14-1

Federal Insurance Contributions Act (FICA).   The FICA tax (a combination of social security and Medicare) helps pay for federal programs for old age and disability benefits, Medicare, and insurance benefits to survivors. During working years, money is set aside from an employee's earnings and placed along with all other employees' contributions to the Social Security fund. When the employee's earnings cease because of disability, retirement, or death, money from this fund is made available to his or her dependents, survivors, or to the employee himself or herself. A combined tax rate of 7.65 percent [6.2 percent for old-age, survivors, and disability insurance (OASDI), also known by the more popular term "Social Security," and 1.45 percent for hospital insurance (Medicare)] is imposed on both employer and employee. The OASDI rate (6.2 percent) applies to wages within the OASDI wage base, which is $68,400 for 1998. The Medicare rate (1.45 percent) applies to all wages with no limit.

EXAMPLE 2

Fran Johnson's earnings prior to this week were $67,800. This week her salary was $500. Her total FICA deduction would be $38.25 ($500 × 7.65 percent). If Fran had earned $68,300 prior to this pay period, only $100 ($68,400 maximum earnings) would be subject to OASDI and the total FICA tax would be only $13.45 ($100 × 7.65 percent + $400 × 1.45 percent).

If an individual works for more than one employer during a year, each employer must withhold and pay taxes on the first $68,400. The employee will be granted a refund from the government if he or she pays taxes on more than the $68,400 base.

Notice that the withholding of any wages represents, from the employer's viewpoint, a liability, because the employer must pay to the government the amount withheld from the employee.

In addition to taxes, or involuntary deductions, there may be a number of voluntary deductions made for the convenience of the employee, such as group insurance premiums, hospitalization programs, savings plans, retirement payments, union dues, and charitable contributions.

EXAMPLE 3

Harold Eccleston earned $580 for the week. Deductions from his pay were federal withholding, $85; FICA, $44.37; insurance, $12; union dues, $18. What is his net pay?

Gross pay		$580.00
Federal withholding	85.00	
FICA	44.37	
Insurance	12.00	
Union dues	18.00	159.37
Net pay		$420.63

14.3 THE PAYROLL SYSTEM

The payroll system generally consists of input data (individual time cards), a payroll register (to compute the payroll each payroll period), individual earnings cards (a detached record for each employee), and a procedure for recording the payroll and the related employer taxes with appropriate liabilities. Most payroll systems are now completely computerized.

(A) Individual Time Card

Although the overall payroll is recorded periodically in a payroll register, it is also necessary to accumulate the earnings and the deductions for each employee separately. These individual records facilitate the preparation of required governmental reports and assist the employer in maintaining control over payroll expenditures. They also act as convenient references to basic employee information such as earnings to date, exemptions, filing status, and employee classification. Information from the payroll register is posted to the individual earnings cards after recording the payroll.

Individual Earnings Record

Name _____   Filing Status _____

Address _____   Exemptions Claimed_____

_____   Position_____

S.S.# _____   Pay Rate_____ Per _____

First Quarter

Payroll Period	Gross			Deductions						Net	
	Reg.	Ot.	Total	FICA	Fed. With.	State With.	Oth. Ded.	Total Ded.		Net Pay	Ck. #
First Quarter											

(B) Payroll Register

A payroll register is a specially designed form used at the close of each payroll period (weekly, biweekly, and so on) to summarize and compute the payroll for the period. Although the design of this form may vary slightly depending on the desired information and the degree of automation, most contain the same basic information.

Refer to the payroll register (Table 14-1) and note that it is broken into five sections:

1. Gross earnings (regular, overtime, total).
2. Taxable earnings (information only), used as a reference in computing FICA tax withheld or paid by the employer and unemployment tax payable by the employer.
3. Deductions from gross pay—a place is provided for each tax withheld and for total deductions.
4. Net pay. This is the employee's take-home pay. This may be checked by adding the total of deductions to the net pay. The result should be the gross pay.
5. Specific accounts to which gross salaries are charged.

EXAMPLE 4

Complete Table 14-1 using the payroll data in Table 14-2. Table 14-3 shows the completed payroll register for the Atlas Company as of June 15.

14.4 RECORDING THE PAYROLL

The payroll entry is generally recorded in the general ledger. Since the payroll register is the input for the entry, it is generally totaled for the payroll period and proved before any entry is made.

EXAMPLE 5

From the summarized data in Table 14-3, record the payroll in general journal form.

Table 14-1 Payroll Register

Date	Name	(1) Gross Pay			(2) Taxable		(3) Deductions						(4) Net		(5) Distribution	
		Reg.	Ot.	Total	FICA	Unemp.	FICA	Fed. With.	State With.	Code	Oth. Ded.	Total Ded.	Net Pay	Ck. No.	Office Salaries	Factory Salaries

Table 14-2 Payroll Data

Name	(Prior to Payroll) Earnings to Date	Gross Pay			Classification	Fed. With.	FICA	State With.	Other Deductions
		Reg.	Ot.	Total					
P. Smith	$3,700	$200	$40	$240	Office	$19.65	$18.36	$ 8.45	Union A $11
S. Jones	8,000	260	0	260	Office	22.40	19.89	9.20	Union A 10
R. Campbell	6,800	285	35	320	Factory	28.00	24.48	12.40	Union A 7

Table 14-3 Payroll Register

Date	Name	Gross Pay			Taxable		Deductions						Net		Distribution	
		Reg.	Ot.	Total	FICA	Unemp.	FICA	Fed. With.	State With.	Code	Oth. Ded.	Total Ded.	Net Pay	Ck. No.	Office Salaries	Factory Salaries
3/15	P. Smith	$200	$40	$240	$240	$240	$18.36	$19.65	$ 8.45	A	$11.00	$57.46	$182.54	44	$240.00	
3/15	S. Jones	260	—	260	260	0*	19.89	22.40	9.20	A	10.00	61.49	198.51	45	260.00	
3/15	R. Campbell	285	35	320	320	200*	24.48	28.00	12.40	A	7.00	71.88	248.12	46		$320.00
	Total	$745	$75	$820	$820	$440	$62.73	$70.05	$30.05		$28.00	$190.83	$629.17		$500.00	$320.00

*Only the first $7,000 is subject to unemployment tax.

General Journal

Date	Description	P.R.	Dr.	Cr.
March 15	Office Salaries Expense		500.00	
	Factory Salaries Expense		320.00	
	FICA Taxes Payable			62.73
	Federal Taxes Payable			70.05
	State Withholding Tax Payable			30.05
	Union Dues Payable			28.00
	Cash			629.17
	To record the payroll for the week ended March 15			

(A) Payroll Taxes Imposed on the Employer (Table 14-4)

Social Security (Federal Insurance Contributions Act).   Not only is Social Security (FICA) withheld from the employee's pay, but a matching amount is paid by the employer. The employer's contribution is generally computed by multiplying the total *taxable* payroll for the current period by 7.65 percent and adding the difference between the total OASDI payroll and the taxable Medicare payroll multiplied by 1.45 percent. The two 7.65 percent contributions (7.65 percent from the employee; 7.65 percent from the employer) are reported quarterly by the employer on federal Form 941 along with federal withholding tax. This tax payment is made at a member bank of the Federal Reserve.

Unemployment Taxes.   Employers are required to pay unemployment taxes to both the federal and state governments under the Federal Unemployment Tax Acts (FUTA) and the State Unemployment Tax Acts (SUTA). Under current legislation, the tax is imposed only on the first $7,000 of each employee's earnings. Although the typical state unemployment tax rate is 5.4 percent, rates vary depending on the state, the nature of the business, and the employer's experience with unemployment. For 1998, the official federal unemployment tax rate was 6.2 percent. However, as long as the employer is up to date on the state tax, the employer is allowed an automatic credit of 5.4 percent no matter what rate the employer actually pays. The effective federal unemployment tax rate is therefore 0.8 percent.

Table 14-4   Payroll Taxes

Tax	Paid by		Rate
	Employee	Employer	
FICA:			
OASDI*	Yes	Yes	6.20% on first $68,400 of wages
Medicare	Yes	Yes	1.45% on all wages
Fed. Income	Yes	No	Varies with exemptions; based on table
Fed. Unemp.	No	Yes	0.8% of first $7,000
State Unemp.	No	Yes	Up to 6.2% of first $7,000

*Also known as Social Security.

(B) Recording the Employer's Taxes

When the payroll entry is recorded, the employer's contribution will also be recorded.

EXAMPLE 6

From the data summarized in the payroll register (Table 14-3), record the employer's taxes for the payroll period. (Assume a 3.4 percent state unemployment tax rate and a 0.8 percent federal rate.)

General Journal

Date	Description	P.R.	Dr.	Cr.
March 15	Payroll Tax Expense		81.21	
	FICA Taxes Payable*			62.73
	State Unemployment Tax Payable**			14.96†
	Federal Unemployment Tax Payable**			3.52
	To record the employer's taxes for the week ended March 15			

*Must match the employees' contribution.

**Note that by reference to the Payroll Register (Taxable Unemployment) only $440 is subject to the tax.

†Based on rate of 3.4%.

Summary

1. Compensation is paid at the rate of time and one-half when an employee works more than _____ hours.

2. The amount of federal income tax withheld from an employee's salary is based on the individual's _____ and _____ .

3. Form _____ will show information as to the number of exemptions an employee is claiming.

4. The rate of FICA tax is _____ percent.

5. FICA is reported _____ by the employer on Form _____ .

6. The payroll _____ is the input for the payroll entry.

7. Generally, all payroll entries are recorded in the _____ journal.

8. The two types of payroll taxes imposed on the employer are _____ and _____ .

9. The payroll tax expense entry is recorded in the _____ journal.

10. The one tax usually paid by the employee and matched by the employer is _____ .

Answers: 1. 40; 2. filing status, number of exemptions; 3. W-4; 4. 7.65; 5. quarterly, 941; 6. register; 7. general; 8. FICA, unemployment; 9. general; 10. FICA

Solved Problems

14.1. Below is a time card for Carol Popich. Complete the hours section of her time card and compute her gross pay. Allow 1 hour for lunch each day.

Time Card

Name	Carol Popich	Pay Rate/Hour	$6.40
Week Ended	9/20/X8		

	Time In	Time Out	Hours
Monday	8:00 A.M.	5:00 P.M.	_____
Tuesday	8:00 A.M.	5:00 P.M.	_____
Wednesday	8:00 A.M.	7:00 P.M.	_____
Thursday	8:00 A.M.	8:30 P.M.	_____
Friday	8:00 A.M.	7:30 P.M.	_____

Approved _____   Total Hours for Week _____

SOLUTION

Time Card

Name	Carol Popich	Pay Rate/Hour	$6.40
Week Ended	9/20/X8		

	Time In	Time Out	Hours
Monday	8:00 A.M.	5:00 P.M.	8
Tuesday	8:00 A.M.	5:00 P.M.	8
Wednesday	8:00 A.M.	7:00 P.M.	10
Thursday	8:00 A.M.	8:30 P.M.	$11\frac{1}{2}$
Friday	8:00 A.M.	7:30 P.M.	$10\frac{1}{2}$

Approved *J.L.*   Total Hours for Week   48

Regular pay: 40 hours × $6.40 =		$256.00
Overtime pay: 8 hours × $9.60* =		76.80
Total gross pay		$332.80

_____

*Time and one-half rate.

14.2. How many exemptions are permitted to be claimed on Form W-4 in the following cases:

(*a*) Taxpayer

(*b*) Taxpayer and (nonworking) spouse

(*c*) Taxpayer and working spouse

(*d*) Taxpayer, spouse, and two children

SOLUTION

(*a*) 1, (*b*) 2, (*c*) 2—if spouse does not claim herself, (*d*) 4—provided spouse does not claim herself

14.3. Based on the Social Security rate of 6.2% (up to $68,400) and the Medicare rate of 1.45% (unlimited), how much will be withheld from the following employees:

	Employee	Amount Earned Prior to Current Payroll	Amount Earned This Week	Amount Withheld for FICA
(*a*)	I. Blanton	$20,000	$400	?
(*b*)	P. Burday	68,200	480	?
(*c*)	M. Fleming	89,100	500	?

SOLUTION

(*a*) $30.60 ($400 × 7.65%)

(*b*) $22.26 ($200 balance × 7.65% + $480 × 1.45%)

(*c*) $5.75 ($500 × 1.45%)

14.4. Complete the table below based on the employer's payroll obligation. Assume a state rate of 3.4 percent and a federal rate of 0.8 percent.

	Employee	Amount Earned This Week	Prior Earnings	FICA	Federal Unemployment	State Unemployment
(*a*)	B. Orzech	$400	$4,300	$28.60	?	?
(*b*)	M. Felson	460	6,800	32.89	?	?
(*c*)	H. Hendricks	500	7,400	35.75	?	?

SOLUTION

	Federal Unemployment	State Unemployment
(*a*)	$3.20	$13.60
(*b*)	1.60*	6.80**
(*c*)	None	None

---

*Federal rate is 0.8% on first $7,000. Balance subject to tax, $200.00.

**State rate is 3.4% on first $7,000. Balance subject to tax, $200.00.

14.5. Judy Bagon worked 44 hours during the first week in February of the current year. Her pay rate is $5.50 per hour. Withheld from her wages were FICA (7.65 percent), federal income tax ($31.00), and hospitalization ($9.00). Determine the necessary payroll entry.

SOLUTION

Salary Expense	253.00*	
FICA Taxes Payable		19.35
Federal Income Tax Payable		31.00
Hospitalization Payable		9.00
Cash		193.65

*40 hours × $5.50 = $220.00 (regular)
    4 hours × 8.25 =   33.00 (overtime)
            Total $253.00

14.6. Based on the information in Prob. 14.5, what is the entry to record the employer's payroll tax if it is assumed that the state tax rate is 3.4 percent, the federal unemployment rate is 0.8 percent, and earnings to date are $1,000?

SOLUTION

Payroll Tax Expense	29.97	
FICA Taxes Payable		19.35
Federal Unemployment Tax Payable		2.02
State Unemployment Tax Payable		8.60

14.7. The total payroll for the Berchid Realty Company for the week ending May 30 was $19,000, all subject to FICA tax; $3,800 was withheld for federal income tax and $1,500 deducted for pensions; and the balance was paid in cash. Present the journal entry necessary to record the payroll for this week, assuming that the FICA tax rate is 7.65 percent.

SOLUTION

Salaries Expense	19,000.00	
FICA Taxes Payable		1,453.50
Federal Income Taxes Payable		3,800.00
Pension Contributions Payable		1,500.00
Cash		12,246.50

14.8. Based on Prob. 14.7, present the employer's payroll tax entry, assuming a state unemployment tax rate of 3.4 percent and federal unemployment tax rate of 0.8 percent, and that of the total payroll, $7,000 was subject to federal and state unemployment.

SOLUTION

Payroll Tax Expense	1,747.50	
FICA Taxes Payable		1,453.50*
State Unemployment Tax Payable		238.00
Federal Unemployment Tax Payable		56.00

*Matched

14.9. For the week ending June 30, the Benezran Company had a gross payroll of $12,000. The amount subject to unemployment compensation tax was $8,000. Present the journal entry to record the employer's payroll tax for the week, assuming the following rates: FICA 7.65 percent, state unemployment 3.4 percent, federal unemployment 0.8 percent.

SOLUTION

Payroll Tax Expense	1,254.00	
FICA Taxes Payable		918.00
State Unemployment Tax Payable		272.00
Federal Unemployment Tax Payable		64.00

14.10. For the week ending July 3, Happy Pools' gross payroll was $37,640, of which $21,370 was subject to unemployment compensation insurance tax. Present the journal entries to record the employer's tax expense for the week. Assume a state unemployment rate of 3.2 percent and a federal rate of 0.8 percent.

SOLUTION

Payroll Tax Expense	3,734.26	
FICA Taxes Payable		2,879.46
State Unemployment Tax Payable		683.84
Federal Unemployment Tax Payable		170.96

14.11. Sooners Fruit Farm employs 20 full-time employees. For the week ending August 5, the gross pay was $14,774, and of that, $12,227 was subject to unemployment insurance tax. Present the journal entry to record the employer's payroll tax expense. Assume a state unemployment rate of 3.3 percent and a federal rate of 0.8 percent.

SOLUTION

Payroll Tax Expense	1,631.52	
FICA Taxes Payable		1,130.21
State Unemployment Tax Payable		403.49
Federal Unemployment Tax Payable		97.82

14.12. Bill King works for Jinx Corporation full-time and Luckey Corporation part-time. His gross pay to date at Jinx is $68,200, and his pay for the week ending November 30 is $500. His pay to date at Luckey Corporation is $12,250, and his pay for the week is $205. How much was withheld from Bill King's pay by each employer?

SOLUTION

Jinx Corp.	$22.55	($200 × 7.65% + $500 × 1.45%)
Luckey Corp.	15.68	($205 × 7.65%)
	$38.23	Total FICA tax withheld

Mr. King will file for a refund on the Social Security tax withheld from his second job because he has reached the $68,400 cap on Social Security tax earnings.

14.13. Yellow Cab Company has 34 employees. For the week ending July 9, their total gross pay was $20,115, all subject to FICA tax, and $11,560 was subject to unemployment insurance tax.

Assume a FICA tax rate of 7.65 percent, a state unemployment rate of 3.4 percent, and a federal rate of 0.8 percent. Present the entry for the employer's payroll tax expense.

SOLUTION

Payroll Tax Expense	2,024.32	
FICA Taxes Payable		1,538.80
State Unemployment Tax Payable		393.04
Federal Unemployment Tax Payable		92.48

14.14. ABC Company has three salespeople who are paid a flat salary of $300 per week, plus a 5 percent commission on their sales. Their sales for the week ending March 26 were Jack, $5,000; Pat, $4,500; and Matt, $5,350. The FICA tax rate is 7.65 percent. What is their FICA tax withheld?

SOLUTION

Jack	$42.08	($5,000 × 5% = $250* + $300** = $550 × 7.65%)
Pat	$40.16	($4,500 × 5% = $225* + $300** = $525 × 7.65%)
Matt	$43.41	($5,350 × 5% = $267.50* + $300** = $567.50 × 7.65%)

*Commission
**Weekly pay

14.15. Low Company has four employees. Their gross pay for the week ending September 5 was Frank, $385; Lyn, $428; Shawn, $454; and Amy, $406. Assuming a FICA rate of 7.65 percent, what is the FICA tax withholding?

SOLUTION

Frank	$29.45	($385 × 7.65%)
Lyn	$32.74	($428 × 7.65%)
Shawn	$34.73	($454 × 7.65%)
Amy	$31.06	($406 × 7.65%)

14.16. Based on the information below, complete the March 28 payroll register for the J. Rakosi Medical Center.

Name	Earnings to Date	Gross Pay			Federal Withholding	Other Deductions
		Reg.	Ot.	Total		
J. Erin	$3,800	$200	$70	$270	$18.10	Union $ 9
M. Ribble	6,950	250	50	300	9.20	Union 11
W. Mondstein	7,200	300	—	300	15.70	Union 14
M. Yamura	8,000	350	—	350	28.40	—

Payroll Register

		Gross Pay			Taxable		Deductions			Net
Date	Name	Reg.	Ot.	Total	FICA	Unemp.	FICA	Fed. With.	Other Ded.	Net Pay

SOLUTION

Payroll Register

		Gross Pay			Taxable		Deductions			Net
Date	Name	Reg.	Ot.	Total	FICA	Unemp.	FICA	Fed. With.	Other Ded.	Net Pay
3/28	J. Erin	200	70	270	270	270	20.66	18.10	U- 9.00	222.24
	M. Ribble	250	50	300	300	50	22.95	9.20	U-11.00	256.85
	W. Mondstein	300	—	300	300	—	22.95	15.70	U-14.00	247.35
	M. Yamura	350	—	350	350	—	26.78	28.40	—	294.82
	Totals:	1,100	120	1,220	1,220	320	93.34	71.40	34.00	1,021.26

14.17. Based on the information in Prob. 14.16, present the payroll entry needed.

SOLUTION

Salaries Expense	1,220.00	
FICA Taxes Payable		93.34
Federal Income Taxes Payable		71.40
Union Dues Payable		34.00
Cash		1,021.26

14.18. Based on the information presented in the payroll register of Prob. 14.16, present the necessary payroll tax expense entry for the employer. Assume a state tax rate of 3.2 percent and a federal rate of 0.8 percent.

SOLUTION

Payroll Tax Expense	106.14	
FICA Taxes Payable		93.34
State Unemployment Tax Payable		10.24*
Federal Unemployment Tax Payable		2.56*

*The total amount of the payroll subject to the $7,000 maximum earned limitation for unemployment insurance is $320. (Erin $270 and Ribble $50.)

14.19. Listed below is the payroll information for four of the employees of the Barlow Company.

Employee	Amount Earned to Date	Gross Pay for Week
M. Jackson	$7,150	$328
J. Jill	6,974	407
R. Hall	5,285	387
R. Mund	6,784	419

The FICA tax rate is 7.65 percent. The state unemployment rate for this company for the present year is 3.1 percent, and the federal rate is 0.8 percent. The cap on wages subject to unemployment tax is $7,000. Present the entry for Barlow's tax expense for these employees for the week.

SOLUTION

FICA	M. Jackson	$ 25.09	($328 × 7.65%)
	J. Jill	31.14	($407 × 7.65%)
	R. Hall	29.61	($387 × 7.65%)
	P. Mund	32.05	($419 × 7.65%)
		$117.89	

State	M. Jackson	$ -0-	
	J. Jill	0.81	($7,000 − $6,974 = $26 × 3.1%)
	R. Hall	12.00	($387 × 3.1%)
	P. Mund	6.70	($7,000 − $6,784 = $216 × 3.1%)
		$ 19.51	

Federal	M. Jackson	$ -0-	
	J. Jill	0.21	($7,000 − $6,974 = $26 × 0.8%)
	R. Hall	3.10	($387 × 0.8%)
	P. Mund	1.73	($7,000 − $6,784 = $216 × 0.8%)
		$ 5.04	

Payroll Tax Expense	142.44	
FICA Taxes Payable		117.89
State Unemployment Tax Payable		19.51
Federal Unemployment Tax Payable		5.04

CHAPTER 15

Property, Plant, and Equipment: Depreciation

15.1 FIXED ASSETS

Tangible assets that are relatively permanent and are needed for the production or sale of goods or services are termed *property, plant, and equipment*, or *fixed assets*. These assets are not held for sale in the ordinary course of business. The broad group is usually separated into classes according to the physical characteristics of the items (e.g., land, buildings, machinery and equipment, furniture and fixtures).

The cost of property, plant, and equipment includes all expenditures necessary to put the asset into position and make it ready for use.

EXAMPLE 1

For a lathe purchased by AB Optical Company, the data were invoice price, $11,000; cash discount, $220; freight-in, $300; trucking, $200; electrical connections and installation, $720. The total cost is $11,000 − $220 + $300 + $200 + $720 = $12,000. Therefore, the entry is

Machinery and Equipment	12,000	
Cash		12,000

15.2 DEPRECIATION AND SCRAP VALUE

Though it may be long, the useful life of a fixed asset is limited. Eventually the asset will lose all productive worth and will possess only salvage value (scrap value). The accrual basis of accounting demands a period-by-period matching of costs against derived revenues. Hence, the cost of a fixed asset (over and above its scrap value) is distributed over the asset's entire estimated lifetime. This spreading of the cost over the periods that receive benefits is known as *depreciation*.

To determine depreciation expense for a fixed asset, we need the following information:

1. *Cost.* The total purchase price of the item, including its initial cost, transportation, sales tax, installation, and any other expense to make it ready for use.

2. *Estimated useful life.* The projected life during which the business expects the asset to function. This may be expressed in years, miles, units of production, or other measures appropriate to the particular equipment. For example, a building or store may be depreciated over a number of years, an automobile by mileage, and a printing press by the number of units it prints or hours it is used.

3. *Residual value.* Also called scrap or salvage value, the estimated value of the asset when it is fully depreciated. When subtracted from the cost of the asset, it produces the "depreciable cost." For example, a $14,000 press with a scrap value of $4,000 has a depreciable cost of $10,000 ($14,000 − $4,000). If the business expects the asset to have no value at the end of the depreciation period, the asset's entire cost ($14,000 for the press) should be depreciated.

Depreciation decreases the fixed asset's book value and also decreases capital. Depreciation is considered an operating expense of the business. It may be recorded by an entry at the end of each month or at the end of the year, usually depending on the frequency of preparing financial statements. Fixed assets are recorded at cost and remain at that figure as long as they are held. The depreciation taken to date is shown as a credit in the offset account Accumulated Depreciation and is deducted from the asset account on the balance sheet, as shown in Example 2 below.

An *offset* (or *contra*) *account* is an account with a credit balance that is offset against (deducted from) an asset account to produce the correct balance sheet book value. The offset account appears in the general ledger directly after its companion account. Generally, every depreciable asset has its own account and an accumulated depreciation account. To determine the asset's book, or carrying, value, the accumulated depreciation account is subtracted from the asset account.

EXAMPLE 2

| Equipment | $10,000 | |
| Less: Accumulated Depreciation | 4,000 | $6,000 |

The book value of the equipment has gone from $10,000 to $6,000.

There is one exception to the above considerations: land. This fixed asset is nondepreciable; it is usually carried on the books permanently at cost.

15.3 METHODS OF DEPRECIATION

The depreciable amount of a fixed asset—that is, cost minus scrap value—may be written off in different ways. For example, the amount may be spread evenly over the years affected, as in the straight-line method. Two accelerated methods, the double-declining-balance method and the sum-of-the-years'-digits method, provide for larger amounts of depreciation in the earlier years. Repairs, on the other hand, are generally lower in the earlier years, so the total cost of depreciation and repairs should be about the same each year. The units-of-production method bases depreciation each period on the amount of output.

(A)   Straight-Line (SL)

The straight-line method is the simplest and most widely used depreciation method. Under this method, an equal portion of the cost of the asset is allocated to each period of use. The periodic charge is expressed as

$$\frac{\text{Cost} - \text{scrap value}}{\text{Useful life (in years)}} = \text{annual depreciation charge}$$

EXAMPLE 3

Cost of machine, $17,000; scrap value, $2,000; estimated life, 5 years.

$$\frac{\$17,000 - \$2,000}{5} = \$3,000 \text{ per year}$$

The entry to record the depreciation would be

Depreciation Expense, Machinery	3,000	
Accumulated Depreciation, Machinery		3,000

In order to have sufficient documentation for an asset's depreciation, a schedule should be prepared showing the asset's cost, depreciation expense, accumulated depreciation, and, most important of all, its "book value." Book value (or "undepreciated cost") is the balance of an asset's cost less its accumulated depreciation to date. Based upon Example 3, the book value at the end of each year would be

	Cost		Accumulated Depreciation		Book Value
19X5	$17,000	–	$ 3,000	=	$14,000
19X6	$17,000	–	$ 6,000	=	$11,000
19X7	$17,000	–	$ 9,000	=	$ 8,000
19X8	$17,000	–	$12,000	=	$ 5,000
19X9	$17,000	–	$15,000	=	$ 2,000

Book value should not be confused with market value. The book value is the difference between cost and accumulated depreciation. Market value is what the asset can actually be sold for on a given date.

As an asset is used, accumulated depreciation increases and book value decreases. The last column shows the asset's book value in any year. In the fifth and final year, 19X9, book value is the same as scrap value. At this point, the asset is said to be fully depreciated.

In the preceding example, we assumed that the machine was purchased at the beginning of the year, permitting depreciation of the machine for the full 12 months. But often, assets are bought during the year. When this happens, the amount of depreciation is recorded not for the entire year, but only for the number of months the asset is used, to the nearest whole month.

If an asset is held for more than half a month, that month is counted. If it is held for less than 15 days in any month, that month is not counted. An asset bought on or before the 15th of the month is considered to be in use and therefore can be depreciated for the entire month. If it is bought on or after the 16th, it cannot be depreciated for that month. Depreciation will begin the following month.

EXAMPLE 4

A truck bought on April 6, 19X8, is depreciated for 9 months, April through December ($\frac{9}{12}$ or $\frac{3}{4}$ of the year). But if it is bought on April 16, depreciation is calculated for only 8 months; May through December ($\frac{8}{12}$ or $\frac{2}{3}$ of the year). After this first, partial year, the truck is depreciated for each remaining full 12-month year until it is fully depreciated.

EXAMPLE 5

The cost of a machine is $25,000. It has scrap value of $5,000 and an estimated life of 5 years. It was purchased on September 18, 19X8. To calculate annual depreciation:

$$\frac{\$25,000 - \$5,000}{5 \text{ years}} = \$4,000 \text{ annual depreciation expense}$$

To calculate depreciation at the end of the first year, determine what fraction of the year the machine was actually used. In this case, it was three months in the first year: October, November, and December. That's because an asset put into use after the 15th day of any month is not included in the depreciation calculation. Thus, the calculation is:

$$\frac{3 \text{ (months of use)}}{12 \text{ (months)}} \times \$4,000 \text{ (annual depreciation)} = \$1,000 \text{ first-year depreciation expense}$$

Entry:

Depreciation Expense—Machine	1,000*	
Accumulated Depreciation—Machine		1,000

*($4,000 × $\frac{1}{4}$) To record depreciation for the last three months of the 1st year of operation.

And one more point: Annual depreciation can also be calculated using a percentage rate instead of years. This percentage is based on the asset's cost and life. It is calculated by dividing the whole number 1.00 by the asset's life in years.

EXAMPLE 6

(a) A building has a projected life of 50 years. (b) A printing press has an estimated life of 5 years. To calculate depreciation using percentage:

(a) $\dfrac{1.00}{50 \text{ (building's life in years)}} = .02 \text{ or } 2\% \text{ annually}$

(b) $\dfrac{1.00}{5 \text{ (press's life in years)}} = .20 \text{ or } 20\% \text{ annually}$

If the printing press was purchased for $12,000 on January 10, 19X5, and had a scrap value of $4,000, what would be the depreciation for each of the five years?

Based on a 20% annual depreciation rate, the depreciation for each of the five years would be the same:

19X5: $12,000 − $4,000 × 20% = $1,600
19X6: $12,000 − $4,000 × 20% = $1,600
19X7: $12,000 − $4,000 × 20% = $1,600
19X8: $12,000 − $4,000 × 20% = $1,600
19X9: $12,000 − $4,000 × 20% = $1,600

(B)   Units-of-Production (UOP)

Units-of-production depreciation is based on an asset's usage. This can be expressed in

(a)   Units produced

(b)   Hours consumed

(c)   Mileage driven

This method is used when an asset's usage varies from year to year.

Units Produced.   Under the first variation of the UOP method, a fixed amount of depreciation is allocated to each unit of output produced by the machine. The per-unit depreciation expense is multiplied by the number of items produced in each accounting period. This depreciation method accurately reflects the depreciation expense for the asset because it is based on the number of units produced in each period. Depreciation per unit is computed in two steps:

$$\frac{\text{Cost of asset} - \text{scrap value}}{\text{Total estimated units of output}} = \text{depreciation per unit}$$

$$\text{Units produced} \times \text{unit depreciation} = \text{annual depreciation expense}$$

EXAMPLE 7

Cost of machine, $17,000; scrap value, $2,000; total estimated units produced during lifetime, 300,000.

First-year production	25,000 units
Second-year production	30,000 units

The depreciation expense for the first and second years would be calculated as

$$\frac{\$17,000 - \$2,000}{300,000} = \$.05 \text{ depreciation per unit}$$

Year 1:   25,000 units × $0.5 = $1,250
Year 2:   30,000 units × $0.5 = $1,500

Entry for first year:

Depreciation Expense, Machine	1,250	
Accumulated Depreciation, Machine		1,250

Entry for second year:

Depreciation Expense, Machine	1,500	
Accumulated Depreciation, Machine		1,500

The machine will continue to be depreciated until the 300,000 units have been produced. Since only production (not time) is considered when using this method, it gives a clearer picture of the machine's true cost.

Hours Used.   In this second variation of UOP, a fixed amount of depreciation is allocated, based on the number of hours a machine is used. (Under straight-line, depreciation expense is based on the passage of time regardless of actual use.)

EXAMPLE 8

Determine the depreciation for the following machines in the first year using straight-line depreciation.

	Machine A	**Machine B**
Cost	$22,000	$22,000
Scrap value	$ 2,000	$ 2,000
Estimated life	5 years	5 years
	(18,000 hours)	(18,000 hours)

Machine A was in use 3,000 hours in the first year.
Machine B was in use 1,000 hours in the first year.

To calculate:

$$\frac{\$22,000 - \$2,000}{5 \text{ years}} = \$4,000 \text{ annual depreciation expense}$$

Machines A and B both have the same annual depreciation cost of $4,000 because the straight-line method does not consider hours of use, but only the estimated life of the machine.

EXAMPLE 9

Using the information in Example 8, determine the depreciation cost of (*a*) machine A and (*b*) machine B using the units-of-production method based on hours used.

$$\frac{\$22,000 - \$2,000}{18,000 \text{ hours}} = \$1.11 \text{ depreciation rate per hour of operation}$$

(*a*) Machine A: 3,000 hours $\times$ $1.11 = $3,330 first-year depreciation expense
(*b*) Machine B: 1,000 hours $\times$ $1.11 = $1,110 first-year depreciation expense

The difference between the first-year depreciation using the straight-line method (Example 8) and that using the units-of-production method (Example 9) is considerable. Under the UOP method, machine B's limited use results in its having 1/3 the depreciation expense of machine A. Under the straight-line method, both machines carry the same depreciation expense, regardless of use. In this case, UOP is the more logical choice for reporting depreciation because it more accurately matches depreciation expense against periodic income. Under UOP, both machines will be fully depreciated when they have completed 18,000 hours of use.

Mileage Driven.   Under the third variation of UOP depreciation, instead of using time to calculate depreciation, the number of miles driven are the "units." The depreciation expense per mile will remain constant over the life of the truck and will be multiplied by the actual miles the truck is driven in each accounting period.

EXAMPLE 10

A truck costing $24,000 with salvage value of $4,000 has an estimated useful life of 80,000 miles. If, in the first year, it is driven 18,000 miles, what is the entry needed to record depreciation expense?

$$\frac{\$24,000 \text{ (cost)} - \$4,000 \text{ (salvage value)}}{80,000 \text{ total estimated miles}} = \$.25 \text{ per mile}$$

18,000 (miles driven) $\times$ $.25 = $4,500   First-year depreciation expense

Depreciation Expense, Truck	4,500	
Accumulated Depreciation, Truck		4,500

Suppose the truck is driven the following numbers of miles:

Year 1: 18,000 miles driven

Year 2: 21,000 miles driven

Year 3: 19,000 miles driven

Year 4: 22,000 miles driven

80,000

If a depreciation table were to be developed for Example 10, using this information below, it would appear as:

Year	A Cost of Truck	Miles Driven	Annual Dep. Exp.	B Accumulated Depreciation	A − B Book* Value
1	$24,000	18,000	$4,500	$ 4,500	$19,500
2	$24,000	21,000	$5,250	$ 9,750	$14,250
3	$24,000	19,000	$4,750	$14,500	$ 9,500
4	$24,000	22,000	$5,500	$20,000	$ 4,000**
		80,000†			

*Book value = cost − accumulated depreciation.

**Salvage value is reached.

†The asset is fully depreciated.

(C)   Declining-Balance (DB)

Declining-balance is an accelerated method of depreciation because a greater amount of depreciation expense is taken in the early years of an asset's life and less is taken in later years. This method is preferred for the following reasons:

1. Technology can make an asset obsolete or inadequate before the asset wears out.

2. Most plant assets decline in value more quickly in their early years than in later years.

3. Often, an asset contributes most to a business during its first years of operation.

4. The expenditure for equipment is made at the beginning of the asset's life.

5. It is good accounting practice to charge more depreciation in the early years of an asset's useful life because in later years repair and maintenance expenses are incurred as the asset gets older.

The double-declining-balance method (DDB) produces the highest amount of depreciation in earlier years. It *does not recognize scrap value*. Instead, the book value of the asset remaining at the end of the depreciation period becomes the scrap value. Under this method, the straight-line rate is doubled and applied to the declining book balance each year. Many companies prefer the double-declining-balance method because of the faster write-off in the earlier years when the asset contributes most to the business and when the expenditure was actually made. The procedure is to apply a *fixed rate* to the declining book value of the asset each year. As the book value declines, the depreciation becomes smaller.

EXAMPLE 11

A $17,000 asset is to be depreciated over 5 years. The double-declining-balance rate is thus 40 percent per year.

Year	Book Value at Beginning of Year	Rate	Depreciation for Year	Book Value at End of Year
1	$17,000	40%	$6,800	$10,200
2	10,200	40%	4,080	6,120
3	6,120	40%	2,448	3,672
4	3,672	40%	1,469	2,203
5	2,203	40%	881	1,322

The $1,322 book value at the end of the fifth year becomes the scrap value. If, however, a scrap value of $2,000 had been estimated, the depreciation for the fifth year would be $203 ($2,203–$2,000) instead of $881.

The date of purchase should also be considered. Up to this point it has been assumed that the equipment was purchased at the beginning of the year, which is usually not a common occurrence. Therefore a change in the computation for the first partial year of service is needed.

EXAMPLE 12

If in Example 11 the equipment had been purchased and placed into use at the end of the ninth month of the fiscal year, the pro rata portion of the first full year's depreciation would be

$$\frac{3}{12}(40\% \times 17,000) = \$1,700$$

The method of computation for the remaining years would not be affected. Thus

$$40\% \ (\$17,000 - \$1,700) = \$6,120$$

would be the depreciation for the second year and $9,180 ($17,000 − $7,820) its book value.

(D)   Sum-of-the-Years'-Digits (SYD)

The fourth method of computing depreciation is sum-of-the-years'-digits. Like DDB, it is an accelerated method that allows more depreciation expense to be recorded in the early years of an asset's life and less in later years. As with DDB, depreciation expense declines over the life of the asset; however, unlike the case with DDB, it declines by the same amount each year.

To determine depreciation expense under SYD, the asset's cost (minus scrap value) is multiplied by a fraction. The numerator of the fraction is the years remaining in the asset's life, but in reverse order. It changes each year. The denominator is the sum of all the digits (hence its name) making up the life of the asset. It remains constant. Here is what the fraction looks like:

$$\frac{\text{Numerator (years in reverse)}}{\text{Denominator (life of asset)}}$$

Example 13 shows how to compute depreciation expense with the SYD method using this fraction.

The years of the asset's lifetime are labeled 1, 2, 3, etc., and the depreciation amounts are based on a series of fractions having the sum of the years' digits as the common denominator. The largest digit is used as the numerator for the first year, the next largest digit for the second year, and so forth.

EXAMPLE 13

Cost of machine, $17,000; scrap value, $2,000; estimated life, 5 years.

The depreciable amount is $17,000 − $2,000 = $15,000. To find the fraction of this amount to be written off each year, proceed as follows:

1. Label the years 1, 2, 3, 4, and 5.
2. Calculate the sum of the years' digits: $S = 1 + 2 + 3 + 4 + 5 = 15$.
3. Convert the sum to a series of fractions:

$$\frac{1}{15} + \frac{2}{15} + \frac{3}{15} + \frac{4}{15} + \frac{5}{15} = 1$$

4. Take the above series of fractions *in reverse order* as the depreciation rates. Thus:

Year	Fraction		Amount		Depreciation
1	5/15	×	$15,000	=	$ 5,000
2	4/15	×	15,000	=	4,000
3	3/15	×	15,000	=	3,000
4	2/15	×	15,000	=	2,000
5	1/15	×	15,000	=	1,000
					$15,000

If the life expectancy of a machine were 5 years as stated above, you could follow step 2 by adding $1 + 2 + 3 + 4 + 5 = 15$. However, for a machine that has a long life expectancy, it is simpler to use the formula

$$S = \frac{N(N+1)}{2} \qquad S = \text{sum}; \ N = \text{number of years}$$

In the above equation:

$$S = \frac{5(5+1)}{2}$$

$$S = \frac{5(6)}{2}$$

$$S = \frac{30}{2} = 15$$

EXAMPLE 14

The life of a piece of equipment is calculated to be 30 years. The sum of the years' digits would be

$$S = \frac{30(30+1)}{2} = 465$$

(E) Partial-Year Depreciation

If an asset is purchased during the year rather than at the beginning, each full year's depreciation must be allocated between the two fiscal years affected to assure accurate reporting and accounting.

EXAMPLE 15

If a machine bought on October 2, 19X8, costing $30,000, with a 10-year life, has a scrap value of $2,500, the depreciation for the first two years would be determined as follows:

Year 1

$$19X8: \quad \$27,500 \times \frac{10}{55} = \$5,000 \times \frac{3^*}{12} = \underline{\underline{\$1,250}} \text{ depreciation expense}$$

Year 2:

$$19X9: \quad \$27,500 \times \frac{10}{55} = \$5,000 \times \frac{9^{**}}{12} = \$3,750 \text{ depreciation expense}$$

$$+$$

$$\$27,500 \times \frac{9}{55} = \$4,500 \times \frac{3}{12} = \underline{\underline{\$1,125}} \text{ depreciation expense}$$

$$= \underline{\underline{\$4,875}} \text{ depreciation expense}$$

---

*Use of the machine for 3 months
**Balance (12 months − 3 months)

(F)   Comparison of Methods

Once you know the four methods of depreciation, the next question is how to select the one that's most appropriate. Under generally accepted accounting principles (GAAP), businesses are encouraged to match the income an asset produces against its expense. This can be accomplished by selecting the correct depreciation method.

The four principal methods of depreciation are compared in Table 15-1. It is assumed that over a 5-year lifetime the asset was in operation for the following numbers of hours: 1,800, 1,200, 2,000, 1,400, 1,600. Cost of asset, $17,000; scrap value, $2,000.

Table 15-1   Annual Depreciation Charge

Year	Straight-Line (SL)	Units-of-Production (UOP)	Double-Declining-Balance (DDB)	Sum-of-the-Years'-Digits (SYD)
1	$ 3,000	$ 3,375	$ 6,800	$ 5,000
2	3,000	2,250	4,080	4,000
3	3,000	3,750	2,448	3,000
4	3,000	2,625	1,468	2,000
5	3,000	3,000	204	1,000
Total	$15,000	$15,000	$15,000	$15,000

Depreciation Method Comparison Chart

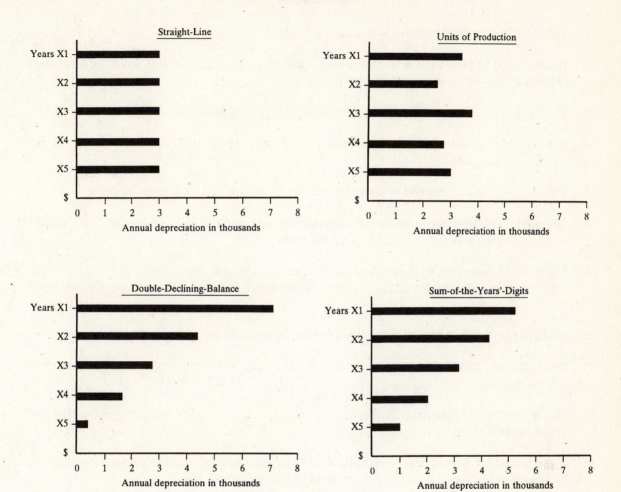

Based upon Table 15-1 and the graphs, we can conclude the following:

(*a*) If the asset is expected to generate income evenly over an extended period of time, the *straight-line method* should be used.

(*b*) If the asset will produce a different number of units each year, or if the machine may wear out early, the *units-of-production method* is preferable because it is based upon usage rather than time. In other words, the more units produced in a single year, the higher the asset's annual depreciation expense.

(*c*) If the asset is expected to generate high income in its early years, the *double-declining-balance method* should be used because it will generate greater depreciation expense in its earlier years, as it can be matched with the early period's higher revenues, or because it is closer to the date of purchase when the major expenditure was made. This accelerated depreciation method reduces tax liability in the early years, making more cash available for the asset's purchase.

(*d*) If the asset is expected to generate high income in its early years, the accelerated method of *sum-of-the-years' digits* is another method of rapid depreciation write-off. Like double-declining-balance, this accelerated depreciation process reduces tax liability in the early years and increases available cash to pay for the asset.

Summary

1. The main reason for depreciation is _____ .

2. Accumulated Depreciation is an example of a(n) _____ account, since the fixed asset remains at cost while the offset builds up.

3. The market value of a fixed asset at the end of its service is known as _____ .

4. The uniform distribution of depreciation over the life of the asset is known as the _____ method.

5. The _____ method is used to write off the asset based on a series of fractions.

6. The method that produces the largest amount of depreciation in the earlier years, then rapidly declines, is known as the _____ method.

7. Under SYD depreciation, (less/more) _____ depreciation expense is recorded in the early years and (less/more) _____ depreciation expense is recorded as the asset gets older.

8. Under SYD, the final year's book value must be the same as its _____ value.

9. When income produced by an asset is the same each year, the recommended method of depreciation is _____ .

10. Where use rather than time is the key factor, _____ is the preferred method of depreciation.

11. If the largest amount of depreciation is taken in the first year of an asset's operation, then the business is using the _____ method of depreciation.

12. Two accelerated methods of depreciation are _____ and _____ .

Answers: 1. aging; 2. offset or contra; 3. scrap or salvage value; 4. straight-line; 5. sum-of-the-years'-digits; 6. double-declining-balance; 7. more, less; 8. scrap; 9. SL; 10. UOP; 11. DDB; 12. SYD, DDB

Solved Problems

15.1. Hacol Company acquired an asset on January 1, 19X8, at a cost of $38,000, with an estimated useful life of 8 years and a salvage value of $2,000. What is the annual depreciation based on the straight-line method?

SOLUTION

Cost	$38,000
Scrap value	2,000
Amount to be depreciated	$36,000

$36,000 \div 8$ years $= \$4,500$ depreciation per year

15.2. For the asset of Prob. 15.1, compute the depreciation for the first 2 years by the sum-of-the-years'-digits method.

SOLUTION

$$S = 8\left(\frac{8+1}{2}\right) = 36$$

Year 1: $\dfrac{8}{36} \times \$36,000 = \$8,000$

Year 2: $\dfrac{7}{36} \times \$36,000 = \$7,000$

15.3. Repeat Prob. 15.2, but using the double-declining-balance method.

SOLUTION

For the depreciation rate, we take twice the straight-line rate; that is,

$$2 \times \frac{100\%}{8 \text{ years}} = 25\% \text{ per year}$$

Therefore,

Year 1: $\$38,000 \times 25\% = \$9,500$
Year 2: $(\$38,000 - \$9,500) \times 25\% = \$7,125$

15.4. A truck was purchased on January 1, 19X8, for $8,500, with an estimated scrap value of $500. It will be depreciated for 8 years using the straight-line method. Show how the Truck account and the related Accumulated Depreciation account would appear on the balance sheet on (*a*) December 31, 19X8; (*b*) December 31, 19X9.

(*a*)

(*b*)

SOLUTION

(*a*)

Truck		$8,500	
Less: Accumulated Depreciation		1,000*	$7,500

(*b*)

Truck		$8,500	
Less: Accumulated Depreciation		2,000**	$6,500

* $\dfrac{\$8,500 - \$500}{8 \text{ years}} = \$1,000$ per year

**$1,000 per year $\times 2$

15.5. Based on Prob. 15.4, what amount will appear in the income statement for Depreciation Expense, Truck (*a*) for the year 19X8? (*b*) For the year 19X9?

SOLUTION

(*a*) $1,000 (1 year's depreciation)

(*b*) $1,000 (1 year's depreciation)

15.6. Equipment costing $9,600, with an estimated scrap value of $1,600, was bought on July 1, 19X8. The equipment is to be depreciated by the straight-line method for a period of 10 years. The company's fiscal year is January through December. Show how the equipment account and the related Accumulated Depreciation account would appear in the balance sheet on (*a*) December 31, 19X8; (*b*) December 31, 19X9.

(*a*)

(*b*)

SOLUTION

(*a*)

Equipment		$9,600	
Less: Accumulated Depreciation		400*	$9,200

* $\dfrac{\$9,600 - \$1,600}{10 \text{ years}} = \$800$ depreciation per year,

$\frac{1}{2}$ year (July 1 to Dec. 31) $\times$ $800 per year = $400

(*b*)

Equipment		$9,600	
Less: Accumulated Depreciation		1,200*	$8,400

*$1\frac{1}{2}$ years $\times$ $800 per year = $1,200

15.7. What amount will appear in the income statement for Depreciation Expense, Equipment (Prob. 15.6) (*a*) for the year 19X8? (*b*) For the year 19X9?

SOLUTION

(*a*) $400 ($\frac{1}{2}$ year's depreciation)   (*b*) $800 (1 year's depreciation)

15.8. A machine was purchased for $28,000 and had an estimated scrap value of $4,000 and an estimated life of 32,000 hours. What would the year-end entry be if the units-of-production method was used, and it was used 7,200 hours in the first year of operation?

SOLUTION

Depreciation Expense, Machine	5,400*	
Accumulated Depreciation, Machine		5,400

* $\dfrac{\$28,000 - \$4,000}{32,000 \text{ hours est. life}} = 0.75 \times 7,200 \text{ hours} = \$5,400$

15.9. See Thru Glass Company purchased a new glass-cutting machine on May 13, 19X8, for $28,000 and put it into use on May 19, 19X8. The machine has an estimated scrap value of $4,000 and will be depreciated by the straight-line method over 5 years. The See Thru Glass Company's year ends on December 31, 19X8. What would the entry be on December 31, 19X8?

SOLUTION

Depreciation Expense, Machine	2,800*	
Accumulated Depreciation, Machine		2,800

*$28,000   Cost
$-4,000$ Scrap value
———
$24,000

$24,000 ÷ 5 years = $4,800 per year
$4,800 ÷ 12 months = $400 per month
$400 × 7 months = $2,800

   Note that the machine was not put into use until after the 15th of the month, so you do not count the month of May.

15.10. Based on the information from Prob. 15.9, what would the entry be if the double-declining-balance method was used?

SOLUTION

Depreciation Expense, Machine	6,533.31*	
Accumulated Depreciation, Machine		6,533.31

*$28,000 × 40% = $11,200
$\dfrac{7}{12}(\$11,200) = \$6,533.31$

15.11. Based on the information from Prob. 15.9, what would the entry be if the sum-of-the-years'-digits method was used?

SOLUTION

Depreciation Expense, Machine	4,666.69*	
Accumulated Depreciation, Machine		4,666.69

*$28,000 cost − $4,000 scrap value = $24,000 × 5/15 = $8,000 per year.
$8,000 ÷ 12 months = $666.67 × 7 months = $4,666.69 depreciation expense for the year.

15.12. A fixed asset costing $60,000, with an estimated salvage value of $5,000, has a life expectancy of 10 years. Compare the results of the various depreciation methods by filling in the tables below. Take twice the straight-line rate as the rate in the double-declining-balance method.

Straight-Line Method

Year	Depreciation Expense	Accumulated Depreciation	Book Value at End of Year
1			
2			
3			
4			

Sum-of-the-Years'-Digits Method

Year	Depreciation Expense	Accumulated Depreciation	Book Value at End of Year
1			
2			
3			
4			

Double-Declining-Balance Method

Year	Depreciation Expense	Accumulated Depreciation	Book Value at End of Year
1			
2			
3			
4			

SOLUTION

Straight-Line Method

Year	Depreciation Expense	Accumulated Depreciation	Book Value at End of Year
1	$5,500*	$ 5,500	$54,500**
2	5,500	11,000	49,000
3	5,500	16,500	43,500
4	5,500	22,000	38,000

*($60,000 − $5,000) ÷ 10 = $5,500

**$60,000 − $5,500 = $54,500

Sum-of-the-Years'-Digits Method

Year	Depreciation Expense	Accumulated Depreciation	Book Value at End of Year
1	$10,000*	$10,000	$50,000
2	9,000	19,000	41,000
3	8,000	27,000	33,000
4	7,000	34,000	26,000

* $\dfrac{\$10(10+1)}{2} = 55;$ $\dfrac{10}{55} \times \$55,000 = \$10,000$

Double-Declining-Balance Method

Year	Depreciation Expense	Accumulated Depreciation	Book Value at End of Year
1	$12,000*	$12,000	$48,000
2	9,600**	21,600	38,400
3	7,680	29,280	30,720
4	6,144	35,424	24,576

*(2 × 10%) × $60,000 = $12,000

**20% × ($60,000 − $12,000) = $9,600

15.13. Klein's Logging Company purchased a new truck for $80,000 on January 1, 19X8, and put it into use on January 3, 19X8. The estimated life is 5 years, with an estimated scrap value of $5,000. From this information, prepare three depreciation schedules, using (*a*) the straight-line method, (*b*) the double-declining-balance method, and (*c*) the sum-of-the-years'-digits method.

(*a*)   Straight-line method

Year	Depreciation Expense	Accumulated Depreciation at End of Year	Book Value at End of Year
1			
2			
3			
4			
5			

(b) Double-declining-balance method

Year	Depreciation Expense	Accumulated Depreciation at End of Year	Book Value at End of Year
1			
2			
3			
4			
5			

(c) Sum-of-the-years'-digits method

Year	Depreciation Expense	Accumulated Depreciation at End of Year	Book Value at End of Year
1			
2			
3			
4			
5			

SOLUTION

(a) Straight-line method

Year	Depreciation Expense	Accumulated Depreciation at End of Year	Book Value at End of Year
1	$15,000	$15,000	$65,000
2	15,000	30,000	50,000
3	15,000	45,000	35,000
4	15,000	60,000	20,000
5	15,000	75,000	5,000*

*Note that at the end of 5 full years, you end up with the estimated scrap value.

(b) Double-declining-balance method

Year	Depreciation Expense	Accumulated Depreciation at End of Year	Book Value at End of Year
1	$32,000	$32,000	$48,000
2	19,200	51,200	28,800
3	11,520	62,700	17,280
4	6,912	69,632	10,368
5	5,368*	75,000	5,000

*Note that at the end of 5 full years, you would have a scrap value of $5,000 because the scrap value had been estimated. Thus depreciation expense of $5,368 ($10,368 − $5,000) is produced for the last year.

(c) Sum-of-the-years'-digits method

$$S = \frac{5(5+1)}{2} = 15$$

Year	Depreciation Expense	Accumulated Depreciation at End of Year	Book Value at End of Year
1	$25,000	$25,000	$55,000
2	20,000	45,000	35,000
3	15,000	60,000	20,000
4	10,000	70,000	10,000
5	5,000	75,000	5,000

CHAPTER 16

Property, Plant, and Equipment: Disposal and Taxation

16.1 ACCOUNTING PROCEDURES FOR DISPOSALS

Plant assets get old, eventually wear out, and must be replaced. When this occurs, the business disposes of the asset. Regardless of the method used, the asset and its related accumulated depreciation must be removed from the accounts upon disposal. The accumulated depreciation account is debited, and the asset is credited for its cost.

Accounting procedures for the disposal of a plant asset vary depending on how the asset is disposed of. Three methods will be described here:

(A) Retiring (discarding) the asset

(B) Selling the asset

(C) Exchanging the asset

(A) Discarding the Asset

When plant assets are no longer needed (and usually are fully depreciated), they may be sold for scrap.

EXAMPLE 1

An item of equipment bought for $15,000 was fully depreciated at the close of the preceding year and is now deemed to be worthless. The entry to record the disposal of the asset is

Accumulated Depreciation	15,000
Equipment	15,000

Sometimes, an asset is fully depreciated but remains in operation. Even though it has completed its estimated useful life for accounting purposes, it may still function for the business. When this occurs, the asset and related accumulated depreciation accounts remain in the ledger to reflect the asset's continued use. Removing them would jeopardize internal accounting controls.

Because the disposal date usually does not coincide with the date when depreciation is recorded, depreciation expense must be brought up to date before writing off the asset. Therefore, before retiring, selling, or trading in the asset, entries must be made for unrecorded depreciation that has accrued since the last depreciation expense was entered.

EXAMPLE 2

A $15,000 asset with accumulated depreciation of $12,600 had been depreciated at the annual rate of 10 percent. If we decide to discard the asset on April 30, an adjusting entry is needed to record the depreciation for the period January 1 to April 30 (4 months), since no entry to record the expense has been made. Therefore, one-third of the annual depreciation of $1,500 ($15,000 × 10%) must be recorded.

Entry 1	Depreciation Expense	500	
	Accumulated Depreciation		500

This entry is necessary to bring the accumulated depreciation up to date of disposal. The entry to record the disposal of the asset would be

Entry 2	Accumulated Depreciation	13,100	
	Loss on Disposal of Fixed Asset	1,900	
	Equipment		15,000

(B) Selling the Asset

Retiring an asset literally means junking it. But a sale, no matter how small, usually involves a cash transaction. If the selling price is greater than the book value (cost less accumulated depreciation), a gain on sale results. If the selling price is less than the book value, there is a loss. If the asset is sold for book value, there is no gain or loss.

The entry to record the sale of an asset is similar to the one for disposal except that an entry must be made to show that compensation (such as cash) has been received. The sale requires entries (1) to bring the depreciation (and hence the book value) up to date, and (2) to record the sale at either a gain (if the selling price exceeds the updated book value) or a loss (if the selling price is below the updated book value).

EXAMPLE 3 Gain on Sale

A $15,000 asset with accumulated depreciation of $12,600 as of December 31, and an estimated straight-line life of 10 years, is sold on the following April 30 for $2,300.

Entry 1	Depreciation Expense	500*	
	Accumulated Depreciation		500

*1/3 × $1,500

Entry 2	Cash	2,300	
	Accumulated Depreciation	13,100	
	Equipment		15,000
	Gain on Disposal of Fixed Asset		400

Proof of gain:	Sale of equipment	$2,300
	Book value	1,900 ($15,000 − $13,100)
	Gain on disposal of fixed assets	$ 400

Gain on disposal of fixed assets would be treated as nonoperating income in the income statement, under the heading "Other Income."

EXAMPLE 4   Loss on Sale

Assume the same information as in Example 3 except that the equipment is sold for $1,600.

Entry 1	Depreciation Expense	500	
	Accumulated Depreciation		500

Entry 2	Cash	1,600	
	Accumulated Depreciation	13,100	
	Loss on Disposal of Fixed Assets	300	
	Equipment		15,000

Proof of loss:	Sale of equipment	$1,600
	Book value	1,900
	Loss on disposal of fixed assets	$(300)

Loss on disposal of fixed assets would be treated as nonoperating expense in the income statement, under the heading "Other Expense."

(C)   Trading the Asset

Instead of either retiring or selling old plant assets, businesses often exchange them for similar assets that are more efficient. This exchange, known as a trade-in, is subtracted from the new asset's price, and the balance that remains (known as the "boot") will be paid based on the terms of the agreement. To record this trade-in, the firm must remove the asset's balance and its related accumulated depreciation account from the books. The trade-in allowance can be greater or less than the book value of the old asset being exchanged. In past years, it was an acceptable practice to recognize the difference between book value and trade-in as a gain or a loss, but today only losses may be recognized.

Nonrecognition of Gain.   The way to record a gain from an exchange of similar assets is to absorb it into the cost of the new asset. This requires several steps:

Step 1. Determine the book value of the old asset by subtracting the up-to-date accumulated depreciation from its cost.

Step 2. Determine the boot (amount to be paid in cash or other assets, such as notes receivable) by subtracting the old asset's trade-in allowance from the new asset's list price.

Step 3. Calculate the depreciable cost (also called "cost basis") of the new asset by adding the book value of the old asset (result of Step 1) to the boot (result of Step 2).

EXAMPLE 5

Data:

Old Equipment				*New Equipment*	
Step 1:				Step 2:	
Cost of equipment		$15,000		Price of new equipment	$20,000
Accumulated depreciation as of				Trade-in allowance	2,500
December 31, previous year	12,600			Cash to be paid	$17,500
Depreciation for the					
current year	500	13,100		Step 3:	
Book value at date of exchange		$ 1,900		Book value	$ 1,900
				Boot	17,500
				New equipment	$19,400

Entry 1	Depreciation Expense		
	Accumulated Depreciation	500	
			500

Entry 2	Accumulated Depreciation	13,100*	
	Equipment (new)	19,400**	
	Equipment (old)		15,000
	Cash		17,500

*$12,600 + $500

**Cost	$20,000
Less: Gain	−600
New equipment	$19,400

Proof of gain:	Trade-in	$2,500
	Book value	1,900
	Gain	$ 600

Even though this transaction yields a gain of $600, generally accepted accounting practices do not permit the business to recognize it. This is based on the concept that income is generated by the sale of items that an asset produces, not from the sale or exchange of the asset itself.

The gain of $600 that is not recognized will be matched by a reduction of $600 in total depreciation expense over the life of the equipment, resulting in lower depreciation expense in future years.

Recognition of Loss.   If less is received for an old asset than is paid for the new one, the loss may be recognized for accounting purposes, but not for tax purposes. In other words, there is one set of rules for financial statements and another set of rules for tax returns. (Federal income tax law does not permit recognition of either gains or losses from an exchange of similar assets.)

EXAMPLE 6

Using the information in Example 5, assume that the trade-in allowance was $1,000 instead of $2,500. The entries that are required would be (1) to bring the depreciation up to date and (2) to record the trade.

Entry 1	Depreciation Expense	500	
	Accumulated Depreciation		500

Entry 2	Accumulated Depreciation	13,100	
	Equipment (new)	20,000	
	Loss on Disposal of Fixed Asset	900*	
	Equipment (old)		15,000
	Cash		19,000

*Equipment (old)	$15,000
Accumulated depreciation	13,100
Book value	$ 1,900
Trade-in	−1,000
Loss on trade-in	$ 900

Nonrecognition of Loss.   Since federal income tax law permits neither gains nor losses on exchanges of similar assets, no "Loss on Trade-In" account may be used for tax purposes, even though it was used for accounting. The new cost will be determined by adding the boot to the book value of the old equipment.

EXAMPLE 7

Based upon the information in Example 6, if no loss is to be recognized, the entry would be

Entry 1	Depreciation Expense	500	
	Accumulated Depreciation		500
Entry 2	Accumulated Depreciation	13,100	
	Equipment (new)	20,900*	
	Equipment (old)		15,000
	Cash		19,000

*Note that the loss of $900 is added to the cost of the new equipment, which is now recorded for tax purposes as Equipment $20,900.

Assets Dissimilar in Nature. For trade-ins of assets that are dissimilar, such as the exchange of a truck for a printing press, both gains and losses are recognized.

EXAMPLE 8

A truck that cost $14,000 and has updated accumulated depreciation of $10,000 is exchanged for a printing press costing $15,000. The truck receives a trade-in allowance of $6,000, with the balance to be paid in cash. What entry is required to record this transaction?

Step 1:	Cost of truck	$14,000
	Less: Accumulated depreciation brought up to date	10,000
	Book value of truck	$ 4,000
Step 2:	Cost of printing press	$15,000
	Less: Trade-in allowance	6,000
	Cash to be paid (boot)	$ 9,000
Step 3:	Book value of truck	$ 4,000
	Less: Trade-in allowance	6,000
	Gain on trade-in (to be recognized)	$ 2,000

Entry:

Printing Press	15,000	
Accumulated Depreciation	10,000	
Truck		14,000
Cash		9,000
Gain on Trade-In		2,000

16.2 DEPRECIATION AND INCOME TAXES

(A) Depreciation as an Expense

The four methods of depreciation are really designed for financial accountability rather than for tax purposes. For example, most companies use the straight-line (SL) method on financial statements for creditors and stockholders. But if they elect to use accelerated depreciation for federal income taxes, they must use different methods. For assets purchased before 1981 that are still in use, the only accelerated methods that may be used are SYD and DDB. (Rules for assets purchased later are explained in this section.) Even though depreciation is an expense that can defer taxes, it is a noncash expense and therefore does not drain cash from business operations.

EXAMPLE 9

Assume that a machine valued at $60,000 with scrap value of $6,000 is to be depreciated over 5 years, and that the company's assumed tax rate is 30 percent. Using the data below, determine (*a*) the net income difference between the SL and SYD methods and (*b*) the tax savings.

	Straight-Line	Sum-of-the-Years'-Digits
Income	$800,000	$800,000
Operating expenses	−600,000	−600,000
Net income before depreciation	$200,000	$200,000
Depreciation expense	− 10,800*	− 18,000**
Net income before income tax	$189,200	$182,000
Income tax expense (30%)	− 56,760	− 54,600
Net income	$132,440	$127,400

---

*$54,000 ÷ 5 years

**$\frac{5}{15} \times$ $54,000

The procedure would be

(*a*)	Net income under SL	$132,440
	Net income under SYD	−127,400
	Net income difference	$ 5,040

(*b*)	Tax savings:	
	Income tax under SL	$56,760
	Income tax under SYD	−54,600
	Tax savings	$ 2,160

(B) Accelerated Cost Recovery System (ACRS)

Although the accelerated methods of depreciation—double-declining-balance and sum-of-the-years'-digits—produce more depreciation expense than straight-line in the early years of an asset's life, many firms wanted even faster write-offs. To meet this demand, in the Economic Recovery Act of 1981, Congress included the Accelerated Cost Recovery System (ACRS). (See Fig. 16-1.) It permitted even faster depreciation write-offs for federal income tax purposes, but only for assets placed into use after 1980. Assets purchased before 1981 were limited to the double-declining-balance or sum-of-the-years'-digits methods. ACRS is easier to compute than double-declining-balance or sum-of-the-years'-digits because it does not recognize scrap value or trade-in or allow partial depreciation for assets bought during the year. Assets purchased under ACRS from 1981 through 1986 were classified according to an estimated recovery period:

Three Years: Autos, light trucks, and machinery used for research.

Five Years: Heavy trucks, ships, aircraft, office furniture and equipment, and any property that does not fall into the other categories.

Accelerated Cost Recovery System

Recovery year	3 years	5 years	10 years	15 years
			Period of recovery	
1	25%	15%	8%	5%
2	38	22	14	10
3	37	21	12	9
4		21	10	8
5		21	10	7
6			10	7
7			9	6
8			9	6
9			9	6
10			9	6
11				6
12				6
13				6
14				6
15				6

Fig. 16-1

Ten Years: Railroad tank cars, residential mobile and prefab homes, and certain public utility property.

Fifteen Years: Other public utility property.

Fifteen–Nineteen Years: Residential and commercial property. (Charts are available from the IRS.)

EXAMPLE 10

A car was purchased in 1984 for $25,000. The depreciation expense allowed each year under ACRS would be computed as follows:

According to the list above, autos fall in the 3-year class of ACRS. Therefore, the following depreciation expense would be recorded for each year:

$$1984: 25\% \times \$25,000 = \$\ 6,250$$
$$1985: 38\% \times \$25,000 = \ \ 9,500$$
$$1986: 37\% \times \$25,000 = \ \ 9,250$$
$$\text{Total depreciation} \qquad \$25,000$$

Keep in mind:

1. At the end of 1986 (the third year), the cost of the auto has been fully recovered.
2. No scrap value was used.
3. Because ACRS allocated depreciation over a much shorter period of time than the asset's true life, it was acceptable only for tax purposes, not for preparing financial statements.

(C) Modified Accelerated Cost Recovery System (MACRS)

Five years after creating ACRS, Congress modified it in the famous Tax Reform Act of 1986. This law permits a Modified Accelerated Cost Recovery System (MACRS) for assets purchased after

December 31, 1986. It kept the four classes of depreciable assets—3-year, 5-year, 10-year, and 15-year—and added four more classes: 7-year, 20-year, 27.5-year, and 31.5-year. It also changed the recovery periods for a number of assets. Cars and light trucks were changed from 3 years to 5 years, and office equipment from 5 years to 7 years. Also, the periods became 7 years for fixtures, equipment, and furniture; 20 years for municipal sewers; 27.5 years for residential rental property; and 31.5 years for nonresidential real property.

In the MACRS table shown in Fig. 16-2, there appears to be an extra year in each class. This extra period is based on "the half-year convention," which assumes that all assets are actually placed in service in the middle of the year and taken out of service in the middle of the year. Thus, neither the first nor the last year of depreciation in any class is considered a full year. An extra year is added to each asset's depreciation expense: A 3-year asset is depreciated over 4 years, a 4-year asset is depreciated over 5 years, and so on.

Modified Accelerated Cost Recovery System

Recovery periods

Recovery year	3 years	5 years	7 years	10 years	15 years	20 years
1	33.3%	20.00%	14.29%	10.00%	5.00%	3.750%
2	44.45	32.00	24.49	18.00	9.50	7.219
3	14.81	19.20	17.49	14.40	8.55	6.677
4	7.41	11.52	12.49	11.52	7.70	6.177
5		11.52	8.93	9.22	6.93	5.713
6		5.76	8.92	7.37	6.23	5.285
7			8.93	6.55	5.90	4.888
8			4.46	6.55	5.90	4.522
9				6.56	5.91	4.462
10				6.55	5.90	4.461
11				3.28	5.91	4.462
12					5.90	4.461
13					5.91	4.462
14					5.90	4.461
15					5.91	4.462
16					2.95	4.461
17						4.462
18						4.461
19						4.462
20						4.461
21						2.231

Note: The 27.5-year class for residential rental property and 31.5-year class for nonresidential real property are not included here for reasons of space. Special rules apply to real estate.

Fig. 16-2

EXAMPLE 11

Year	3-Year Depreciation Rate*
1	33.33%
2	44.45%
3	14.81%
4	7.41%
	100.00%

*Spread over four years because of the "half-year convention."

EXAMPLE 12

A truck was purchased in May 1987 for $25,000. Since the light truck was purchased after December 31, 1986, it falls in the 5-year class of MACRS depreciation. Using the MACRS table in Fig. 16-2, the depreciation would be calculated as follows:

Depreciation Calculations Under MACRS

Year	Rate	Depreciable Cost	Annual Depreciation Expense
1987	20.00% ×	$25,000 =	$ 5,000
1988	32.00% ×	$25,000 =	8,000
1989	19.20% ×	$25,000 =	4,800
1990	11.52% ×	$25,000 =	2,880
1991	11.52% ×	$25,000 =	2,880
1992	5.76% ×	$25,000 =	1,440
Total depreciation			$25,000

Note that because of the "half-year convention," 5-year depreciation is spread over 6 years.

Summary

1. Depreciation is considered a(n) _____ expense because it does not drain cash from operations.

2. The rapid write-off system introduced in the Economic Recovery Act is known by the initials _____ , which stands for _____ .

3. The rapid write-off system that replaced the ACRS is known by the initials _____ , which stands for _____ .

4. Assets purchased before 1981 were allowed to use either the _____ or _____ depreciation methods, since ACRS did not exist at that time.

5. Under MACRS, all assets are assumed to be placed into production in the _____ of the first year.

6. The business term for an exchange of similar assets is _____ .

7. The balance to be paid after subtracting the trade-in allowance from the price of the new asset is called the _____ .

8. Generally accepted accounting principles do not permit recognition of a (gain/loss) _____ in the exchange of similar assets.

9. For accounting purposes, an exchange of similar assets cannot result in a(n) _____ .

10. If a trade-in produces a (gain/loss) _____ , it may be recognized for accounting purposes but not for tax purposes.

Answers: 1. noncash; 2. ACRS, Accelerated Cost Recovery System; 3. MACRS, Modified Accelerated Cost Recovery System; 4. DDB, SYD; 5. middle; 6. trade-in; 7. boot; 8. gain; 9. gain; 10. loss

Solved Problems

16.1. As of December 31, 19X8, accumulated depreciation of $9,000 has been recorded on equipment that originally cost $14,000. What is the entry to record the disposal of the asset if the equipment was discarded with no salvage value?

SOLUTION

Accumulated Depreciation, Equipment	9,000	
Loss on Disposal of Fixed Assets	5,000	
Equipment		14,000

The book value of $5,000 is considered a loss because there is no salvage value.

16.2. For Prob. 16.1, what entry would be recorded if the equipment were sold for $6,000?

SOLUTION

Accumulated Depreciation, Equipment	9,000	
Cash	6,000	
Equipment		14,000
Gain on Disposal of Fixed Assets		1,000*

*Cost	$14,000	Cash sale	$6,000
Accumulated depreciation	9,000	Book value	5,000
Book value	$ 5,000	Gain	$1,000

16.3. Based on Prob. 16.2, what entry would be recorded if the equipment were sold for $4,000?

SOLUTION

Accumulated Depreciation, Equipment	9,000	
Cash	4,000	
Loss on Disposal of Fixed Assets	1,000	
Equipment		14,000

16.4. Renee-Chris Company traded in a cutting machine for a new one priced at $2,600, receiving a trade-in allowance of $600 and paying the balance in cash. The old machine cost $1,800 and had an accumulated depreciation of $1,400. What is the entry to record the acquisition of the new machine?

SOLUTION

Accumulated Depreciation, Machine	1,400	
Machine (new)	2,400*	
Machine (old)		1,800
Cash		2,000

*Price of new machine	$2,600		Equipment (old) book value	$ 400
Less: Unrecognized gain	200	or	Cash paid	2,000
Cost of new machine	$2,400		Cost of new equipment	$2,400

16.5. Based on the information above, assume that the trade-in allowance had been $100 instead of $600. What is the entry to record the acquisition of the new machine?

SOLUTION

Accumulated Depreciation, Machine	1,400	
Machine (new)	2,600	
Loss on Disposal of Fixed Assets	300	
Cash		2,500
Machine (old)		1,800

16.6. Equipment that was acquired at a cost of $5,000 has an accumulated depreciation of $3,800. It is traded in for similar equipment costing $8,400, and a trade-in allowance of $1,500 is received. Present the entry to record the acquisition of the new equipment.

SOLUTION

Accumulated Depreciation	3,800	
Equipment (new)	8,100*	
Equipment (old)		5,000
Cash		6,900

*Trade-in allowance	$1,500	Price of new equipment	$8,400
Book value	1,200	Less: Unrecognized gain	300
Gain	$ 300	Cost of new equipment	$8,100

16.7. The four transactions below were selected from the ledger of J. B. Adam regarding the disposal of some of his fixed assets. Depreciation is considered to be recorded only to the end of the prior year. Present journal entries for each transaction. (*Note*: If an item is disposed of before the 15th, do not count the month.)

(*a*)   Mar. 3   Discarded four typewriters, realizing no scrap value. Total cost, $3,000; accumulated depreciation as of Dec. 31, $2,000; annual depreciation, $360.

(*b*)   Mar. 29   Sold office furniture for cash, $1,600. Total cost, $8,000; accumulated depreciation through Dec. 31, $6,800; annual depreciation, $600.

(*c*)   May 2   Traded in an old automobile for a new one priced at $4,000, receiving a trade-in allowance of $1,400 and paying the balance in cash. Data on the old automobile: cost, $3,900; accumulated depreciation, $2,700; annual depreciation, $960.

(*d*)   May 5   Traded in dictating equipment costing $1,000, with $800 accumulated depreciation as of Dec. 31. The annual depreciation is $240. Received a trade-in allowance of $100, paying the balance in cash for a new dictating unit at $1,400.

(*a*)   (1)

        (2)

(*b*)   (1)

        (2)

(c) (1)

(2)

(d) (1)

(2)

SOLUTION

(a) (1)

Depreciation Expense	60	
Accumulated Depreciation		60
[2 months × $30 per month = $60]		

(2)

Accumulated Depreciation	2,060	
Loss on Disposal of Fixed Assets	940	
Typewriters		3,000

(b) (1)

Depreciation Expense	150	
Accumulated Depreciation		150
[3 months × $50 per month = $150]		

(2)

Accumulated Depreciation	6,950	
Cash	1,600	
Office Equipment		8,000
Gain on Disposal of Fixed Assets		550

(c) (1)

Depreciation Expense		320	
Accumulated Depreciation			320
[4 months × $80 per month = $320]			

(2)

Accumulated Depreciation		3,020	
Automobile (new)		3,480*	
Cash			2,600
Automobile (old)			3,900

*Price of auto (new)	$4,000	Trade-in	$1,400
Less: Unrecognized gain	520	Book value	880
Auto to be recorded at	$3,480	Gain	$ 520

(d) (1)

Depreciation Expense		80	
Accumulated Depreciation			80
[4 months × $20 per month = $80]			

(2)

Equipment (new)		1,400	
Accumulated Depreciation		880	
Loss on Disposal of Fixed Assets*		20	
Equipment (old)			1,000
Cash			1,300

*Book value	$120
Trade-in	100
Loss	$ 20

16.8. The transactions below were selected from the records of the Allie & Hallie Restaurant regarding the disposal of some of its fixed assets. Depreciation is considered to be recorded only to the end of the year, December 31. Record the entries for each transaction.

(a) Apr. 2   Sold refrigerators for cash, $600. Total cost, $4,000; accumulated depreciation, $3,600; annual depreciation, $600.

(b) Apr. 18   Discarded mixer, realizing no scrap value. Total cost, $10,500; accumulated depreciation, $9,360; annual depreciation, $720.

(c) May 4   Traded in a freezer case costing $13,000 with accumulated depreciation of $10,000, receiving $2,500 trade-in allowance. The annual depreciation was $600. The cost of the new freezer was $16,500, and the balance was paid in cash.

(d) Aug. 8   Traded in a delivery van costing $6,000 with accumulated depreciation of $4,200. The annual depreciation was $1,800. Received a trade-in allowance of $1,900. The price of the new van was $9,800, and the balance was paid by a note.

(a)

(b)

(c)

(d)

SOLUTION

(a)	(1)	Depreciation Expense	150	
		Accumulated Depreciation		150
		[3 months × $50 per month = $150]		
	(2)	Accumulated Depreciation	3,750	
		Cash	600	
		Equipment		4,000
		Gain on Disposal of Fixed Assets		350

(b)	(1)	Depreciation Expense	240	
		Accumulated Depreciation		240
		[4 months × $60 per month = $240]		
	(2)	Accumulated Depreciation	9,600	
		Loss on Disposal of Fixed Assets	900	
		Equipment		10,500

(c)	(1)	Depreciation Expense	200	
		Accumulated Depreciation		200
		[4 months × $50 per month = $200]		
	(2)	Accumulated Depreciation	10,200	
		Equipment (new)	16,500	
		Loss on Disposal of Fixed Assets	300	
		Equipment (old)		13,000
		Cash		14,000

(d)	(1)	Depreciation Expense	1,050	
		Accumulated Depreciation		1,050
		[7 months × $150 per month = $1,050]		
	(2)	Equipment (new)	8,650*	
		Accumulated Depreciation	5,250	
		Equipment (old)		6,000
		Notes Payable		7,900

*Trade-in	$1,900	Price of equipment (new)	$9,800
Book value ($6,000 − $5,250)	750	Less: Gain	1,150
Gain (to be deducted		Equipment (new)	$8,650
from price of new equip.)	$1,150		

or

Proof: Paid for by:
Book value of old equipment	$ 750	($6,000–$5,250)
Notes payable	7,900	
Cost of new equipment	$8,650	

16.9. An automobile bought in 1982 for $28,000 has a scrap value of $4,000 and an estimated life of 3 years. Determine depreciation expense for each of the 3 years under the Accelerated Cost Recovery System.

1982	
1983	
1984	

SOLUTION

$$
\begin{array}{llll}
1982: & 25\% \times \$28,000 = & \$\ 7,000 \\
1983: & 38\% \times \$28,000 = & \$10,640 \\
1984: & 37\% \times \$28,000 = & \underline{\$10,360} \\
& & \underline{\underline{\$28,000}}
\end{array}
$$

16.10. Office furniture purchased for $10,000 has a scrap value of $2,000. Determine the depreciation expense for each year under ACRS.

Year 1	
2	
3	
4	
5	

SOLUTION

Since this is office furniture, it falls into the 5-year class. Therefore:

$$
\begin{array}{llll}
\text{Year 1:} & 15\% \times \$10,000 = & \$\ 1,500 \\
\text{Year 2:} & 22\% \times \$10,000 = & 2,200 \\
\text{Year 3:} & 21\% \times \$10,000 = & 2,100 \\
\text{Year 4:} & 21\% \times \$10,000 = & 2,100 \\
\text{Year 5:} & 21\% \times \$10,000 = & \underline{2,100} \\
& & \underline{\underline{\$10,000}}
\end{array}
$$

(Scrap value is not considered in the computation under ACRS.)

16.11. A light truck bought in 1994 for $20,000, with scrap value $5,000, is to be depreciated under the Modified Accelerated Cost Recovery System. What is the depreciation expense for each year?

1994	
1995	
1996	
1997	
1998	
1999	

SOLUTION

Under MACRS, light trucks were reclassified to a 5-year recovery from the prior 3-year recovery class. The following computation for depreciation is based on figures from the 5-year class (see Fig. 16-2).

$$
\begin{array}{llll}
1994: & 20.00\% \times \$20,000 = & \$\ 4,000 \\
1995: & 32.00\% \times \$20,000 = & 6,400 \\
1996: & 19.20\% \times \$20,000 = & 3,840 \\
1997: & 11.52\% \times \$20,000 = & 2,304 \\
1998: & 11.52\% \times \$20,000 = & 2,304 \\
1999: & 5.76\% \times \$20,000 = & \underline{1,152} \\
& & \underline{\underline{\$20,000}}
\end{array}
$$

(Scrap value is not considered under MACRS.)

16.12. (*a*) A heavy truck bought in 1983 was purchased for $40,000. Determine the amount of the write-off each year for tax purposes.

(*b*) A light truck was bought on June 25, 1985, for $12,000. Compute each year's depreciation for income tax purposes.

(*c*) An asset bought in 1996 for $21,000 falls in the 3-year class for depreciation. What amount of depreciation will be taken in each year?

(*a*) 1983 _____
     1984 _____
     1985 _____
     1986 _____
     1987 _____

(*b*) 1985 _____
     1986 _____
     1987 _____

(*c*) 1996 _____
     1997 _____
     1998 _____
     1999 _____

SOLUTION

(*a*) Since the heavy truck was purchased in 1983, it falls under the 5-year class of ACRS.

$$
\begin{array}{llr}
1983: & 15\% \times \$40,000 = & \$\ 6,000 \\
1984: & 22\% \times \$40,000 = & 8,800 \\
1985: & 21\% \times \$40,000 = & 8,400 \\
1986: & 21\% \times \$40,000 = & 8,400 \\
1987: & 21\% \times \$40,000 = & \underline{\ \ 8,400} \\
& & \underline{\$40,000}
\end{array}
$$

(*b*) The year 1985 falls under ACRS. Since the asset is a light truck, it is placed in the 3-year class. Even though the truck was bought in the middle of the year, the figures in the ACRS table are not prorated because under ACRS a business may not take partial depreciation for assets bought during the year. Instead, a smaller percentage depreciation is allowed in the first year on the assumption that the asset was used for less than the full year.

$$
\begin{array}{llr}
1985: & 25\% \times \$12,000 = & \$\ 3,000 \\
1986: & 38\% \times \$12,000 = & 4,560 \\
1987: & 37\% \times \$12,000 = & \underline{\ \ 4,440} \\
& & \underline{\$12,000}
\end{array}
$$

(*c*) Since the asset was bought in 1996, it falls under the Modified Accelerated Cost Recovery System. The table shows four years of figures instead of three because under MACRS all assets are treated as though they were bought in the middle of the first year and sold in the middle of the last year.

$$
\begin{array}{llr}
1996: & 33.33\% \times \$21,000 = & \$\ 7,000 \\
1997: & 44.45\% \times \$21,000 = & 9,334 \\
1998: & 14.81\% \times \$21,000 = & 3,110 \\
1999: & 7.41\% \times \$21,000 = & \underline{\ \ 1,556} \\
& & \underline{\$21,000}
\end{array}
$$

Examination IV

Chapters 12–16

1. The total amount of earnings shown on the Jamison Company payroll on April 15 was $20,000, subject to FICA (7.65 percent). Total payroll deductions included: hospitalization, $1,000; and pension, $2,500. Present the general journal entry needed to record this payroll.

2. Below is the payroll information for three of the employees of the Ernst Company.

Employee	Amount Earned to Date	Gross Pay for Week
A	$4,000	$100
B	5,800	250
C	8,000	200

   The company is located in a state that imposes an unemployment insurance tax of 2 percent on the first $7,000. Federal unemployment tax is 0.8 percent; FICA tax is 7.65 percent. Present the journal entry necessary to record the employer's payroll tax expenses.

3. A 60-day, 12 percent, $3,000 note received in settlement of an account, dated June 1, is discounted at 12 percent on July 1. What are the entries needed to record the information (a) on June 1? (b) on July 1?

4.

Accounts Receivable		Sales	
100,000			400,000

Allowance for Uncollectible Accounts	
	300

   For the balances given above, what is the adjusting entry to record the provision for uncollectible accounts, if the uncollectible expense is estimated as

   (a) One percent of sales?

   (b) $3,600, by the balance sheet method?

5. Transactions for the Blaky Company for the month of January, pertaining to the establishment of a petty cash fund, were as follows:

   Jan. 1 Established an imprest petty cash fund for $75
       31 Examination of the petty cash box showed: Office Supplies, $10; Transportation, $20; Freight, $15; Charity, $6; Miscellaneous Expense, $15

   What are the journal entries necessary to record the petty cash information?

6. Based on the following information, (a) prepare a bank reconciliation and (b) journalize the adjusting entries.

   1. Balance per bank statement, $2,121.21

2. Checkbook balance, $3,315.24

3. Deposit in transit not recorded by bank, $788.37

4. Outstanding checks:

Check Number	Amount
312	$21.12
314	$131.21
315	$127.22
317	$57.45
321	$9.34

5. The bank debited the account $740 for half-payment of a $1,400 note plus interest, $700 for principal, $40 interest.

6. A check for $212.80 for supplies was inadvertently posted as $221.80

7. Bank service charge, $21

7. The Washington Company acquired an asset on January 1, 19X8, at a cost of $28,000, with an estimated useful life of 10 years and a salvage value of 500. Find the annual depreciation for the first 2 years, using (a) the straight-line method, (b) the sum-of-the-years'-digits method, (c) the double-declining-balance method.

8. As of December 31, 19X8, accumulated depreciation of $10,000 has been recorded on equipment that had originally cost $15,000. What is the entry to record the disposal of the assets (a) if the equipment was discarded and no funds were received for it? (b) If it was sold for $8,000?

9. Saltman Company traded in an electric motor for a new one priced at $5,200, receiving a trade-in allowance of $600 and paying the balance in cash. For the old motor, the cost and accumulated depreciation were $3,800 and $3,400, respectively. What is the entry needed to record the acquisition?

10. Equipment purchased on July 1, 19X8, for $5,500 has an estimated scrap value of $1,000. The equipment will be depreciated the straight-line method for a period of 5 years. The company's fiscal year begins January 1. Show how the equipment and the related accumulated depreciation would appear in the balance sheet on (a) December 31, 19X8, and (b) December 31, 19X9.

11. Based on the data above, what amount would appear in the income statement for Depreciation Expense, Equipment (a) for the year 19X8, and (b) for the year 19X9?

Answers to Examination IV

1.

Salary/Expense	20,000	
FICA Taxes Payable		1,530
Hospitalization Payable		1,000
Pension Contributions Payable		2,500
Cash		14,970

2.

Employee	FICA	State Unemployment	Federal Unemployment
A	$ 7.65 (7.65% × $100)	$2.00 (2% × $100)	$0.80 (0.008 × $100)
B	19.13 (7.65% × $250)	5.00 (2% × $250)	2.00 (0.008 × $250)
C	$15.30 (7.65% × $200)	—	—
	$42.08	$7.00	$2.80

Payroll Tax Expense	51.88	
FICA Taxes Payable		42.08
State Unemployment Tax Payable		7.00
Federal Unemployment Tax Payable		2.80

3.

$3,000.00	Principal
60.00	Interest income
$3,060.00	Maturity value
30.60	Discount
$3,029.40	Net proceeds

(a)

Notes Receivable	3,000.00	
Accounts Receivable		3,000.00

(b)

Cash	3,029.40	
Interest Income		29.40
Notes Receivable		3,000.00

4. (a)

Uncollectible Accounts Expense	4,000	
Allowance for Uncollectible Accounts		4,000

(b)

Uncollectible Accounts Expense	3,300*	
Allowance for Uncollectible Accounts		3,300

---

*$3,600 − $300 = $3,300; the balance in the allowance account must be taken into consideration.

5.

Petty Cash	75	
Cash		75

Transportation Expense	20	
Freight Expense	15	
Charity Expense	6	
Office Supplies Expense	10	
Miscellaneous Expense	15	
Cash		66

6. (*a*)   ***Bank Reconciliation***

Balance per bank statement	$2,121.21	Checkbook balance	$3,315.24
Add: Deposit in transit	788.37	Error in recording check	9.00
	$2,909.58		$3,324.24
Less: Outstanding checks	346.34	Less: Note plus interest	740.00
			$2,584.24
		Less: Service charge	21.00
Adjusted bank balance	$2,563.24	Adjusted bank balance	$2,563.24

(*b*)   ***Adjusting Entries***

Cash	9	
Supplies		9
Notes Payable	700	
Interest Expense	40	
Cash		740
Miscellaneous Expense	21	
Cash		21

7.

	First Year	Second Year
(*a*)	$2,750	$2,750
(*b*)	5,000	4,500
(*c*)	5,600	4,480

8. (*a*)

Accumulated Depreciation, Equipment	10,000	
Loss on Disposal of Fixed Asset	5,000	
Equipment		15,000

(*b*)

Accumulated Depreciation, Equipment	10,000	
Cash	8,000	
Equipment		15,000
Gain on Disposal of Fixed Asset		3,000

9.

Accumulated Depreciation	3,400	
Equipment (new)	5,000*	
Equipment (old)		3,800
Cash		4,600

*Price of new machine	$5,200	
Less: Unrecognized gain	200	($600 trade-in − $400 value)
New machine	$5,000	

10. (*a*)

	Equipment	$5,500	$5,050
	Less: Accumulated Depreciation	450*	

$$\frac{*\$5,500 - \$1,000}{5 \text{ years}} = \$900 \text{ depreciation per year}$$

1/2 year (July 1–December 31) × $900 per year = $450

(*b*)

	Equipment	$5,500	
	Less: Accumulated Depreciation	1,350*	$4,150

*1.5 years × $900 per year = $1,350

11. (*a*) $450 (1/2 year's depreciation)

   (*b*) $900 (1 year's depreciation)

Final Examination

1. Journalize the following adjusting data as of December 31:

   (a) Merchandise inventory, January 1, $46,000; December 31, $48,000.

   (b) Office supplies physically counted on December 31 were $1,250. The original balance of supplies on hand was $2,100.

   (c) Prepaid insurance before adjustment, $3,850. It was found that $2,700 had expired during the year.

   (d) Salaries for a 5-day week ending on Friday were $3,500. The last payday was on the previous Friday, December 28.

   (e) The company holds a $6,000, 9 percent, 60-day note receivable dated December 16 of the year just ended.

2. The total payroll for the Madison Bridge Company for the week ending March 30 was $12,000. Deductions made: $2,800, federal income tax; $900, hospitalization; the balance was paid in cash.

   (a) Present the journal entry to record the payroll, assuming that the FICA tax is 7.65 percent.

   (b) Present the employer's payroll tax entry, assuming state unemployment tax of 2 percent and federal unemployment tax of 0.8 percent. Of the total payroll, $5,000 was subject to state and federal unemployment taxes.

3. Record the following transactions in the books of Richard Johnson:

   (a) Sept. 5   Received an $8,000, 90-day, 12 percent note in settlement of the M. Ribble account and immediately discounted it at 12 percent at the bank.

   (b) Dec. 4   M. Ribble dishonored the note, and a protest fee of $2 was imposed.

   (c) Dec. 31   M. Ribble paid her obligation, including the protest fee.

4. Prepare a bank reconciliation statement based on the information below;

   (a) Bank balance, $3,400.

   (b) Checkbook balance, $3,120.

   (c) Outstanding checks, $1,140.

   (d) Deposits in transit, $1,800.

   (e) A $1,000 note was collected by the bank; interest, $15; service charge, $5.

   (f) A $16 check was returned for not sufficient funds.

   (g) Check 12 for $82 was incorrectly recorded in check stubs as $28.

5. Inventory information for product 248 is given below:

Jan. 1	Balance	15 units @	$10	per unit
Mar. 17	Purchase	12 units @	11	per unit
Apr. 29	Purchase	8 units @	12	per unit
Aug. 19	Purchase	12 units @	14	per unit
Aug. 29	Purchase	5 units @	16	per unit
Sept. 18	Purchase	6 units @	20	per unit

After taking a physical count, we find that there are 20 units on hand. Determine the ending inventory cost by (*a*) first-in–first-out; (*b*) last-in–first-out; (*c*) weighted average.

6. P&C Printing Company traded in its old press for a new one priced at $18,000, receiving a trade-in allowance of $1,500 and paying the balance in cash. The old press cost $12,500 and had accumulated depreciation of $11,800. (*a*) What is the entry to record the acquisition of the new machine? (*b*) What entry would be needed if the trade-in had been only $500?

7. The abbreviated income statement of Fran and Robert for December 31, 19X8, appears below:

Sales (net)	$240,000
Less: Cost of Goods Sold	105,000
Gross Profit	$135,000
Less: Expenses	65,000
Net Income	$ 70,000

The profit and loss agreement specifies that

1. Interest of 5 percent is to be allowed on capital balances (Fran, $25,000; Robert, $15,000).
2. Salary allowances to Fran and Robert are to be $6,000 and $4,000, respectively.
3. A bonus equal to 20 percent of net income is to be given to Fran without regard to interest or salary.
4. Remaining profits and losses are to be divided in the ratio of capital balances. (*a*) Present the distribution of net income. (*b*) Present the journal entry required to close the books.

8. The trial balance on the work sheet of the Roseman Corporation as of December 31 is as follows:

Roseman Corporation
Work Sheet
Year Ended December 31, 19X8

Account Title	Trial Balance Dr.	Trial Balance Cr.	Adjustments Dr.	Adjustments Cr.	Income Statement Dr.	Income Statement Cr.	Balance Sheet Dr.	Balance Sheet Cr.
Cash	22,000							
Accounts Receivable	6,500							
Merchandise Inventory	38,100							
Supplies	4,200							
Prepaid Insurance	8,000							
Equipment	15,100							
Accumulated Deprec.		4,400						
Accounts Payable		18,200						
Capital Stock		20,000						
Retained Earnings		17,000						
Dividends	2,400							
Sales		98,200						
Purchases	42,100							
Purchase Returns		300						
Salaries Expense	11,200							
Rent Expense	4,500							
Misc. Gen. Expense	4,000							
	158,100	158,100						
Income Summary								
Supplies Expense								
Insurance Expense								
Deprec. Expense								
Salaries Payable								
Net Income								

(a) Prepare an eight-column work sheet, using the following additional information for year-end adjustments: (1) merchandise inventory on December 31, $42,000; (2) supplies inventory, December 31, $4,000; (3) insurance expired during the year, $2,000; (4) depreciation for the current year, $800; (5) salaries accrued at December 31, $400.

(b) Prepare all necessary adjusting and closing entries.

(c) Prepare the income statement, the retained earnings statement, and the balance sheet for the Roseman Corporation.

Answers to Final Examination

1. *(a)*

Income Summary	46,000	
Merchandise Inventory		46,000
Merchandise Inventory	48,000	
Income Summary		48,000

(b)

Office Supplies Expense	850	
Office Supplies		850

(c)

Insurance Expense	2,700	
Prepaid Insurance		2,700

(d)

Salaries Expense	700	
Salaries Payable		700
(Monday, Dec. 31: $3,500 \div 5$)		

(e)

Interest Receivable	22.50	
Interest Income		22.50

2. *(a)*

Salaries Expense	12,000	
FICA Taxes Payable		918
Federal Income Taxes Payable		2,800
Hospitalization Payable		900
Cash		7,382

(b)

Payroll Tax Expense	1,058	
FICA Taxes Payable		918
State Unemployment Tax Payable		100
Federal Unemployment Tax Payable		40

3. *(a)*

Notes Receivable	8,000.00	
Accounts Receivable, M. Ribble		8,000.00
Cash	7,992.80	
Interest Expense	7.20	
Notes Receivable		8,000.00

(b)

Accounts Receivable, M. Ribble	8,242.00	
Cash		8,242.00

(c)

Cash	8,242.00	
Accounts Receivable, M. Ribble		8,242.00

4.

Bank Reconciliation Statement

Bank balance	$3,400		Checkbook balance		$3,120
Add: Deposits in transit	1,800		Add: Notes receivable	$1,000	
	$5,200		Interest income	15	1,015
					$4,135
Less: Outstanding checks	1,140				
			Less: Service charge	$ 5	
			NSF	16	
			Error	54	75
Bank balance corrected	$4,060		Checkbook balance corrected		$4,060

5. (*a*) First-in–first-out

Sept. 18:	6 units @ $20 =	$120
Aug. 29:	5 units @ 16 =	80
Aug. 19:	9 units @ 14 =	126
Total units	20	$326

(*b*) Last-in–first-out

Jan. 1:	15 units @ $10 =	$150
Mar. 17:	5 units @ 11 =	55
Total units	20	$205

(*c*) Weighted average

15 units @ $10 =	$150		
12 units @ 11 =	132		
8 units @ 12 =	96		
12 units @ 14 =	168		
5 units @ 16 =	80		
6 units @ 20 =	120		$746 ÷ 58 = $12.86 per unit*
Total units	58	$746	$12.86 × 20 units = $257.20

*Rounded

6. (*a*)

Accumulated Depreciation	11,800	
Machine (new)	17,200	
Machine (old)		12,500
Cash		16,500

(*b*)

Accumulated Depreciation	11,800	
Machine (new)	18,000	
Loss on Disposal of Fixed Assets	200	
Machine (old)		12,500
Cash		17,500

7. (a)

	Fran	Robert	Total
Interest	$ 1,250	$ 750	$ 2,000
Salary	6,000	4,000	10,000
Bonus	14,000		14,000
	$21,250	$ 4,750	$26,000
Balance	27,500*	16,500*	44,000
Net income	$48,750	$21,250	$70,000

*$25,000	Fran	25/40 × $44,000 = $27,500
15,000	Robert	15/40 × $44,000 = $16,500
$40,000	Total	

(b)

Income Summary	70,000	
Fran, Capital		48,750
Robert, Capital		21,250

8. (a)

Roseman Corporation
Work Sheet
Year Ended December 31, 19X8

Account Title	Trial Balance Dr.	Trial Balance Cr.	Adjustments Dr.	Adjustments Cr.	Income Statement Dr.	Income Statement Cr.	Balance Sheet Dr.	Balance Sheet Cr.
Cash	22,000						22,000	
Accounts Receivable	6,500						6,500	
Merchandise Inventory	38,100		(1) 42,000	(1) 38,100			42,000	
Supplies	4,200			(2) 200			4,000	
Prepaid Insurance	8,000			(3) 2,000			6,000	
Equipment	15,100						15,100	
Accumulated Deprec.		4,400		(4) 800				5,200
Accounts Payable		18,200						18,200
Capital Stock		20,000						20,000
Retained Earnings		17,000						17,000
Dividends	2,400						2,400	
Sales		98,200				98,200		
Purchases	42,100				42,100			
Purchase Returns		300				300		
Salaries Expense	11,200		(5) 400		11,600			
Rent Expense	4,500				4,500			
Misc. Gen. Expense	4,000				4,000			
	158,100	158,100						
Income Summary			(1) 38,100	(1) 42,000	38,100	42,000		
Supplies Expense			(2) 200		200			
Insurance Expense			(3) 2,000		2,000			
Depreciation Expense			(4) 800		800			
Salaries Payable				(5) 400				400
			83,500	83,500	103,300	140,500	98,000	60,800
Net Income					37,200			37,200
					140,500	140,500	98,000	98,000

(b)

Adjusting Entries

(1)

Merchandise Inventory	42,000	
Income Summary		42,000
Income Summary	38,100	
Merchandise Inventory		38,100

(2)

Supplies Expense	200	
Supplies		200

(3)

Insurance Expense	2,000	
Prepaid Insurance		2,000

(4)

Depreciation Expense	800	
Accumulated Depreciation		800

(5)

Salaries Expense	400	
Salaries Payable		400

Closing Entries

(1)

Sales Income	98,200	
Purchase Returns	300	
Income Summary		98,500

(2)

Income Summary	65,200	
Purchases		42,100
Salaries Expense		11,600
Rent Expense		4,500
Misc. General Expense		4,000
Supplies Expense		200
Insurance Expense		2,000
Depreciation Expense		800

(3)

Income Summary	37,200	
Retained Earnings		37,200

(4)

Retained Earnings	2,400	
Dividends		2,400

(c)
Roseman Corporation
Income Statement
Year Ended December 31, 19X8

Sales			$98,200
Cost of Goods Sold			
Merchandise Inventory, Jan. 1		$38,100	
Purchases	$42,100		
Less: Purchase Returns	300	41,800	
Goods Available for Sale		$79,900	
Less: Merchandise Inventory, Dec. 31		42,000	
Cost of Goods Sold			37,900
Gross Profit			$60,300
Operating Expenses			
Salaries Expense		$11,600	
Rent Expense		4,500	
Insurance Expense		2,000	
Supplies Expense		200	
Depreciation Expense		800	
Misc. Gen. Expense		4,000	
Total Operating Expenses			23,100
Net Income			$37,200

Roseman Corporation
Retained Earnings Statement
Year Ended December 31, 19X8

Retained Earnings, January 1, 19X8		$17,000
Net Income	$37,200	
Less: Dividends	2,400	
Increase in Retained Earnings		34,800
Retained Earnings, December 31, 19X8		$51,800

Roseman Corporation
Balance Sheet
December 31, 19X8

ASSETS

Current Assets		
Cash	$22,000	
Accounts Receivable	6,500	
Merchandise Inventory	42,000	
Supplies	4,000	
Prepaid Insurance	6,000	
Total Current Assets		$80,500
Fixed Assets		
Equipment	$15,100	
Less: Accumulated Deprec.	5,200	9,900
Total Assets		$90,400

LIABILITIES AND EQUITY

Liabilities

Current Liabilities

Accounts Payable	$18,200	
Salaries Payable	400	
Total Current Liabilities		$18,600
Equity		
Capital Stock	$20,000	
Retained Earnings, December 31, 19X8	51,800	
Total Equity		71,800
Total Liabilities and Equity		$90,400

Index